Alan Taylor has been a journalist for over 30 years. He was deputy editor and managing editor of *The Scotsman*, and for 15 years was Writer-at-Large for the *Sunday Herald*. He was a Booker Prize judge in 1994 – the only year a Glaswegian has won. He has contributed to numerous publications, including *The Times Literary Supplement*, *The New Yorker* and *The Melbourne Age*. Co-founder and editor of *The Scottish Review of Books*, he has edited three acclaimed anthologies – *The Assassin's Cloak* (2000), *The Secret Annexe* (2004) and *The Country Diaries* (2009).

Glasgow

THE AUTOBIOGRAPHY

Edited by Alan Taylor

BIRLINN

This edition first published in 2017 by
Birlinn Limited
West Newington House
10 Newington Road
Edinburgh
EH9 1QS

2

www.birlinn.co.uk

First published in hardback in 2016

A full list of copyright permissions appears on p. 297

ISBN 978 1 78027 481 2

British Library Cataloguing-in-Publication Data
A catalogue record for this book is available from the British Library

Typeset by Hewer Text UK Ltd, Edinburgh
Printed and bound by MBM Print SCS Ltd, Glasgow

CONTENTS

ACKNOWLEDGEMENTS

Whoever it was who said that of the making of books there is no end had a point. The existence of *Glasgow: The Autobiography* is dependent on countless other books, most of which one trusts are cited in the endmatter. I am grateful to their authors who have added to the ever-growing cairn of knowledge about this rambunctious city. Anyone who aspires to study Glasgow must urgently make acquaintance with the Mitchell Library, one of Scotland's great municipal institutions, and in particular the Glasgow Room. Its staff personify why public libraries are rightly revered and must be protected from those who either through ignorance, ideology or incompetence would do them harm.

Two other libraries deserve also be hymned. The first is Edinburgh Central Library where in the reference library I spent the best part of a decade as a research assistant. Working on this book I often haunted the Scottish Department, grateful to be allowed to borrow items I needed to spend more time with. The second is the National Library of Scotland wherein is contained our collective memory. Its staff have been unfailingly helpful and patient, not least when guiding this techno-naif through fields pocked with mines that may not lead to physical impairment but which can surely scar one mentally. The NLS's café deserves special mention for it is here that twenty-first-century men (and women) of genius are to be found daily hunched over a steaming bowl of lentil soup and putting the world to rights, among them historian and Hibs supporter Ian S. Wood, architectural expert David Black and Mario Relich, poet and sage.

It is a privilege to have Birlinn as the publisher of *Glasgow: The Autobiography*. Its venerable HQ, in Newington, Edinburgh, within a stone's throw of Arthur's Seat, not only accommodates a thrum of employees but appears also to function as a B&B for writers who for whatever reason – better not to speculate – find themselves in need of a bed for the night. Hugh Andrew runs the show with the air of a man who in an earlier incarnation must have been a spinner of plates. Like me, my editor, Andrew Simmons, is an Italophile, which has added to the pleasure of us working together. My gratitude to Andrew is on a par with that of Pavarotti's to his favourite pizza chef. Finally, I am indebted beyond measure to my wife, Rosemary Goring, who, when the going got tough – I'm referring specifically to the index – dragged me rejoicing over the finishing line.

Alan Taylor
July 2017

INTRODUCTION

In the considered and utterly impartial opinion of the blithe souls who live there, Glasgow is without doubt the greatest city in the universe. It must be said at the outset that the evidence offered for this is more heart-felt than empirical. Glaswegians, however, are unshakeable in their view that they reside in a northern Shangri-la, albeit a rain-soaked, pewter-clouded version, and are amazed and outraged when anyone dares question the obviousness of this assumption. In Glasgow, its champions point out, you will find spectacular architecture, verdant gardens, high culture, sensational shopping, buskers galore, peerless panhandlers and all human life rubbing along more or less harmoniously. 'For me,' as Jack House, one of several contenders for the title 'Mr Glasgow', wrote, 'Glasgow was the greatest town in the world from the moment I realised I was seeing it.'

As the mantra goes, people are what make Glasgow. Humour is the glue that binds them. Even in the worst of times, of which there have been a few, Glaswegians are not inclined to take themselves too seriously and accept whatever unjust gods throw at them with the forbearance of an audience tortured by the routine of a comedian who has forgotten his punchline. They know that Glasgow has a reputation as a place where such performers have been known to die an embarrassing and excruciating death and, to a degree, they are happy to play along with it, because it would be unmannerly to do otherwise. 'What do I have to do to make you laugh?' asked one frustrated comedian of the po-faced rabble in the stalls. 'Try cracking a joke!' cried a clown in the front row.

It sometimes seems there are as many Glasgows as there are Glaswegians, and I do not mean those towns called Glasgow in Kentucky, Montana and goodness knows where else. In the beginning was the Dear Green Place, which took its name from the Gaelic, Gles Chu. Or so we have been led to believe. Glasgow then was little more than a sylvan hamlet situated at the point where the Molendinar burn flowed into the River Clyde, hence the saw: 'The Clyde made Glasgow and Glasgow made the Clyde.' Why the Clyde is so called is another mystery the solution to which may be also be found in Gaeldom. There is, for example, the Gaelic name Cluaidh, but what it means seems to have confounded toponymists, etymologists, lexicographers and anyone else with a fancy handle. Was there a woad-smeared, cudgel-bearing chiel from the isles called Cluaidh? Perhaps. But if there was he is yet to poke his head above the parapet. Just as plausible, however, is the theory that the Clyde is derived from 'clut', which among the ancient Celts meant 'the cleansing one'.

There is no lack of other theories, none any less valid – or more verifiable – than those already mentioned. What we can be certain of is that the Dear Green Place owes its primacy to a fine novel of the same name by Archie Hind which appeared as recently as 1966. In it, the author repeats the legend of St Mungo, Glasgow's patron saint, recovering from the waters of the Molendinar a lost ring from the belly of a salmon. But even as we savour that magical image, Hind reminds us this was all in the distant past and that, 'The little valley of the Molendinar is now stopped with two centuries of refuse – soap, tallow, cotton waste, slag, soda, bits of leather, broken pottery, tar and caoutchouc – the waste products of a dozen industries and a million lives, and it is built over with slums, yards, streets and factories.'

This is a description of the Glasgow that grew out of the Industrial Revolution, which led to it being titled the Second City of Empire. It was a dirty, teeming, pulsating, enterprising, inventive, unequal metropolis into which poured immigrants from the Scottish Highlands and Ireland. Meanwhile other Glasgows continued to emerge. The aforementioned Mr House recalled that it had been dubbed – by a Russian grand duke no less – 'the centre of intelligence of Europe', but no reliable source has been found for this extravagance. Then there is, in novelist William McIlvanney's felicitous phrase, the 'city of the stare' where you have no idea where the next assault on your privateness is coming from. This is a place that 'in spite of its wide vistas and areas of dereliction often seemed as spacious as a rush-hour bus'. No Mean City is yet another label which has attached itself, leech-like, to Glasgow. It, too, is indebted to a novel. First published in 1935, and reprinted frequently thereafter, *No Mean City* (from the Bible in which the apostle Paul announces: 'I am a Jew of Tarsus in Cilicia, a citizen of no mean city . . .') was a collaborative effort by a journalist, Herbert Kingsley Long, and an unemployed worker, Alexander McArthur. Set in the slum underworld where razor gangs ran amok, it made such an impression that eight decades later Glasgow is still bedevilled by its legacy.

Growing up in the douce east, I knew of this Glasgow only by its fearsome reputation. Untempered by personal knowledge, a teacher said that should we ever feel the need to go west we ought to be aware that we would be unlikely to return in one piece and that if we did we could expect to have scars of which a musketeer would have been proud. Glasgow, she added, in the superior tone of Jean Brodie, was an uncivilised, uncouth backwater where violence was by and large the norm and unchecked by the forces of law and order. In my young mind's eye, it was Dodge City incarnate. It took no great leap of the imagination to picture bandy-legged loons bursting into saloons, demanding whisky and rye and eager to engage in fisticuffs. Moreover, it was where things were made. Furnaces burned round the clock and chimney stacks rose high into the sky belching acrid, asphyxiating smoke. Dickens's Coketown, with its vile-smelling river, black and thick with dye, was how I saw it. There, runty men with no teeth and a fag stuck behind an ear got their hands dirty so that we, in Scotland's pen-pushing, paper-driven, white-collar capital, didn't have to.

I was so in thrall to what my teacher told me that when finally I left school and was offered a job in Glasgow I didn't give it a second's serious thought. For all I knew it was no more safe than a war zone, which was exactly how it was invariably portrayed by the ever-evil media. It was an untamed territory divided by unswerving loyalty to football teams: Rangers and Celtic, blue and green, Protestant and Catholic, Huns and Tims, who year in, year out cleared the trophy board much to the chagrin to those of us whose sympathies lay with less successful teams. It was said that if you dared to wear the wrong colour in the wrong part of the city you could expect terrible retribution. What, I wondered, if you happened to be colour blind? Would you be spared? Nor was it wise to park a green car in the vicinity of Ibrox, Rangers' ground, or a blue one near Parkhead, Celtic's home turf, for they would surely be vandalised.

This was alien to those of us who grew up in the environs of Edinburgh where class, not religion, was what divided society. It was not until 1977, when Alan Spence's epiphanic collection of short stories, *Its Colours They Are Fine*, was published, that I began to comprehend the depth to which sectarianism influenced the lives of countless Glaswegians. Spence took his title from 'The Sash', the rousing Protestant anthem. Born in Glasgow in 1947, he wrote about a childhood that was primitive in its richness and roughness. 'Gypsies ur worse than cathlicks!' says Aleck, a young Protestant boy, adding: 'Nae kiddin. They havnae a fuckin clue.' Such pronouncements come naturally to Aleck, who has grown up in the kind of culture that is manna to anthropologists. The way Aleck speaks (''Mon wull go up tae mah hoose'n clean it aff'), what he eats (sausages and egg and fried bread is a favourite meal), what he reads (Oor Wullie, The Broons, Merry Mac's Fun Parade), where he plays (waste ground, tenement closes, back streets), all contribute to a sense of otherness. Little wonder, therefore, that when visitors arrived in Glasgow they often reacted as if they had travelled deep into the Amazonian jungle and encountered a lost tribe speaking in a tongue they struggled to comprehend and enjoying rituals fathomable only to initiates.

In the second part of Spence's book, however, adult life intrudes and the innocence and unquestioning of youth gives way to aspects of 'adult' life – an Orange walk, a wedding, violence at a dance-hall, an old woman living alone in a tower block, an old man who seeks refuge and warmth in the Kibble Palace. In the story that gives the collection its title, the main character, Billy, is preparing for 'the Walk', which is always held on the Saturday nearest the 12th of July, the anniversary of the 1690 Battle of the Boyne, which was won by William of Orange, aka King Billy. Spence writes,

> Billy's own walk was a combination of John Wayne and numberless lumbering cinema-screen heavies. He'd always been Big Billy, even as a child. Marching in the Walk was like being part of a liberating army. Triumph. Drums throbbing.

> Stirring inside. He remembered newsreel films of the Allies marching into Paris. At that time he'd been working in the shipyards and his was a reserved occupation, 'vital to the war effort', which meant that he couldn't join up. But he had marched in imagination through scores of Hollywood films. From the sands of Iwo Jima to the beachheads of Normandy. But now it was real, and instead of 'The Shores of Tripoli', it was 'The Sash My Father Wore'.

This is what Billy might call a celebration of tradition, a remembrance of a glorious past, keeping a flame alive. For others though, the Orange Parades, with their flute bands, Lambeg drums and banners, are provocative and intimidating, evidence of an aspect of Glasgow life they would rather was swept away. What cannot be denied, however, is that without them Glasgow would be a little less, well, Glaswegian. Of all the cities I have visited, none is as immediately characterful as Glasgow, as sure of itself, and at one with itself. You can be standing in a supermarket queue and chances are the person behind you will comment on the contents of your basket. In a pub, it is by no means unusual for a total stranger to offer to buy you a drink. This happened to me not so long ago and when I politely declined, my would-be benefactor asked 'Whit's wrang wi' yi?', in the tone of an aggressive doctor attempting to get to the bottom of a nasty stomach bug. In an attempt to divert the conversation, I said that I was from Edinburgh. 'That explains everythin',' said the stranger, turning his attention elsewhere. On another occasion, early in my acquaintance with Glasgow, I was in the Horseshoe Bar in Drury Street in whose Gents I was approached by a man in a flat cap who, apropos nothing in particular, asked if I knew how many wonders in the world there are. I hazarded seven and started to list them. I got as far the Hanging Gardens of Babylon when I was imperiously interrupted. 'Naw,' said Mr Flat Cap contemptuously, 'there's eight.' 'Really. What's the eighth?' I asked. 'That's for me to know and you to find out,' he said with a wink, and was gone before I could quiz him further.

Such encounters added to the frisson whenever I visited Glasgow, which I did more often after I started writing for the *Herald*. Back then, it was based in Albion Street, in the heart of the

Merchant City. The HQ was a brutalist block which, in an earlier era, had housed the *Scottish Daily Express*, which in its pomp, so legend had it, was able in pursuit of a hot story to put more planes in the air than the Luftwaffe. On the ground level was the no-frills Press Bar. Once I was bidden there by my editor, a fellow who was so tall that when he stood next to me I couldn't see where he stopped. As we got down to business one of the worse-for-wear regulars inveigled himself into our colloquy and was decked for his impertinence. The editor carried on talking as if nothing untoward had happened. When I pointed out that there was a barely conscious fellow lying on the floor he said, 'He shouldn't have interrupted me when I was talking.' In the toilet there was another regular who appeared to have passed out mid-micturition. Concerned for his wellbeing I informed a barman who gave me a 'what am I supposed to do about it' shrug and continued polishing a glass. Throughout the afternoon people came and went as their duties demanded. A fêted contributor studied his watch, drained his nip, donned his fedora and breezed out the door. Apparently, he had a column to write. Less than an hour later he reappeared, having met his deadline, and resumed where he had left off.

In those days, as we entered the 1980s, Glasgow was a byword for decline. Many of the industries from which its grandeur had sprung were on their uppers and there was a feeling that its future was bleak. It was in a dark, dank, menacing place which the rain, which seemed to start as soon as you reached Harthill, midpoint on the M8 between Edinburgh and Glasgow, did nothing to temper. The news was full of strikes and closures, empty order books and unemployment. The Clyde, which had been as noisy as a nursery, fell quiet as one yard after another shut its gates. The Tories, led by Margaret Thatcher, were in power and impervious to the protests of left-leaning Scots. (Consequently, when Thatcher died in 2013 some Glaswegians regretted no statue had been erected to her so that they could tear it down, while others held street parties.) In 1981 I attended the launch for a novel at the Third Eye Centre – the predecessor of the Centre for Contemporary Arts – in Sauchiehall Street. The novel was *Lanark* by Alasdair Gray. In hindsight, it was one of those rare moments when a work of art is the agent for change. Ten years and more in the writing, it marked Gray's debut. Part of *Lanark* is autobiographical, following its author's upbringing in the 1930s and 1940s initially in a tenement in Bridgeton then in Riddrie, part of the first tier of what's known as the three-tiered Addison Act. Unlike the two tiers that were to follow it, people were not piled on top of one another but were placed in low-density, semi-detached houses with gardens.

Duncan Thaw, Gray's hero, progresses through school to art college, where he encounters a fellow student called Kenneth McAlpin, who has a moustache – a sure sign of social superiority – and lives in Bearsden, which is as alien to Duncan as Marseilles. On a morning ramble he and McAlpin venture into Cowcaddens to do some drawing. At the top of a hill they look across the city.

> Travelling patches of sunlight went from ridge to ridge, making a hump of tenements gleam against the dark towers of the city chambers, silhouetting the cupolas of the Royal Infirmary against the tomb-glittering spine of the Necropolis. 'Glasgow is a magnificent city,' said McAlpin. 'Why do we hardly ever notice that?' 'Because nobody imagines living here,' said Thaw. McAlpin lit a cigarette and said, 'If you want to explain that I'll certainly listen.'

What follows is an impassioned analysis of why Glasgow is not comparable to great cultural centres such as Florence, Paris, London and New York, to all of which strangers can relate because they've 'already visited them in paintings, novels, history books and films'. In contrast, Glasgow is by and large invisible, existing only as a music-hall song – presumably the drunks' anthem, 'I belong to Glasgow' – and a few bad novels, one of which is doubtless *No Mean City*. 'What is Glasgow to most of us?' asks Thaw/Gray. 'A house, the place we work, a football park or golf course, some pubs and connecting streets. That's all. No, I'm wrong, there's also the cinema and library.'

The period in which this scene is set is the mid-1950s, when Glasgow was undoubtedly in the doldrums and suffering from what looked like terminal decay. What used to be the place which made anything that was required to carry you from cradle to grave was so no longer, as cheap goods from the Far East saturated the market and caused local companies to bring down the shutters. Thaw's mission, and that of Gray, his creator, is through paint and print 'to give Glasgow a more imaginative life'. The irony was that when *Lanark* appeared many of the sentiments expressed in its pages were interpreted as a comment on the city as it stood at that moment. And to a degree that was understandable. Glasgow had yet to export a positive identity; it was still mired in many observers' minds in a macho past where brawn triumphed over brain. It was of course a highly misleading image, but it persisted and proved remarkably durable. Tourists were few and many of those who did come arrived with their prejudices as part of their luggage.

One welcome counterpoint to the prevailing view was offered in 1983 by the acerbic American novelist and travel writer Paul Theroux, whom few tourist boards would adopt as a copywriter. Ostensibly following Britain's coastline, he alighted in Glasgow after sojourning in Troubles-torn Belfast, an experience he was relieved to put behind him. In contrast, Theroux, much to his surprise, found Glasgow 'peaceful, even pretty'. 'The slums were gone, the buildings washed of their soot; the city looked dignified – no barricades, no scorchings. Well, I had just struggled ashore from that island of antiquated passions.' Coincidentally, 1983 proved to be an *annus mirabilis* for the city, for it was in that year that the 'Glasgow's Miles Better' campaign was launched. Inspired by 'I ♥ New York', dreamed up six years earlier to encourage tourists to visit the Big Apple, which had become a muggers' playground, it was initially greeted with scepticism by many wags who asked, 'Miles better than what?' What Glasgow has never lacked, however, are people to hymn it and the slights and criticisms were brushed off with the contempt a heifer shows to ticks. The slogan soon entered the bloodstream and there was a discernible improvement in the mood of the natives and a measurable influx of visitors keen to see what all the fuss was about.

High on the list of the attractions they wanted to visit was the Burrell Collection, which opened the same year. It had been amassed by Sir William Burrell, scion of a family whose business was in shipping. When his father, also named William, died, William Junior and his brother George took over. Through astute buying and selling of their merchant fleets, the brothers amassed considerable fortunes. When in 1916 they finally disposed of their assets, Sir William was able to devote himself to building up his art collection, filling his Berwickshire castle with an extraordinary collection of paintings, sculptures, ceramics, carpets, tapestries, glassware, needlework and artefacts from around the globe. In the 1930s, he decided that he would like it all to be housed under one roof held in public ownership. It is said that he first offered it to the Tate Gallery, London, but it spurned the opportunity for lack of space. In 1944, Burrell handed it over to Glasgow. But worried about the damaging effects of the former Dear Green Place's polluted air on his precious objects he quixotically stipulated that it must be housed on a site not less than sixteen miles from Wellington's statue – the one invariably decorated with a traffic cone – in Royal Exchange Square, and not more than four miles from Killearn, Stirlingshire. In 1963, five years after their benefactor's death, the Burrell trustees agreed to allow the collection to be housed in a building within the Pollok estate, a mere three miles south of the city centre. An international competition was announced to find architects to design a building specifically to contain Burrell's gallimaufry. It was finally opened by the Queen in 1983 to a thunderclap of applause.

The Burrell was a signal that Glasgow was emerging from its begrimed past. Another was the Glasgow Garden Festival in 1988. The words 'garden' and 'Glasgow', like 'cuisine' and 'Mexico', had rarely been spied in the same sentence. Yet again this was a travesty of the truth, for where else is called the Dear Green Place? Indeed, Glasgow has what might be termed an embarrassment of parks and gardens, including Kelvingrove Park, which in the late nineteenth and early twentieth centuries hosted three major exhibitions, and the Botanic Gardens, among whose treasures is a fine collection of exotic orchids. The Garden Festival, however, was located not in a park but on a 100-acre site in what had been Prince's Dock on the south bank of the Clyde. Nearly four and a half million people attended its attractions. Two years thereafter came Glasgow's reign as European City of Culture, the third such place, after Athens and Florence no less, to hold that title. Even ten years earlier that would have been – *pace* Gray's *Lanark* – unthinkable and to many observers, especially residents of Edinburgh, the 'Festival City', it still was. Though some criticised the organisers for paying too little attention to Glasgow's indigenous art and artists, there is no doubt that its tenure as City of Culture raised its profile and radically altered attitudes towards it. 'Glasgow used to be perceived as a violent post-industrial city and now it is celebrated as a creative and cultural centre of European importance,' was the judgement of Robert Palmer, who orchestrated the year-long programme of events. His assertion is borne out by many studies which have all shown that Glasgow 1990 had a dramatic impact in building city confidence. Moreover, had it not happened it is unlikely that the 2014 Commonwealth Games would have been given to Glasgow.

But the resilience of an unsavoury image – however misrepresentative – ought not to be underestimated. Nor is there any point in drawing curtains on a past that was undoubtedly grim. Countless impoverished Glaswegians lived in squalid, overcrowded, insanitary conditions and were as a consequence thrust into behaviour which we now deem antisocial. Infant mortality rates were on a par with those in the Third World and any men who reached three score and ten years, as the psalmist insisted was the norm, must have been fitness fanatics or have led very careful and prosperous lives. Districts like the Gorbals and Townhead were barely fit for human habitation and those who had the wherewithal escaped as fast as they could.

One such was Ralph Glasser. The son of immigrant Jews from Russia, Glasser grew up in the Gorbals between the wars. After years of night study, he won a scholarship to Oxford, to take up which he had to cycle hundreds of miles. When I met him many years later, he looked what he was: an eminent scholar and author, a psychologist and an economist. But as he spoke I could tell by his accent immediately where he came from. In his book *Growing Up in the Gorbals*, an unvarnished account of his childhood first published in 1986, Glasser relates how he left school when he was about eleven to work in a garment factory. His 'only true home' was the Mitchell Library, which allowed him to read the gamut of literature or philosophy and to dream of a brighter future. Yet as his career developed, and as he travelled around the world, he knew that while he might have 'escaped' the Gorbals and Glasgow, he was not free of them, and never would be. As a young man he was desperate to leave but as he grew older he began to appreciate the 'presiding genius' of his birthplace and that to have thought of it as a 'malign influence' was wrong.

In any case, on revisiting the city, Glasser soon discovered that it had changed utterly. In *A Gorbals Legacy* (2000), he wrote,

> Now, even the physical Gorbals I knew has been destroyed, including much of the old street plan. When I go back it is almost impossible to identify the ground where former landmarks stood – Gorbals Cross and the darkly sculptured monument named after it, bearing under a clock the City of Glasgow arms and the motto 'Let Glasgow flourish by the preaching of the word', and stone benches on its walls where men in mufflers and cloth caps gathered on Saturday mornings to smoke and talk about the world; Cumberland Street railway bridge with its broad arches, workshop caverns for upholsterers, metal workers, machine shops; and the old Main Street library. On a visit to Glasgow a few years ago, when journalists wanted to have me photographed at Gorbals Cross, we drove round fruitlessly till I realised that these Glasgow men were lost. I got out of my car, stood on an unknown pavement and, helped by a sighting on the steeple of a surviving church, led them to where Gorbals Cross had stood. I was photographed standing on a windy piece of wilderness, Gorbals Cross. The true Gorbals is in the heart. Its demons will probably stay there forever, waiting to receive *their* quittance.

This is a reminder that Glasgow, like all cities, is inchoate. As a former Lord Provost told me, it will never be finished; change is the one thing of which you can be certain. Even in the short time I've known it Glasgow has undergone a spectacular transformation. The Merchant City, where I live, is unrecognisable from the area I used to walk through to get to the *Herald*. People, too, come and go, as they must, memory of them kept alive in the names of streets, buildings, institutions, shops: Archibald Ingram, John Glassford of Dougalston, John Anderson, Kate Cranston, George Hutcheson and many, many others. *Glasgow: The Autobiography* is an attempt to tell the city's story through the words of those who witnessed it happening. By its very nature it is incomplete and subjective, but I hope that what emerges as one year succeeds another is a portrait that is sympathetic and true to its subject. With that uppermost in mind, I have selected material from diverse sources, including memoirs, newspapers and journals, historical documents, dictionaries, encyclopedias, travelogues, poetry and fiction, official reports and evidence given in court. The authors come from near and far. Many were born and bred in Glasgow, and were disinclined ever to leave. Others came and went in a day and were glad to see the back of it. It is often said of cities that they are characters in their own right. Glasgow's character, readers will find, is much more complex than the stereotype. It envelops you in its embrace, it doesn't attempt to be other than what it is, it loves to put on a show, it is resilient, optimistic, kindly, ambitious, it likes a good time, it won't be put down or put upon, it is inferior to nowhere. There is, too, an edge to it which may be a legacy of its history of dissent and the championing of the underdog, of Red Clydeside and the World War One rent strikes and the award to Nelson Mandela of the 'Freedom of the City' when he was still incarcerated on Robben Island. It was encapsulated by Billy Connolly, without doubt the greatest comedian ever to come out of Anderston, in the aftermath of a terrorist attack on Glasgow Airport in 2007. It was in part thwarted by a baggage handler called John Smeaton who, spotting what was going on while puffing on a cigarette, leapt into action and set about one of the suicide bombers even as he attempted to blow himself up. 'What were they thinking about, bringing terror to Glasgow?' said Connolly, barely able to speak for laughing. It was one of those moments, added the Big Yin, that makes you swell with pride, that makes you want to tell the world you are a Glaswegian. 'I come from there. That's where I come from. Don't you forget it.' Expletives have been deleted to protect readers of a sensitive nature.

PROLOGUE

GLASGOW GOT ITS NAME

John and Julia Keay

How did Glasgow come to be called Glasgow? The likelihood, as John and Julia Keay point out below, is that it is Celtic in origin and probably Gaelic. Over the years its spelling has become anglicised but its pronunciation by locals often depends on which social class they belong to. 'Glesca' is preferred by those who do not wish to appear pretentious while those who dwell in rather more refined areas – Bearsden, Milngavie, Kelvingrove, etc – are apt to opt for 'Glass-go'. Scots language experts suggest that 'folk in the wast o Scotland ken it as Glesga or Glesca, and folk fae the east maistly caw it Glesga or Glesgae'. All of which may prove mystifying to visitors to the city who are often bamboozled by the native speakers. Not for nothing has Glaswegian been called the most impenetrable dialect in the United Kingdom. The story of the city's origins is similarly obscure and freighted with myth.

The etymology of the name of Scotland's largest city is warmly disputed. Its derivation is surely Celtic and probably Gaelic, but with anglicised spellings varying widely from *glas-chu* to *glas-cun*, the component words are uncertain, let alone their precise meaning. In the heyday of the 19th-century industrialisation *glas* was taken to mean 'grey', leading to such seemingly appropriate translations as 'the grey blacksmith' ('gow' suggesting *gobha*, a smith) or 'the grey hound ferry' *cu*, a dog). Currently the favoured derivations are more pastoral and cultural, with *glas* taken to indicate 'green' or 'church'. Hence the popular 'dear green place', 'green hollow', 'dear stream', 'green cloister', 'dear cloister', 'church within the enclosed space', 'church of Cun(tigernus) [Kentigern]', etc.

A gift to the image-makers, such uncertainty accords well with the city's occasional need to reinvent itself.

1597–1700

AN ARCHBISHOP'S SEAT

WITCHCRAFT, 1597
John Spottiswoode

The first recorded witchcraft cases in Glasgow date from 1597 and were described by John Spottiswoode, Archbishop of St Andrews (1565–1639), in his History of the Church and State of Scotland, *published in 1655. In 1563, an Act regarding 'witchcraft, sorcery and necromancy' was passed by the Scottish Parliament. These were punishable by death and judges were expected to be unsparing of those who practised them. The goal was to eradicate evil in all its supposed forms. Around 80 per cent of the victims of witchcraft accusations and trials were women. It is estimated that there were 1,337 executions for witchcraft in Scotland. The last execution for this crime was that of Janet Horne in Dornoch in 1727.*

This summer there was a great business for the trial of witches. Amongst others one Margaret Atkin [the great witch of Balwearie], being apprehended upon suspicion, and threatened with torture, did confess herself guilty. Being examined touching her associates in that trade, she named a few, and perceiving her dilations find credit, made offer to detect all of that sort, and to purge the country of them, so she might have her life granted. For the reason of her knowledge, she said, 'That they had a secret mark all of that sort, in their eyes, whereby she could surely tell, how soon she looked upon any, whether they were witches or not' and in this way she was so readily believed, that for the space of three or four months she was carried from town to town to make discoveries of that kind. Many were brought in question by her dilations, especially at Glasgow, where divers innocent women, through the credulity of the minister, Mr John Cowper, were condemned and put to death. In the end she was found to be a mere deceiver . . . and was sent back to Fife.

HEAD COVERING, 1604
Glasgow Kirk Session

The influence of the Church of Scotland – the Kirk – has been incalculable and far-reaching. John Knox (1513–72) is often believed to have been at the root of much misogyny, famously inveighing against 'the monstrous regiment [rule] of women'. Whether he is deserving of the considerable opprobrium that has been heaped upon him is debateable. What is clear, however, is that the history of Presbyterianism – like that of virtually all religions – has been male-dominated and that many of its more oppressive, and ridiculous, edicts have been directed at women.

No woman, married or unmarried, come within kirk doors, to preachings or prayers, with their plaids about their heads . . . The session considering that great disorder hath been in the kirk, by women sitting with their heads covered in time of sermon, sleeping that way, ordains intimation to be made that none sit with their heads covered with plaid in time of sermon.

A CLOSET LINED WITH IRON, 1 JULY, 1636
Sir William Brereton

An English writer and politician, Sir William Brereton (1604–61) was a commander in the Parliamentary army in the English Civil war. Born in Manchester, he studied at Oxford. Interested in field sports, he built a duck decoy at Dodleston, Cheshire, which proved to be something of a commercial success. In 1636, he travelled through north-eastern England and lowland Scotland and thereafter to Ireland, recording his impressions as he went.

We came to the city of Glasgow, which is thirty-six miles from Edinburgh, eighteen from Failkirke. This is an archbishop's seat, an ancient university, one only college consisting of about one hundred and twenty students, wherein are four schools, one principal, four regents. There are about six or seven hundred communicants, and about twenty thousand persons in the town, which is famous for the church, which is fairest and stateliest in Scotland, for the Toll-boothe and Bridge.

The church I viewed this day, and found it a brave and ancient piece. It was said, in this church this day, that there was a contribution throughout Europe (even Rome itself contributed) towards the building thereof. There is a great partition or wall 'twixt the body of the church and the chancel; there is no use of the body of the church, only divine service and sermon is used and performed in the quire or chancel, which is built and framed church-wise; and under this quire there is also another church, which carries the same proportion under this, wherein also there is two sermons every Lord's day.

The Toll-boothe, which is placed in the middle of the town, and near unto the cross and market-place, is a very fair and high-built house, from the top whereof, being leaded, you may take a full view and prospect of the whole city. In one of these rooms or chambers sits the council of this city; in other of the rooms or chambers preparation is made for the lords of the council to meet in these stately rooms. Herein is a closet lined with iron: walls, top, bottom, floor, and door, iron; wherein are kept the evidences and records of the city: this made, to prevent the danger of fire. This Toll-booth said to be the fairest in this kingdom: the revenues belonging to this city are about £1000 per annum. This town is built: two streets, which are built like a cross, in the middle of both which the cross is placed, which looks four ways into four streets, though indeed they be but two straight streets; the one reaching from the church to the bridge, a mile long – the other which crosseth, that is much shorter.

We lodged in Mr David Weyme's house; his wife's name is Margrett Cambell (the wives in Scotland never change, but always retain, their own names), no stabling hereunto belonging; in the town we were constrained to provide stabling. I paid 5*d.* for pease straw, for my straw; no hay would be gotten. We paid for victuals, dinner, and breakfast, seven persons, two rix-dollars.

O GLASGOW!, 1685
John Barclay

Glasgow has been the source of poetic inspiration from an early date. Before 597 St Columba, the great missionary of the Hebrides, paid a visit to the aged St Mungo at his cell on the banks of the Molendinar river. In memory of their conversation, in that green and holy place, it is said that the two old men exchanged staves and Columba composed a hymn. John Barclay, minister of Cruden in Aberdeenshire, composed the following lines which appeared, incongruously, in Skene's Succinct Survey of the Famous City of Aberdeen *in 1685.*

Glasgow, to thee thy neighb'ring towns give place.
'Bove them thou lift thine head with comely grace.
Scarce is the spacious earth can any see
A city that's more beautiful than thee.
Towards the setting sun thou'rt built, and finds
The temperate breathings of the western winds.
To thee the winter colds not hurtful are,
Nor scorching heats of the Canicular.
More pure than amber is the river Clyde,
Whose gentle streams do by thy borders glide.
And here a thousand sail receive commands
To traffic for thee unto foreign lands.
A bridge of polished stone doth here vouchsafe
To travellers o'er Clyde a passage safe.
Thine orchards full of fragrant fruits and buds
Come nothing short of the Corcyran woods,
And blushing roses grow into thy fields
In no less plenty than sweet pasture yields.
Thy pastures, flocks; thy fertile ground, the corn;
Thy waters, fish; thy fields the woods adorn.
Thy buildings high and glorious are, yet be
More fair within than they are outwardly.
Thy houses by thy temples are outdone –
Thy glitt'ring temples of the fairest stone.
And yet the stones of them however fair,
The workmanship exceeds, which is more rare.
Not far from thee the place of Justice stands,

Where senators do sit and give commands.
In midst of thee Apollo's court is plac't,
With the resort of all the muses grac't
To citizens in the Minerva arts
Mars valour, Juno stable wealth, impairts.
That Neptune and Apollo did, 'tis said,
Troy's famed walls rear, and their foundations laid;
But thee, O Glasgow! we may justly deem
That all the gods have been in esteem,
Which in the earth and air and ocean are,
Have join'd to build with a propitious star.

1701–1750

PRETENDING TO BE GENTLEMEN

A FISHY TALE, 1702
Thomas Morer

Thomas Morer (1651–1715) was an English chaplain to a Scottish army regiment. In 1778, five years after James Boswell and Samuel Johnson journeyed to the Western Isles, Boswell lent Johnson a copy of Morer's A Short Account of Scotland, *published in 1702. Johnson was far from impressed. 'It is sad stuff, Sir, miserably written, as books in general then were. There is now an elegance of style universally diffused. No man now writes so ill as Martin's* Account of the Hebrides *is written. A man could not write so ill, if he should try. Set a merchant's clerk now to write, and he'll do better.' The bridge referred to by Morer was erected in 1350 (in place of the wooden bridge by which William Wallace crossed the river to attack the bishop's palace) and widened and modernised in 1770.*

Glasgow is as factious as it is rich. Yet the most considerable persons for quality are well disposed to the church. But the disaffected make up that defect with number, and sometimes call the hill men or field conventiclers to assist them.

Over the river Clyde is a very fine bridge, with a great number of arches; and on the other side is a little town, which is to the suburbs of Glasgow, as Southwark is to London. The sight of the river and the arms of Glasgow (being a fish with a ring in his mouth) put me in mind of this story, as the inhabitants report it.

A young lady being courted by a gentleman living not far from Glasgow, was presented with a ring, which after marriage, going over the river, she accidentally let fall into the water. A while after, the husband missing the ring grew jealous, and suspected she had given it to some other man whom she fancied better. This created great discontent, nor could the archbishop himself reconcile them, though he earnestly and often endeavour'd it; till one day walking in a green by the river-side, and seeing the fishermen drawing their nets, it so happened that the bishop made a purchase of the draught, and in the mouth of one of the fishes found the ring, which had occasioned so much animosity and quarrels between the man and his wife. The bishop immediately carries the ring to the husband, convinces him of his wife's innocency, and so without much difficulty reconciles them again. And from the strangeness of the event, from this time forward, was made the arms of the town.

CLEANEST AND BEAUTIFULLEST CITY IN BRITAIN . . . 1726
Daniel Defoe

Best known as the author of Robinson Crusoe *(1719), Daniel Defoe (1660–1731) was born in London. Throughout his life he travelled widely. He was a prolific writer and pamphleteer, whose work included polemics, novels, biographies and curiosities such as* The Complete Englishman, *which did not appear until 1890.* A Tour Through the Whole Island of Britain, *from which the present extract is taken, was published in three volumes between 1724 and 1726. Previously, he was employed by Robert Harley, a prominent politician. In exchange for securing his release from prison, Defoe agreed to act as Harley's emissary, travelling throughout Britain on fact-finding missions. Two years before the 1707 Union, Defoe spent considerable time in Scotland spying on Harley's behalf, from where he wrote: 'I am perfectly unsuspected as corresponding with anybody in England. I converse with Presbyterian, Episcopal-Dissenter, papist and Non-Juror, and I hope with equal circumspection. I flatter you will have no complaints of my conduct. I have faithful emissaries in every company and I talk to everybody in my own way. To the merchants I am about to settle here in trade, building ships etc. With the lawyers I want to purchase a house and land to bring my family and live upon it (God knows where there is money to pay for it). Today I am going into partnership with a Member of Parliament in a glass house, tomorrow with another in a salt work . . . I am all to everyone that I may gain some.' It is worth noting that Glasgow, like most Scottish burghs, voted against the Union and that its 'rabble' took to the streets to make its opposition known.*

With the division of Cunningham, I quitted the shire of Ayre, and the pleasantest country in Scotland, without exception: joining it to the north, and bordering on the Clyde itself, I mean the river, lies the little shire of Renfrew, or rather a barony, or a sheriff-dom, call it as you will.

It is a pleasant, rich, and populous, though small country, lying on the south bank of the Clyde; the soil is not thought to be so good as in Cunningham: but that is abundantly supplied by the many good towns, the neighbourhood of Glasgow, and of the Clyde, and great commerce of both. We kept our route as near along the coast as we could, from Irwin; so that we saw all the coast of the Firth of Clyde, and the very opening of the Clyde itself, which is just at the west point, or corner of this country, for it comes to a narrow point just in that place. There are some villages and fishing towns within the mouth of the Clyde, which have more business than large port towns in Galloway and Carrick: but the first town of note is called Greenock; 'tis not an ancient place, but seems to be grown up in later years, only by being a good road for ships, and where the ships ride that come into, and go out from Glasgow, just as the ships for London do in the downs. It has a castle to command the road, and the town is well built, and has many rich trading families in it. It is the chief town on the west of Scotland for the herring fishing; and the merchants of Glasgow, who are concerned in the fishery, employ the Greenock vessels for the catching and curing the fish, and for several parts of their other trades, as well as carrying them afterwards abroad to market.

Their being ready on all hands to go to sea, makes the Glasgow merchants often leave their ships to the care of these Greenock men; and why not? for they are sensible they are their best seamen; they are also excellent pilots for those difficult seas.

The country between Pasely and Glasgow, on the bank of Clyde, I take to be one of the most agreeable places in Scotland, take its situation, its fertility, healthiness, the nearness of Glasgow, the neighbourhood of the sea, and altogether, I may say, I saw none like it.

I am now come to the bank of the Clyde: the Clyde and the Tweed may be said to cross Scotland in the south, their sources being not many miles asunder; and the two Firths, from the Firth of Clyde to the Firth of Forth, have not an interval of above twelve or fourteen miles. Nor can I refrain mentioning how easy a work it would be to form a navigation, I mean a navigation of art from the Forth to the Clyde, and so join the two seas, as the King of France has done in a place five times as far, and five hundred miles as difficult, namely from Thouloze to Narbonne. What an advantage in commerce this would be, opening the Irish trade to the merchants of Glasgow, making a communication between the west coast of Scotland, and the east coast of England, and even to London itself; nay, several ports of England, on the Irish Sea, from Liverpool northward, would all trade with London by such a canal.

I am now crossed the Clyde to Glasgow, and I went over dry-footed without the bridge; on which occasion I cannot but observe how different a face the river presented itself in, at those two several times when only I was there; at the first, being in the month of June, the river was so low, that not the horses and carts only passed it just above the bridge, but the children and boys playing about, went everywhere, as if there was no river, only some little spreading brook, or wash, like such as we have at Enfield-Wash, Chelston-Wash in Middlesex. But my next journey satisfied me, when coming into Glasgow from the east side, I found the river not only had filled up all the arches of the bridge, to the infinite damage of the inhabitants, besides putting them into the greatest consternation imaginable, for fear of their houses being driven away by the violence of the water, and the whole city was not without apprehension that their bridge would have given way too, which would have been a terrible loss to them, for 'tis as fine a bridge as most in Scotland.

Glasgow is, indeed, a very fine city; the four principal streets are the fairest for breadth, and the finest built that I have ever seen in one city together. The houses are all of stone, and generally equal and uniform in height, as well as in front; the lower storey generally stands on vast square Doric columns, not round pillars, and arches between give passage into the shops, adding to the strength as well as beauty of the building; in a word, 'tis the cleanest and beautifullest, and best-built city in Britain, London excepted.

Glasgow is a city of business; here is the face of trade, as well foreign as home trade; and I may say, 'tis the only city in Scotland, at this time, that apparently increases and improves in both. The Union has answered its end to them more than any other part of Scotland, for their trade is new-formed by it; and, as the Union opened the door to the Scots in our American colonies, the Glasgow merchants presently fell in with the opportunity; and though, when the Union was making, the rabble of Glasgow made the most formidable attempt to prevent it, yet, now they know better, for they have the greatest addition to their trade by it imaginable; and I am assured, that they send near fifty sail of ships every year to Virginia, New England, and other English colonies in America, and are every year increasing.

NOTHING BUT GOOD LOOKS AND FINE CLOTHES, 1743
Alexander Carlyle

Alexander Carlyle (1722–1805), who was nicknamed 'Jupiter' because of his imposing demeanour, was born in East Lothian and educated at the universities of Edinburgh, Glasgow and Leiden. From 1748 until his death he was minister at Inveresk on the outskirts of Musselburgh. He had a wide circle of friends, including David Hume, Adam Smith and Tobias Smollett. Unlike many of his fellow clergy he was fond of the theatre, liked to dance and was a keen card player. Unsubstantiated rumours suggest that he once rode naked over the links at Musselburgh. His remembrance of Glasgow, which appeared in his posthumously published popular Autobiography, *while fond and colourful, also displays the sense of innate superiority that is an enduring Edinburgh trait.*

The city of Glasgow at this time, though very industrious, wealthy, and commercial, was far inferior to what it afterwards became, both before and after the failure of the Virginia trade.

The modes of life, too, and manners, were different from what they are at present. Their chief branches were the tobacco trade with the American colonies, and sugar and rum with the West India. There were not manufacturers sufficient, either there or at Paisley, to supply an outward-bound cargo for Virginia. For this purpose they were obliged to have recourse to Manchester. Manufacturers were in their infancy. About this time the inkle manufactory was first begun by Ingram & Glasford, and was shown to strangers as a great curiosity. But the merchants had industry and stock, and the habits of business, and were ready to seize with eagerness, and prosecute with vigour, every new object in commerce or manufactures that promised success.

Few of them could be called learned merchants; yet there was a weekly club, of which Provost Cochrane was the founder and a leading member, in which their express design was to inquire into the nature and principles of trade in all its branches, and to communicate their knowledge and views on that subject to each other. I was not acquainted with Provost Cochrane at this time, but I observed that members of this society had the highest admiration of his knowledge and talents. I became well acquainted with him twenty years afterwards, when Drs Smith and Wight were members of the club, and was made sensible that too much could not be said of his accurate and extensive knowledge, of his agreeable manners, and colloquial eloquence. Dr Smith acknowledged his obligations to this gentleman's information, when he was collecting materials for his *Wealth of Nations*; and the junior merchants who have flourished since his time, and extended their commerce far beyond what was then dreamt of, confess, with respectful remembrance, that it was Andrew Cochrane who first opened and enlarged their views.

It was not long before I was well established in close intimacy with many of my fellow-students, and soon felt the superiority of an education at the College of Edinburgh; not in point of knowledge, or acquirements in the languages or sciences, but in knowledge of the world, and a certain manner and address that can only be attained in the capital. It must be confessed that at this time they were far behind in Glasgow, not only in their manner of living, but in those accomplishments and that taste that belong to people of opulence, much more to persons of education. There were only a few families of ancient citizens who pretended to be gentlemen; and a few others, who were recent settlers there, who had obtained wealth and consideration in trade. The rest were shopkeepers and mechanics, or successful pedlars, who occupied large warerooms full of manufactures of all sorts, to furnish a cargo to Virginia. It was usual for the sons of merchants to attend the college for one or two years, and a few of them completed their academical education. In this respect the females were still worse off, for at that period there was neither a teacher of French nor of music in the town. The consequence of this was twofold; first, the young ladies were entirely without accomplishments, and in general had nothing to recommend them but good looks and fine clothes, for their manners were ungainly. Secondly, the few who were distinguished drew all the young men of sense and taste about them; for, being void of frivolous accomplishments, which in some respects make all women equal, they trusted only to superior understanding and wit, to natural elegance and unaffected manners.

The manner of living, too, at this time, was but coarse and vulgar. Very few of the wealthiest gave dinners to anybody but English riders, or their own relations at Christmas holidays. There were not half-a-dozen families in town who had menservants; some of those were kept by the professors who had boarders. There were neither post-chaises nor hackney-coaches in the town, and only about three or four sedan-chairs for carrying midwives about in the night, and old ladies to church, or to the dancing assemblies once-a-fortnight.

The principal merchants, fatigued with the morning business, took an early dinner, and then resorted to the coffeehouse or tavern to read the newspapers, which they generally did in companies of four or five in separate rooms, over a bottle of claret or a bowl of punch. But they never stayed supper, but always went home by nine o'clock, without company or further amusement. At last an arch fellow from Dublin, a Mr Cockaine, came to be master of the chief coffeehouse, who seduced them gradually to stay supper by placing a few nice cold things at first on the table, as relishers to the wine, till he gradually led them on to bespeak fine hot suppers, and to remain till midnight.

There was an order of women at that time in Glasgow, who, being either young widows not wealthy, or young women unprovided for, were set up in small grocery-shops in various parts of the town, and generally were protected and countenanced by some creditable merchant. In their back shops much time and money were consumed; for it being customary then to drink drams and white wine in the forenoon, the tipplers restored much to those shops, where there were bedrooms; and the patron, with his friends, frequently passed the evening there also, as taverns were not frequented by persons with affected characters of strict decency.

1751–1800

WHAT TO DO WITH DUNG

THE SARACEN'S HEAD, 1755
Robert Tennant

Prior to the 1750s, according to one nineteenth-century chronicler, Glasgow 'possessed no inns for the accommodation of travellers, except small public houses to which stabling was attached, and the signboard of these petty hostelries generally bore the well-known intimation to wayfarers of "Entertainment for men and horses here".' The first purpose-built inn in the city was the Saracen's Head, built in 1755, with stones recycled from the nearby medieval archbishop's palace. The land was donated by Glasgow magistrates. It had thirty-six rooms and a large meeting room which could accommodate one hundred people. It soon acquired a good reputation and was used by judges on the circuit. In 1779, the 'Sarrie Heid', as it soon became known, hosted a charity dinner, attended by members of the nobility and country gentry who were pleasantly surprised to see 'fifteen or sixteen elegant young cooks, with white aprons' acting as waitresses. Robert Tennant, its original owner, told the Glasgow Courant*:*

The bed-chambers are all separate, none of them entering through another, and so contrived that there is no need of going out of doors to get to them. The beds are all very good, clean and free from bugs.

THE HUNT FOR THOMAS DIDDY, *c.* 1770s
Advert in a Glasgow paper

Glasgow's – and Scotland's – role in the slave trade has long been under-acknowledged, ignored and brushed under the carpet. While it is true that few vessels left Scottish ports for Africa to participate in this abhorrent business, and that Scots were at the forefront of the abolitionist movement, there can be no doubt that Scots in general and Glaswegians in particular were no innocent bystanders as human beings were treated like animals and traded like commodities.

From his master's house in Glasgow, on the morning of Saturday 3d current, A NEGRO MAN. He is about 35 years of age, and 5 feet 9 or 10 inches high, pretty broad and stout made, broad faced, and somewhat yellowish complexioned. The white of his eyes are remarkably tinged with black, and he has a fairly gloomy aspect. His dress when he ran off, was an olive-coloured thickset coat, jacket and breeches, a black wig tied behind, and silver buckles in his shoes: but as they were all good, it is probable he would change them for worse, and thereby supply himself with cash.

His name is THOM, but sometimes he assumes the name of THOMAS DIDDY.

A Reward of FIVE GUINEAS, and payment of all reasonable charges, is hereby offered to secure said Negro in any jail in Scotland, so he may be kept safe, and delivered to his Master's order. The money to be paid by Mr John Alston merchant in Glasgow, upon notice being sent to him of the Negro's being secured.

All shipmasters are hereby cautioned against carrying the said Negro abroad; and if any person harbours him, or assists him in making his escape, they will be prosecuted therefor.

BEST OF THE SECOND-RATE, 1771
Thomas Pennant

Hailing from Wales, Thomas Pennant (1726–98) combined his interests in the natural world and travelling, about which he wrote copiously. His travel writings were admired by Samuel Johnson and James Boswell, though the latter disapproving of his portrait of Scotland. Pennant, remarked Johnson, is 'the best traveller I ever read; he observes more things than any one else does'. This, thought Boswell, 'was too high praise of a writer who had traversed a wide extent of country in such haste'.

Reach Glasgow; the best built of any second-rate city I ever saw: the houses of stone, and in general well built, and many in good taste, plain and unaffected. The principal street runs east and west, is near a mile and a half long, but unfortunately not straight; yet the view from the cross, where the two other great streets fall into this, has an air of vast magnificence. The tolbooth is large and handsome, with the apt motto on the front:

> *Haec domus odit, amat, punit, conservat, honorat,*
> *nequitiam, pacem, crimina, jura, probos.*

Next to the exchange: within is a spacious room, with full-length portraits of all our monarchs since James I, and an excellent one, by Ramsay, of Archibald, Duke of Argyle, in his robes as Lord of Sessions. Before the exchange is a large equestrian statue of King William. This is the finest and broadest part of the street: many of the houses are built over arcades, but too narrow to be walked in with any conveniency. Numbers of other streets cross this at right angles.

The market-places are great ornaments to the city, the fronts being done up in very fine taste, and the gates adorned with columns of one or other of the orders. Some of these markets are for meal, greens, fish or flesh: there are two for the last which have conduits of water out of several of the pillars, so that they are constantly kept sweet and neat. Before these buildings were constructed, most of those articles were sold in the public streets; and even after the market-places were built, the magistrates with great difficulty compelled the people to take advantage of such cleanly innovations.

Near the meal-market is the public granary, to be filled on any apprehension of scarcity.

The guardhouse is in the great street; where the inhabitants mount guard, and regularly do duty. An excellent police is observed here; and proper officers attend the markets to prevent abuses.

A MEDIOCRITY OF KNOWLEDGE, 1773
Samuel Johnson

James Boswell (1740–95) had long hoped to bring his hero, Samuel Johnson (1709–84), to his native Scotland and, in particular, to the Western Isles. Finally, in the autumn of 1773, he realised his ambition. The pair set off from Edinburgh – 'a city too well known to admit description' – and crossed the Firth of Forth, heading up the north-east coast before travelling westward, via Banff, Elgin and Inverness (where the intrepid duo bade 'farewell to the luxury of travelling'), to the Highlands and Islands about which Johnson wrote with his usual forthrightness. Glasgow was one of the last stops on a journey that provided a template for countless future wayfarers.

To describe a city so much frequented as Glasgow, is unnecessary. The prosperity of its commerce appears by the greatness of many private houses, and a general appearance of wealth. It is the only episcopal city whose cathedral was left standing in the rage of the Reformation. It is now divided into many separate places of worship, which, taken all together, compose a great pile, that had been some centuries in the building, but was never finished; for the change of religion intercepted its progress, before the cross isle was added, which seems essential to a Gothick cathedral.

The college has not had a sufficient share of the increasing magnificence of the place. The session was begun; for it commences on the tenth of October, and continues to the tenth of June, but the students appeared not numerous, being, I suppose, not yet returned from their several homes. The division of the academical year into one session, and one recess, seems to me better accommodated to the present state of life, than that variegated of time by terms and vacations derived from distant centuries, in which it was probably convenient, and still continued in the English universities. So many solid months as the Scotch scheme of education joins together, allow and encourage a plan for each part of the year; but with us, he that has settled himself to study in the college is soon tempted into the country, and he that has adjusted his life in the country, is summoned back to his college.

Yet when I have allowed to the universities of Scotland a more rational distribution of time, I have given them, so far as my inquiries have informed me, all that they can claim. The students, for the most part, go thither boys, and depart before they are men; they carry with them little fundamental knowledge, and therefore the superstructure cannot be lofty. The grammar schools are not generally well supplied; for the character of a school-master being there less honourable than in England, is seldom accepted by men who are capable to adorn it, and where the school has been deficient, the college can effect little.

Men bred in the universities of Scotland cannot be expected to be often decorated with the splendours of ornamental erudition, but they obtain a mediocrity of knowledge, between learning and ignorance, not inadequate to the purposes of common life, which is, I believe, very widely diffused among them, and which countenanced in general by a national combination so invidious, that their friends cannot defend it, and actuated in particulars by a spirit of enterprise so vigorous, that their enemies are constrained to praise it, enables them to find, or to make their way to employment, riches, and distinction.

HAVE YOU EVER SEEN BRENTFORD? 1773
James Boswell

In his journal of the tour of the Western Isles he undertook with Samuel Johnson, James Boswell was as keen to relay what his companion was doing and saying as to describe the people and places visited. But though he was in awe of Johnson, Boswell was a brilliant and colourful reporter and his biography of Johnson, which drew heavily on his infamous journal, is one of the main reasons why the great polymath is still remembered. Boswell was born in Edinburgh, the eldest son of Lord Auchinleck. He studied law at Glasgow but his passion was for literature and making friends with the famous. He first met Dr Johnson in a bookshop in London in 1763. When he told Johnson that he came from Scotland, he was told: 'That, Sir, I find, is what a great many of your countrymen cannot help.'

On our arrival at the Saracen's Head . . . I was made happy by good accounts from home; and Dr Johnson, who had not received a single letter since we left Aberdeen, found here a great many, the perusal of which entertained him much. He enjoyed in imagination the comforts which we could now command, and seemed to be in high glee. I remember, he put a leg on each side of the grate, and said, with mock solemnity, by way of soliloquy, but loud enough for me to hear it, 'Here am I, an *English* man, sitting by a *coal* fire.'

The professors of the university being informed of our arrival, Dr Stevenson, Dr Reid and Mr Anderson, breakfasted with us. Mr Anderson accompanied us while Dr Johnson viewed this beautiful city. He had told me that, one day in London, when Dr Adam Smith was boasting of it, he turned to him and said, 'Pray, sir, have you ever seen Brentford?'

DUNG-MOVING, 1781
Glasgow Mercury

An extract from an advertisement placed by the magistrates of Glasgow, who were clearly determined to force their fellow citizens to clean up their act.

That all proprietors of houses in this city shall, as soon as the season will admit, remove all water-barges, and fix and erect rones and pipes for the purpose of conveying the water from the eaves of of their respective buildings; so constructed as to prevent loose slates from falling upon the streets; and it is recommended to those the inhabitants who have already conveyed down their water in this manner that they will cause their pipes to be lengthened so as to prevent inconvenience to the public in rainy weather.

That all persons using ladders for repairing houses shall remove the same every evening before sunset, and no mason or slater, or any person working on the roofs of the houses in this city, shall throw over rubbish of any kind without keeping a person as a watch to prevent danger to the inhabitants.

That the person or persons having properties in dunghills in the closes opposite to which the dung of the street is laid down, shall remove the same in twelve hours after it is collected by the scavengers, and no dung going to the country will be suffered to remain on the street after sunset on any pretext whatsoever.

That all boys shall be discharged by their parents and masters from playing tops, shinty, or using any diversion whatever upon the flags [flagstones] that may be incommodious to the inhabitants; they are likewise discharged from playing shinty on the Green.

That no person shall shake carpets, or throw water or nastiness over any of the windows of this city.

That all boys, or others, who shall be detected at any time, throwing stones, making bonfires, crying for illuminations, or attempting to make any disturbance on the streets of this city, calculated to endanger public peace, shall be punished with the utmost severity. On all such occasions parents and masters are to be accountable for their children or apprentices, and a reward is hereby offered of Five Pounds sterling to any person who shall detect or discover boys, or others, guilty of these practices, to be paid on conviction of the offenders.

That as the poor who have a right to the charity of the city are amply provided for, it is earnestly recommended to the inhabitants to give their assistance in suppressing and discouraging vagrant and public beggars.

That all horses going to water shall on no pretence be rode hard, nor shall any person be permitted to gallop through the streets or avenues of this city.

1801–1850

HAUNTS OF VAGRANCY

GLASGOW GREEN, 23 AUGUST, 1803
Dorothy Wordsworth

Accompanied by her brother William, and for a short period by Samuel Taylor Coleridge, Dorothy Wordsworth (1771–1855) travelled north from their home in the Lake District on a tour of Scotland which took them through the Scottish Lowlands and south-western Highlands. As summer slid into autumn they covered over 660 miles. On their return home, Dorothy recorded with warmth and poetic imagery her impressions in a journal she entitled Recollections of a Tour Made in Scotland, A.D. 1803.

A cold morning. Walked to the bleaching ground [Glasgow Green], a large field bordering on the Clyde, the banks of which are perfectly flat, and the general face of the country is nearly so in the neighbourhood of Glasgow. This field, the whole summer through, is covered with women of all ages, children, and young girls spreading out their linen, and watching it while it bleaches. The scene must be very cheerful on a fine day, but it rained when we were there, and though there was linen spread out in all parts, and great numbers of women and girls were at work, yet there would have been many more on a fine day, and they would have appeared happy, instead of stupid and cheerless. In the middle of the field is a wash-house, whither the inhabitants of this large town, rich and poor, send or carry their linen to be washed. There are two very large rooms, with each a cistern in the middle for hot water; and all round the rooms are benches for the women to set their tubs upon. Both the rooms were crowded with washers; there might be a hundred or two, or even three; for it is not easy to form an accurate notion of so great a number; however, the rooms were large, and they were both full. It was amusing to see so many women, arms, head, and face all in motion, all busy in an ordinary household employment, in which we are accustomed to see, at the most, only three or four women employed in one place. The women were very civil. I learnt from them the regulations of the house; but I have forgotten the particulars. The substance of them is, that 'so much' is to be paid for each tub of water, 'so much' for a tub, and the privilege of washing for a day and, 'so much' to the general onlookers of the linen, when it is left to be bleached. An old man and woman have this office, who were walking about, two melancholy figures.

The shops of Glasgow are large, and like London shops, and we passed by the largest coffee-shop I ever saw. You look across the piazza of the Exchange, and see to the end of the coffee-room, where there is a circular window, the width of the room. Perhaps there might be thirty gentlemen sitting on the circular bench at the window, each reading a newspaper. They had the appearance of figures in a fantoccine, or men seen at the extremity of the opera-house, diminished into puppets.

INDESCRIBABLY UNDERBRED, 1818
Elizabeth Grant of Rothiemurchus

Born in Edinburgh, the daughter of a Highland landowner, Elizabeth Grant (1797–1885) spent her formative years in London, holidaying in Scotland in summer. In 1814, the family returned permanently to Edinburgh. She is known chiefly for her diary, Memoirs of a Highland Lady *(1898) and its sequel,* The Highland Lady in Ireland.

Glasgow was not a place to improve in. We were there once, I forget in what year. My father went to collect evidence in some political business, my Mother and I with him, as a cloke I suppose. We were at Aunt Leitch's pretty new house in St Vincent Street, and she took a great deal of trouble for us in making up parties at home, engagements abroad, and even directed an Assembly. We were not very refined in manners in Edinburgh, some of us, but there were brains with us, abilities of a high order, turned to a more intellectual account than could be the general employment of them in a mere manufacturing seaport town, for into that had Glasgow sunk. Its college, as to renown, was gone; its merchants no longer the Cadets of the neighbouring old County families, but their clerks of low degree shot up into the high places. 'Some *did* remain who in vain mourned the *better* days when they were young,' but as a whole the Society was indescribably underbred.

THE NATIONAL JEALOUSY OF THE ENGLISH, 1818

Sir Walter Scott

The influence and importance of Sir Walter Scott (1771–1832) is incalculable. Born in Edinburgh, he is forever associated with the Borders, where he built a house, Abbotsford, on the banks of the Tweed near Melrose. Called to the Bar in 1792, he combined a career in the law with writing. His first fame came as a poet but it is as a novelist that he is best remembered. His first novel, Waverley, *appeared anonymously in 1814, but his secret was soon out. Many others followed and drew admirers from across the globe. The following extract is taken from* Rob Roy *(1817), which is set immediately before the Jacobite rising of 1715. One of its main characters, and a great favourite with readers, is Bailie Nicol Jarvie of Glasgow.*

We now pursued our journey to the northwestward, at a rate much slower than that at which we had achieved our nocturnal retreat from England. One chain of barren and uninteresting hills succeeded another, until the more fertile vale of Clyde opened upon us, and with such dispatch as we might we gained the town, or, as my guide pertinaciously termed it, the city of Glasgow. Of late years, I understand, it has fully deserved the name, which, by a sort of political second sight, my guide distinguished it. An extensive and increasing trade with the West Indies and American colonies, has, if I am rightly informed, laid the foundation of wealth and prosperity, which, carefully strengthened and built upon, may one day support an immense fabric of commercial prosperity; but, in the earlier time of which I speak, the dawn of this splendour had not arisen. The Union had, indeed, opened to Scotland the trade to the English colonies; but, betwixt want of capital, and the national jealousy of the English, the merchants of Scotland were as yet excluded, in a great measure, from the exercise of the privileges which that memorable treaty conferred upon them. Glasgow lay on the wrong side of the island for participating in the east country or continental trade, by which the trifling commerce as yet produced in Scotland chiefly supported itself. Yet, though she then gave small promise of the commercial eminence to which, I am informed, she seems now likely one day to attain, Glasgow, as the principal central town of the western district of Scotland, was a place of considerable rank and importance. The broad and brimming Clyde, which flows so near its walls, gave the means of an inland navigation of some importance. Not only the fertile plains in its immediate neighbourhood, but the districts of Ayr and Dumfries regarded Glasgow as their capital, to which they transmitted their produce, and received in return such necessaries and luxuries as their consumption required.

The dusky mountains of the Western Highlands often sent forth wilder tribes to frequent the marts of St Mungo's favourite city. Hordes of wild, shaggy, dwarfish cattle and ponies, conducted by Highlanders, as wild, as shaggy, and sometimes as dwarfish as the animals they had in charge, often traversed the streets of Glasgow. Strangers gazed with surprise on the antique and fantastic dress, and listened to the unknown and dissonant sounds of their language, while the mountaineers, armed even while engaged in this peaceful occupation with musket and pistol, sword, dagger, and target, stared with astonishment on the articles of luxury of which they knew not the use, and with avidity which seemed somewhat alarming upon the articles which they knew and valued. It is always with unwillingness that the Highlander quits his deserts, and at this early period it was like tearing a pine from its rock to plant him elsewhere. Yet even then the mountain glens were over-peopled, until thinned occasionally by famine or by the sword, and many of their inhabitants strayed down to Glasgow – there formed settlements – there sought and found employments, though different, indeed, from those of their native hills. This supply of a hardy and useful population was of consequence to the prosperity of the place, furnished the means of carrying on the few manufactures which the town already boasted, and laid the foundation of its future prosperity.

The exterior of the city corresponded with these promising circumstances. The principal street was broad and important, decorated with public buildings, of an architecture rather striking than correct in point of taste, and running between rows of tall houses, built with stone, the fronts of which were occasionally richly ornamented with mason-work, a circumstance which gave the street an imposing air of dignity and grandeur, of which most English towns are in some measure deprived, by the slight, unsubstantial, and perishable quality and appearance of the bricks with which they are constructed.

GLASGOW INVADES EDINBURGH, 1819

Henry Thomas Cockburn

Towards the end of 1819 economic distress was acute and there were many popular disturbances throughout Britain. These were called the 'Radical War'. There were few such disturbances in Scotland, but a rumour spread that 'the Radical Army' would march from Glasgow and 'capture' Edinburgh on the last night of the year. The following extract shows just how seriously this supposed threat was taken. Henry Cockburn (1779–1854) was Edinburgh born, bred and educated. He was called to the Bar in 1800 and in 1830 he became Solicitor-General for Scotland. A year later he was elected Rector of Glasgow University. He was the author of Memorials of His Time *(1856), from which the following is taken.*

The perfect facility with which a party of forty or fifty thousand weavers could march from Glasgow, and seize upon the Banks and Castle of Edinburgh, without ever being heard of till they appeared in our streets, was demonstrated. Our magistrates therefore invited all loyal citizens to congregate, with such arms as they had, at various assigned posts. I repaired to the Assembly rooms in George Street, with a stick, about eight in the evening. The streets were as quiet as an ordinary Sunday; but their silence was only held by the excited to forebode the coming storm. There seemed to be nobody abroad except those who, like myself, were repairing to their forlorn hopes. On entering the large room, I found at least 400 or 500 grown gentlemen, pacing about, dressed coarsely, as if for work, according to taste or convenience, with bludgeons, fowling pieces, dirks, cane-swords, or other implements. A zealous banker laboured under two small swivels set on stocks, one under each arm. Frivolity, though much provoked, and a good deal indulged in corners, was reproved as unbecoming the crisis. At last, about ten p.m., the horn of the Glasgow coach was heard, and the Lord Provost sent us word from the council chamber that we might retire for the night. We never met again.

THE RITUAL OF PUNCH-MAKING, 1819
J.G. Lockhart

Born in Lanarkshire, the son of a Church of Scotland minister, John Gibson Lockhart (1794–1854) spent his boyhood in Glasgow, where he graduated from the High School to college. Aged 13, he went up to Balliol College, Oxford, where in 1813 he took a first in classics. In 1820 he married Sophia, the eldest daughter of Sir Walter Scott, whose first and fabled biographer he subsequently became. A caustic wit and occasionally savage critic, his book, Peter's Letters to his Kinsfolk *(1819) makes fun at the expense of the Edinburgh intellectuals and the bourgeoisie.*

The sugar being melted with a little cold water, the artist squeezed about a dozen lemons through a wooden strainer, and then poured in enough water almost to fill the bowl. In this state, the liquor goes by the name of sherbet, and a few of the connoisseurs in his immediate neighbourhood were requested to give their opinion of it – for in the mixing of the sherbet lies, according to the Glasgow creed, at least one half of the whole battle. This being approved by an audible smack of the lips of the umpires, the rum was added to the beverage, I suppose, in something about the proportion of one to seven. Last of all, the maker cuts a few limes, and running each section rapidly round the rim of his bowl, squeezed in enough of this more delicate acid to flavour the whole composition. In this consists the true *tour de maitre* of the punch-maker.

Glasgow punch should be made of the coldest spring water taken from the spring. The acid ingredients above mentioned will suffice for a very large bowl.

AN INVINCIBLE NOSE, 1819
Robert Southey

The son of a Bristol linen-draper, Robert Southey (1774–1843) was brought up by an eccentric aunt who indulged his love of reading. He was appointed poet laureate in 1813, a position he grew to loathe and for which he received much mockery from among others Lord Byron. He wrote copiously, prose as well as poetry, on subjects as diverse as the history of Brazil, the Peninsular War and Admiral Nelson. He also liked to travel and was often drawn, as this excerpt from his Journal of a Tour of Scotland *shows, to things usually overlooked.*

A City like Glasgow is a hateful place for a stranger, unless he is reconciled to it by the comforts of hospitality and society. In any other case the best way is to reconnoitre it, so as to know the outline and outside, and to be contented with such other information as books can supply. Argyle Street is the finest part; it has a mixture of old and new buildings, but is long enough and lofty enough to be one of the best streets in G. Britain. The Cathedral is the only edifice of its kind in Scotland which received no external injury at the Reformation. Two places of worship have been neatly fitted up within. I observed, however, three things deserving of reprobation. The window in one of these kirks had been made to imitate painted glass, by painting on the glass, and this of course had a paltry and smeary appearance. The arches in those upper passages which at Westminster we used absurdly to call the nunneries, and of which I do not know the name, are filled up with an imitation of windows: these are instances of the worst possible taste. The other fault belongs to the unclean part of the national character; for the seats are so closely packed that any person who could remain there during the time of service in the warm weather, must have an invincible nose. I doubt even whether any incense could overcome so strong a smell.

I was much struck with the picturesque appearance of the monuments in the Church yard – such large ones as we have in our churches, being here ranged along the wall, so that even on the outside their irregular outline makes an impressive feature in the scene. They were digging a grave near the entrance of the Church; had it been in any other situation, I should not have learnt a noticeable thing. A frame consisting of iron rods was fixed in the grave, the rods being as long as grave was deep. Within this frame the coffin was to be let down and buried, and then an iron cover fitted on to the top of the rods, and strongly locked. When there is no longer any apprehension of danger for the resurrection-men, the cover is unlocked and the frame drawn out: a month it seems is the regular term. This invention, which is not liable to the same legal obligations as the iron coffins, is about two years old. The price paid for its use is a shilling a day.

THE ROGUERIES OF THE BROOMIELAW, 1825
John Gibson Lockhart

It is often said that Sir Walter Scott invented tourism in Scotland. But long before his novels and poems sent folk flocking to the Trossachs, Glaswegians had discovered the delight of a trip down the Clyde. Here John Gibson Lockhart, Scott's son-in-law and biographer, recalls a memorable occasion when the 'Wizard of the North' experienced Glasgow hospitality at first hand. Broomielaw, situated on the north bank of the Clyde immediately west of Glasgow Bridge, means a 'gorse or broom-covered slope'.

A voyage down the Firth of Clyde is enough to make anybody happy; nowhere can the home tourist, at all events, behold, in the course of one day, such a succession and variety of beautiful, romantic, and majestic scenery: on one hand, dark mountains and castellated shores – on the other, rich groves and pastures, interspersed with elegant villas and thriving towns – the bright estuary between, alive with shipping, and diversified with islands.

It may be supposed how delightful such a voyage was in a fine day of July, with Scott, always as full of glee on any trip as a schoolboy; crammed with all the traditions and legends of every place we passed; and too happy to pour them out for the entertainment of his companions on deck. After dinner, too, he was the charm of the table. A worthy old Bailie of Glasgow sat by him, and shared fully in the general pleasure; although his particular source of interest and satisfaction was, that he had got into such close quarters with a live Sheriff and Court of Session, – and this gave him the opportunity of discussing sundry knotty points of police law, as to which our steerage passengers might perhaps have been more curious than most of those admitted to the symposium of the cabin. Sir Walter, however, was as ready for the rogueries of the Broomielaw, as for the mystic antiquities of Balclutha, or the discomforture of the Norsemen at Largs, or Bruce's adventures in Arran. I remember how this new acquaintance chuckled when he, towards the conclusion of our first bowl of punch, said he was not surprised to find himself gathering much instruction from the Bailie's conversation on his favourite topics, since the most eminent and useful of the police magistrates of London (Colquhoun) had served his apprenticeship in the Town Chamber of Glasgow. The Bailie insisted for a second bowl, and volunteered to be the manufacturer; 'for', quoth he (with a sly wink), 'I am reckoned a fair hand, though not equal to *my father the deacon*.' Scott smiled in acquiescence, and the ladies having by this time withdrawn, said he was glad to find the celebrated beverage of the city of St Mungo had not fallen into desuetude. The Bailie extolled the liquor he was brewing, and quoted Sir John Sinclair's Code of Health and Longevity for the case of a gentleman well known to himself, who lived till ninety, and had been drunk upon it evry night for half-a-century. But Bailie *** was a devout elder of the kirk, and did not tell his story without one or two groans that his doctrine should have such an example to plead. Sir Walter said, he could only hope that manners were mended in other respects since the days when a popular minister of the last age (one Mr Thom), renowned for satirical humour, as well as for high-flying zeal, had demolished all his own chances of a Glasgow benefice, by preaching before the Town-Council from this text in Hosea: 'Ephraim's drink is sour, and he hath committed whoredom continually.' The Bailie's brow darkened (like Nicol Jarvie's when they *misca'd Rab*); he groaned deeper than before and said he feared 'Tham o' Govan a ne'erdoweel.' He, however, refilled our glasses as he spoke; and Scott, as he tasted his, said, 'Weel, weel, Bailie, Ephraim was not so far wrong as to the matter of drink.'

MOLLY'S HISTORY, 1826

The Glasgow Room of the Mitchell Library is the greatest repository of the city's history, much of which was of an ephemeral nature. The story of Molly the Stuffer is to be found in the collection, in a broadsheet which appeared in 1826 and which was reprinted in Elspeth King's indispensable The Hidden History of Glasgow's Women *(1993).*

Account of the Life and Transactions of M---y G--- otherwise Molly the Stuffer, who died in the Gorbals of Glasgow, on Tuesday the 1st of August last, and who kept a Lodging House there, giving an account of the numerous scenes she was engaged in with various Lodgers who frequented her house for near 30 years, consisting of Beggars, Fortune-tellers, Rowly powly Gentry, and a host of other travelling characters, to the number of 50,000, who have, at times, been with her since she began lodgings.

The above woman was born near Lisburn in Ireland. At an early period of life, she left her native country and came to Scotland, where she, for some time, earned a livelihood, by making stiffeners for the neck, by which she gained a little money. Being of a pushing temper, and careful habits, she resolved upon bettering her condition, if possible, and accordingly took up a Lodging House in the Gorbals of Glasgow, where she continued from its commencement to the day of her death, a period of nearly 30 years, during which period, on a moderate calculation, she has afforded shelter to 50,000 stragglers, who have comfortably dozed under her hospitable roof, except when assailed by the yells of drunkards, or the moving phalanx of black and grey horsemen, aided by infantry, clothed in red, who often made an attack on their bodies, and disturbed their peaceful slumber.

Every person who had 3d. to pay for a bed, had an open door at Molly's; the beggar here could lay down his wallets, and take repose for the night; the tinker could range town and country with his vice and other implements, and return in the evening to his lodgings; the Fair attenders, with all their implements, consisting of puppets, E O tables, dice, gingerbread and sweetmeat baskets, could safely deposit them into the hands of Molly, who paid particular attention to their various articles. It would require sheets to give a definition of the motley group who attended this lodging house; travellers told one another where she resided, which soon made her a favourite all over the country, and made them flock to her hospitable roof, when their travels led them that way.

Molly, though a courageous woman, had her own to do amongst them to preserve order. In the evenings, many high words took place for the use of the fire, one wanting his pot on, another his pan, and a third his kettle, till, in the general scuffle, the contents were emptied on the floor, or on their bodies. Another party now claims the right, and the fizzing of bacon is heard, when some of the rest claiming the turn before the bacon party, wheel it off, and, in the scuffle, gravy and bacon descends to the ashes, and a scramble ensues for the fragments. Thus it goes on, either by one party or another, the whole evening, till Molly's tongs, or some other weapon, comes across the back of some of the most outrageous.

Molly's situation was not to be envied – she had many duties to perform – but none was ever fitter for a situation of the kind. The drunkard she could advise to bed – the known thief she kept out – and if there were any in her house, of whom she was suspicious, she at the expense of rest, watched them narrowly, for she had great responsibility on her.

Molly was about 60 years of age when she died, was several times married, and it is said, had earned some little. She was kind, hospitable and charitable, and was respected (notwithstanding her vocation) in the neighbourhood where she resided. The stranger never wanted food or a bed, though he had no money, did Molly but know the circumstances.

BREAD, BEEF AND BEER, 1832
William Cobbett

In bygone times travellers in Scotland rarely had a good word to say about its food and drink. No one was more scathing than Samuel Johnson, whose definition of 'oats' – 'A grain, which in England is generally given to horses, but in Scotland supports the people' – still rankles. William Cobbett (1763–1835) was clearly a more charitable, open-minded and enlightened fellow. The son of a farmer, he was born in Surrey. A political radical, he was a champion of the poor. He travelled widely, teaching, farming and writing. Latterly, he became a Member of Parliament. His book, Rural Rides *(1830) is a delightful picture of a world disappearing almost as fast as Cobbett could record its passing.*

When we got to Glasgow, we alighted at a hotel; and though I was engaged to take up my quarters at the house of Mr David Bell, Clyde Buildings, as I had not breakfasted, I therefore set to that work at the inn, without loss of time, upon everything that is good, but particularly upon some *tender* beef-steaks; a thing I have not met with before in more than one out of ten beef-steak jobs in my life: and, I may as well stop here to observe, that which I have omitted before, that all the beef that I have tasted in Scotland has been excellent. It appears to come from the little oxen which the Highlands send down in such droves; and a score of which, please God to give me life, I will have next year in Surrey. I should suppose that these little oxen, when well fatted, weigh about twenty score, which is about the weight of a Hampshire hog eighteen months or two years old. The joints are, of course, small compared with the general run of beef in London. A sirloin appears to be no very great deal larger than a loin of large veal, rump and all. The meat is exceedingly fine in grain; and these little creatures will grow fat where a Devonshire or Lincolnshire ox would half starve. My project is to get a score of them, let them run upon the common till the corn-tops and blades are fit to cut, then feed them with them; after that with mangel-wurzel or Swedish turnips, and have them fat as butter in the months of March, April and May.

So much for the meat of Scotland; and now I am talking about victuals, let me observe first, that the wheaten bread, of which there is an abundance in all the towns, is just about as good as it is in London; that, besides this, there are oatcakes made very thin, which are very nice things of the bread kind, it being understood that I am speaking of such as are made in the houses of gentlemen, merchants, and persons who do not rigidly adhere to the saving of expense; for there are some of these cakes which rank with the '*brose*' mentioned in the former part of this article. Then the oatmeal, when ground and dressed in a nice manner, is made into porridge, just in the same manner as the Americans make the cornmeal into *mush*, and it is eaten with milk in just the same manner. Every morning but one, when I was at Edinburgh, it formed the principal part of my breakfast; and I greatly preferred it, and should always prefer it, to toasted bread and butter, to muffins, to crumpets, to bread and butter, or to hot rolls. This is the living in Scotland, along with plenty of eggs, very fine butter, and either Ayrshire or English cheese; and everywhere you see a sufficiency of good victuals (including poultry and game); you see it without ostentation; you see it without being compelled to sit whole hours over it; you see everything good, and everything sensibly done with regard to the victuals; and as to the drink, just as in England, you always see ten times too much of it; and I very believe that I shall be the first human being who ever came to Scotland and went out of it again, without tasting wine, spirits, beer, or cider. Everyone drinks too much; and it is not just to reproach the working people with drunkenness, if you, whose own bodily exertions do not tend to provoke thirst, set them the mischievous example, by indulging in drinks, until habit renders it a sort of necessary of life.

WILLIE WINKIE, c. 1832
William Miller

Born in Briggait in 1810, William Miller spent his early years in Parkhead, then a rural village east of the city. He had hoped to become a surgeon but a severe illness when he was 16 put paid to that ambition. He was then apprenticed to a wood-turner, a skill at which he excelled. He began early to contribute poetry to periodicals but it was the appearance of 'Willie Winkie', 'John Frost' and 'The Sleepy Bairn' in the third and fourth series of Whistle Binkie *that made his name. His poems were not published in book form till 1863, under the title of* Scottish Nursery Songs and Poems. *Latterly, Miller wrote little. He died in Glasgow in 1872, where he is buried and where, in his memory, there is a monument to him in the Necropolis. 'Willie Winkie' has been described as 'the greatest nursery song in the world'.*

Wee Willie Winkie rins through the toun,
Up stairs and doun stairs in his nicht goun,
Tirlin' at the window, cryin' at the lock,
'Are the weans in their bed, for it's now ten o'clock?'

'Hey, Willie Winkie, are ye comin' ben?
The cat's singin' grey thrums to the sleepin' hen,
The dog's speldert on the floor, and doesnae gie a cheep,
But here's a waukrife laddie that winna fa' asleep.'

Onything but sleep, you rogue, glowerin' like the moon,
Rattlin' in an airn jug wi' an airn spoon,
Rumblin', tumblin' roun' about, crawin' like a cock,
Skirlin' like a kenna-what, waukenin' sleepin' folk.

'Hey, Willie Winkie, the wean's in a creel,
Wamblin' aff a body's knee like a very eel,
Ruggin' at the cat's lug, and ravelin' a' her thrums –
Hey, Willie Winkie – see there he comes!'

Wearied is the mither that has a stourie wean,
A wee stumpie stousie that canna rin his lane,
That has a battle aye wi' sleep afore he'll close an e'e;
But a kiss frae aff his rosie lips gies strength anew to me.

COCK-FIGHTING, 1835
The New Statistical Account of Scotland

In the pursuit of diversion human beings are often cruel, especially to animals which cannot retaliate. Cockfighting, as this entry in the New Statistical Account of Scotland *shows, was for a while one of the most popular pastimes, though it was frowned on by the Kirk. Like other pastimes – golf, pitch and toss, prize-fighting, horse-racing – it was connected to gambling. It was made illegal in Scotland from 1850, although it continued underground long after that.*

In former times cock-fighting was so prevalent in this part of the country, that on certain holidays, school-boys provided cocks, and the fight was superintended by the master. But as civilisation advanced, this practice gradually disappeared, and at length the amusement in the estimation of many came under the denomination of cruelty to animals. During the latter part of the last and the beginning of the present century, cock-fighting in this city was conducted in a clandestine manner. In 1807, our cock-fighting amateurs, finding a vacant temporary building in Queen Street, made preparations for fighting a main, but when the sport had just commenced, a portion of the city and county magistrates made their appearance and dismissed the meeting. Since that period mains have occasionally been fought here without interference of the authorities. Of late, however, the desire for this amusement has so much increased, that in this year a spacious building has been erected for a cock-pit in Hope Street, on the joint stock principle. This building, which is seated for about 280 persons, has suitable accommodation for the judges, handlers, and feeders, and is inferior in nothing to the Westminster pit, but in its dimensions. The company who frequent the Glasgow cock-pit do not belong to the 'exclusives'; for here we have all grades, from the senator to the journeyman butcher.

A RECKONING, 1835
The New Statistical Account of Scotland

This extract from The New Statistical Account of Scotland *gives a cold-blooded summation of criminal activity and the penalties the perpetrators paid for their recividism.*

The average number of delinquents committed yearly during five years, ending on the 31st December 1834, was 667. From 1765 to 1830, 89 persons were executed in Glasgow, of which number 5 were females. During the first 12 years there were only 6 persons executed, whilst in the last 12 there were 37. During 66 years previously to 1831, there were 26 in which there were no executions, 15 in which there was 1 each year; ten, 2; seven, 3; four, 4; one, 5; and two in which there were 6. From the 29th of September 1830, to the 20th of January 1834, 12 persons have been executed in Glasgow, viz. 11 males, and 1 female; of whom 6 were for murder, 1 for rape, 1 for hamesucken, 1 for robbery, and 3 for housebreaking and theft. From the 4th of May 1818, to the 8th of October 1834, 6 persons received sentence of death, but had their punishment commuted to transportation for life, viz. 4 males and 2 females; of 1 for murder, 1 for hamesucken and rape, 1 for robbery, and 1 for housebreaking and theft; the two females were for issuing forged bank notes.

LESS WET THAN EDINBURGH, 1840
James Cleland

It has long been the view of smug east coasters that rain in Scotland falls mainly in the west, Glasgow being no exception. Perhaps that's why it is such a green place. But it seems that this is one of those myths urgently in need of debunking, for actually more rain falls in Edinburgh. Possibly. Incidentally, Dr Thomas Thomson (1773–1852), ever the contrarian, opposed the ideas of James Hutton (1726–97), the founding father of geology. Thomson also gave silicon its name. Born in Crieff, he was inspired to study medicine by Joseph Black (1728–99), the first scientist to discover that there are gases other than air. He was a

Fellow of the Royal Society of Edinburgh and is buried at the Glasgow Necropolis.

Dr. Thomson, Professor of Chemistry in this University, gives as a reason for the greater quantity of rain falling at Edinburgh than at Glasgow: 'that the latter place is about twenty miles inland from the west coast, and is therefore beyond the immediate influence of the Atlantic, which renders some parts of the north-west of England so rainy, while its distance from the east coast, and the high land between it and Edinburgh screen it from those violent rains, when the east wind blows, which are so common in Edinburgh. The distance from the hills from Glasgow is farther from Edinburgh, and it is in some degree screened by high grounds both on the east and west.'

QUANTITY OF RAIN: A Rain Gauge, constructed by the celebrated Crichton of Glasgow, is placed on the top of the Macfarlane Observatory in the College Garden. The Observatory is situated at some distance from houses or trees. The gauge stands about 80 feet above the Clyde at high water mark at Hutcheson's Bridge. The situation, therefore, with the exception of its height above the river, is favourable. The late Rev. Dr. Couper, Professor of Astronomy in this University, took the charge of the gauge, and prepared an annual table from the date of his induction in 1803 to 1836, with the exception of the two last years, which were drawn up since his decease by one of his sons. Dr. Couper found that the yearly average of rain which fell during 30 years was 22.175 inches. The smallest quantity which fell in any year was 14.468 in 1803, and the largest 27.801 in 1811.

GLASGOW OBSERVATORY, 1841
Thomas de Quincey

The author of Confessions of an English Opium-Eater, *de Quincey (1785–1850) lived most of his later life in Edinburgh trying to evade his many creditors. He visited Glasgow on several occasions and stayed for a spell with J.P. Nichols, Professor of Astronomy at Glasgow University. The two met in Edinburgh where de Quincey, as ever on his uppers, introduced himself and asked, 'Dr. Nichol, can you lend me two-pence?' Nichol took this in good part and invited de Quincey to his home in Glasgow. Befitting his position, Nichol lived in the Glasgow Observatory on Garnet Hill. Apparently, de Quincey was not enamoured of Glasgow but was enchanted by his temporary abode.*

What makes the Glasgow Observatory so peculiarly interesting is its position, connected with and overlooking so vast a city . . . How tarnished with eternal canopies of smoke, and of sorrow, how dark with agitations of many orders, is the mighty town below! How serene, how quiet, how lifted above the confusion, and the roar, and the strifes of earth, is the solemn observatory that crowns the heights overhead! And duly, at night, just when the toil of overwrought Glasgow is mercifully relaxing, then comes the summons to the labouring astronomer!

WRETCHED, DISSOLUTE, LOATHSOME AND PESTILENTIAL, 1842

Captain Miller, Superintendent of Police

As Glasgow's population multiplied – it increased tenfold in a century, from 30,000 in the mid-eighteenth century to around 400,000 by the 1850s – so too did its social problems, as is demonstrated in this report to both Houses of Parliament on sanitary conditions.

It is of great moment, as affecting the state of crime, that the health of the lower classes of the community be strictly adhered to. In the very centre of the city there is an accumulated mass of squalid wretchedness, which is probably unequalled in any other town in the British dominions. In the interior part of the square, bounded on the east by the Salt-market, on the west by Stockwell-street, on the north by Trongate, and on the south by the river, and also in certain parts of the east side of High-street, including the Vennals, Havannah and Burnside, there is concentrated everything that is wretched, dissolute, loathsome, and pestilential. These places are filled by a population of many thousands of miserable creatures. The houses in which they live are unfit even for sties, and every apartment is filled with a promiscuous crowd of men, women and children, all in the most revolting state of filth and squalor. In many of the houses there is scarcely any ventilation: dunghills lie in the vicinity of the dwellings; and from the extremely defective sewerage, filth of every kind constantly accumulates. In these horrid dens the most abandoned characters of the city are collected, and from thence they nightly issue to disseminate disease, and to pour upon the town every species of crime and abomination. In such receptacles, so long as they are permitted to remain, crime of every sort may be expected to abound, and unless the evil is speedily and vigorously checked, it must of necessity increase. The people who dwell in these quarters of the city are sunk to the lowest possible state of personal degradation, in whom no elevated idea can be expected to arise, and who regard themselves, from the hopelessness of their condition, as doomed to a life of wretchedness and crime. Much might be done to relieve the misery, and to repress the crime of this destitute population, by compelling attention to personal cleanliness, so as to remove and prevent disease, by placing the lodging-houses for the destitute under proper regulations; by preventing the assemblage of a large number of persons in one apartment; by opening and widening the thoroughfares, and forming new streets wherever practicable; by causing the houses to be properly ventilated, and all external nuisances removed; and by an improved plan of sewerage for carrying away all impurities. Were it possible to adopt measures something similar to these, the health of the community would be greatly improved; and by breaking up the haunts of vagrancy, a happy check would be given to the spread of profligacy and crime.

1851–1900

CITY OF MERCHANTS

THE TRIAL OF MADELEINE SMITH, 30 JUNE, 1857
The Illustrated London News

Did Madeleine Smith poison her lover Pierre Emile L'Angelier? An Edinburgh jury was unconvinced and decided the case against her was 'Not Proven', a unique Scottish verdict which has been interpreted as 'go away and don't do it again'. Smith was the daughter of a Glasgow architect who had fallen headlong for L'Angelier, the son of a French nurseryman who happened to be working in Glasgow. In the course of their affair the couple exchanged dozens of passionate, explicit letters. When she transferred her affections to another man, L'Angelier refused to return Smith's letters. Subsequently, he died from a huge dose of arsenic which could have killed a hippopotamus. In court it was revealed that Smith had been buying arsenic from a local chemist. So she had a motive and the means to kill her lover. But did she? We will never know. The trial, which was held in Edinburgh because it was believed Smith would not get a fair hearing in Glasgow, attracted international coverage. The following extract, from The Illustrated London News, *is of its opening day.*

One writer describes her appearance as more than ordinarily prepossessing. Her features, he says, express great intelligence and energy of character. Her profile is striking, the upper part of her face exhibiting considerable prominency, while the lower part is cast in a most delicate mould, and her complexion is soft and fair. Her eyes are large and dark and full of sensibility. She looks younger than her reputed age of 21, but at the same time, her countenance betrays the effect of confinement and anxiety, in an air of languor and weariness, which her natural spirits and strength of mind in vain attempt to conceal. She was elegantly but simply attired in a white straw bonnet, trimmed with white ribbon and mounted with a figured black veil, which, however, she did not make use of to conceal her face with. She had on a visite [short cloak] trimmed with lace; her gown was of brown silk. She held in her gloved hands a cambric handkerchief and a bottle of smelling salts. Her figure seemed to be less than the middle size, and girlish and slight.

Her portrait has thus been sketched by another pen: Miss Smith is about five feet two inches in height. She has an elegant figure, and can neither be called stout nor slim. She looks older than her years, which are twenty-one. I should have guessed her age to be twenty-four. Her eyes are deep-set, large, and some think beautiful; but they certainly do not look prepossessing. Her brow is of the ordinary size, and her face inclines to the oval. Her nose is prominent but is too long to be taken as a type for the Romans, and too irregular to remind one of Greece. Her complexion, in spite of prison life, is clear and fresh – indeed, blooming – unless the colour with which it was suffused was the effect of internal excitement and nervousness. Her cheeks are well coloured and the insinuation that a rosy hue is imparted by artificial means, made by some portions of the press, does not seem well founded. Her hair, of which she has a rich profusion, is quietly arranged in the fashion prevalent before the Eugenie style. She was dressed simply, yet elegantly. She wore a brown silk dress, with black silk cloak, with a small straw bonnet, trimmed with a white riband, of the fashionable shape, exposing the whole front of the head. She also had lavender coloured gloves, a white cambric handkerchief, a silver-topped smelling bottle in her hand, which she never used, and a wrapper thrown over her knee. Altogether she had a most attractive appearance, and her very aspect and demeanour seemed to advocate her cause.

During the whole day's proceedings the prisoner maintained a firm and unmoved appearance, her keen and animated expression and healthful complexion evincing how little, outwardly at least, she had suffered by the period of her imprisonment and the horror of her situation. Though, on once looking round, a dark veil was thrown over her face, the interest she took in the proceedings was yet evident. Her head never sank for a moment, and she even seemed to scan the witnesses with a scrutinising glance. Her perfect self-possession, indeed, could only be accounted for either by a proud consciousness of innocence, or by her possessing an almost unparalleled amount of self-control. She even sometimes smiled with all the air and grace of a young lady in the drawing-room, as her agents came forward at intervals to communicate with her.

The indictment charged the prisoner with intent to murder, and with murder; and it set forth that on the 19th or 20th of February last, the prisoner, in the house in Blythswood Square, Glasgow, occupied by her father, did wickedly and feloniously administer to Emile L'Angelier, now deceased, a quantity or quantities of arsenic or other poisons in cocoa or coffee, or some other article of food or drink, with intent to murder the deceased, and that he having taken the said arsenic or other poison so administered by her, did in consequence thereof suffer severe illness; that on the 22d or 23d of February she repeated the crime, and also on the 22d or 23d of March, and that he died on the latter day in consequence of the said arsenic or other poisons having been taken by him, and was thus murdered by the said Madeleine Smith.

A SUBURB OF THE DEAD, 1857
George Blair

Though Jews are renowned for their wanderlust they appear not to have discovered Glasgow until relatively recently. Their eventual arrival coincided with the exponential expansion of the city in the early nineteenth century, since when the contribution of Jews to the city's cultural and commercial growth has been considerable. Initially, many of the new immigrants came from Germany and Holland but as the nineteenth century progressed greater numbers arrived from Poland and Russia, fleeing persecution and pogroms. Between 1890 and the start of the First World War the Jewish population increased from around 2,000 to almost 6,000, most of whom lived south of the river. Today, Newton Mearns is regarded as the main Jewish centre in the west of Scotland. The following extract is taken from Biographic and Descriptive

Sketches of Glasgow Necropolis *by George Blair, a Church of Scotland minister.*

Some allowance must be made for olden prejudice, even though they do not rest on any valid principle, and therefore it is perhaps well that the burying-ground of the Jews has been placed in this sequestered corner [of the Necropolis], which may be regarded as a suburb of a beautiful city of the dead. Although the position is a partial separation, it is not an exclusion, and perhaps the arrangement is equally satisfactory to both Jew and Christian.

A beautiful gateway and ornamental column, erected at the expense of the Merchants' House, mark the spot where the children of Abraham are interred . . .

. . . Here, in this northern section of a remote island, mingling with people of whom it was once said, '*penitus toto divisos orbe Britannos*' ['Britons totally divided from the whole world'], these descendants of the Mesopotamian patriarch actually slumber in a quiet place of sepulture near a magnificent Cathedral devoted to Christian worship, and not far from a monument erected to the memory of John Knox. Everything is Christian around them, and here, in a corner of the city of the dead, is a little group of Jews, slumbering peacefully together in a place of rest at last, after being strangers and sojourners in a land to which they have given a religion, and from which they receive only a grave.

NOT WAVING BUT DROWNING, 3 MARCH, 1860
Glasgow Sentinel

In the days when the Clyde was clean there was no need for those living near its banks to go far to fetch water. Increasingly, however, it became polluted and it became imperative that uncontaminated water be piped directly into people's homes. Bringing fresh water from Loch Katrine in the Trossachs thirty-four miles from Glasgow was one of the great feats of the Victorian era, the benefits of which Glaswegians still enjoy today. Why anyone wants to buy bottled water when they can turn on their taps and drink water that tastes like nectar defies common sense. The entire project took only three years to complete but along the way there were one or two hiccups . . .

Considerable excitement was occasioned at Maryhill on Tuesday evening by the bursting of one of the large pipes by which the water from Loch Katrine is conveyed to Glasgow. The pipe burst in Main Street, nearly opposite the branch office of the Union Bank. The water for some time discharged itself into the air to a height of about 20 feet, causing great destruction of property and danger of life. In a short time every corner around for a considerable distance was entirely flooded, and so strong was the current running toward the Kelvin through Gairbraid farm steading, that in the court-yard it was impossible to pass through it. The whole of the out-houses in connection with the farm were completely flooded, particularly a byre, in which were about 40 cows, and which had a beautiful stream running down its centre. The private house of Mr Renwick, the occupier of the farm, also suffered very much; indeed in several rooms the water stood two feet deep. Mr Renwick had a beautiful garden lying to the south of the house, which has been completely destroyed. The water took this way on its course to the Kelvin, cutting up the garden fearfully – in some cases the channels thus formed were three or four feet deep – and carrying the greater part of the surface of the garden a considerable distance, as far, indeed, as the avenue leading to Beechbank Cottage, the residence of J.L. Ewing Esq. The soil thus removed from the garden choked up the avenue to the height of from three to four feet, so that to get out of his own house Mr Ewing had to go a round-about way and climb over his garden wall.

Several other families in the neighbourhood suffered severely, being forced to leave their houses; and the horses in some stables had to be removed to another resting-place for the night. The scene about half past ten was indeed pitiful and alarming. Right and left might be seen poor families labouring away with bucket and broom, doing all they could to bale out the water from their houses. The man stationed at Maryhill to take charge of the works was immediately on the spot to turn off the water. The Water Company's local engineer was prompt in his attendance. An hour, however, elapsed before the water subsided, and when it did so it left a large hole in the centre of the street where the disruption had taken place. A great many people were, of course, walking about the spot, eager to see what damage had been done; and the rest were some females. One who was walking carelessly along went right into the hole, up to the neck in water; and had it not been for the timeous assistance of some gentlemen, it is quite possible that the poor girl might have been drowned, as the hole was about five feet deep, with an insecure bottom; at all events, she could not have had much relish for her cold bath on such an evening.

THE FIRST FOOTBALL MATCH, 1868
Robert Gardner

Scots, as the American academic Arthur Herman has pointed out, invented the modern world. But one thing he neglected to mention was football. This letter, from Robert Gardner, Secretary of the Thistle football club to Queen's Park, offers cast-iron proof that the first proper match of the beautiful game was played in Glasgow on 1 August 1868.

Dear Sir,

I duly received your letter dated 25th inst. on Monday Afternoon, but as we had a Committee Meeting called for this evening at which time it was submitted, I could not reply to it earlier. I have now been requested by the Committee, on behalf of our Club, to accept the Challenge you kindly sent, for which we have to thank you, to play us a friendly Match at Football on our Ground, Queen's Park, at the hour you mentioned, on Saturday, first proximo, with Twenty players on each side. We consider, however, that Two-hours is quite long enough to play in weather such as the present, and hope this will be quite satisfactory to you. We would also suggest that if no Goals be got by either side within the first hour, that Goals be then exchanged, the ball, of course, to be kicked off from the centre of the field by the side who had the original Kick-off, so that both parties may have the same chance of wind and ground, this we think very fair and can be arranged on the field before beginning the Match. Would you also be good enough to bring your ball with you in case of any break down, and thus prevent interruption. Hoping the weather will favour the Thistle and Queen's.

I remain,
Yours very truly,
(Sgs.) Robt. Gardner
Secy.

A PENNYWORTH O' LIVER, 1869
Anonymous

It is hard now to imagine just how desperate and degrading living conditions were in the Victorian era for poor people. Compounding all of this was the rapaciousness of landlords who took great pains to ensure that their tenants kept up with their rent.

Hovels with earthen floors earned rents of six shillings a month. In Oaklands Street there were tenanted cellars that never engaged daylight. At St Andrews Lane there were no conveniences, and the human excreta was thrown over the windows, so that the window sills, the walls and the bottom of the court were 'covered with human ordure'. At Creilly's Crescent the children were 'quite dwarfed and attenuated to mere skeletons, their crooked limbs and wasted bodies and little claw-like hands all combine to give them a weird appearance'. The proprietor of Creillys' desirable mansions was a Sauchiehall Street banker who personally called for the rents, and was 'very civil to those who pay promptly, but sharper than a serpent's tooth to unfortunates who may not be able at the moment to pay up'. In 102 Main Street, Gorbals, were 46 houses, the tenants of which were all apparently liable to pay poor's rate, for we read of reports by Sheriff's officers for the poor's rate 'with expenses added'. In one house the sole article of furniture, a chest valued at 4s. 10d is seized; in another case a woman complained that 'they cam' an' took my pot aff the fire wi a pennyworth o' liver in't for poor's rate'.

A NOBLE PARK, 1872
John Tweed

Does Glasgow have more green space than elsewhere in these islands? Who would argue otherwise? For this we have to thank City Fathers who, in the nineteenth century, had such enthusiasm for setting up parks that they could eventually claim to have created more public open spaces per head of population than any other UK city. Glasgow Green was Glasgow's first public park and its most variously used, as the publisher and local historian John Tweed describes. Comprising some 136 acres, it has been used for golf, bagpiping, bowling, hockey, tennis and goodness knows what else. It is here, too, that Glasgow Rangers have their roots.

This noble park, which we enter at its east end below Rutherglen Bridge, is the largest and, in spite of the attention lavished on its new-born rivals, is in some respects perhaps the finest of which Glasgow can boast. It lacks the undulating and wooded beauty of the West-end Park, and the blooming parterres of the Queen's; but it can boast of noble elms, its well-kept footpaths, its three-mile drive, and its incomparable fields for many sports, and then, gentle reader, it serves also the purposes of a bleaching field! But that is not all; the Clyde washes its banks from Rutherglen Bridge to Jail Square; and here on summer evenings, skimming over the broad river's bosom, are crowds of skiffs, punts and jolly-boats, pulled by the rising aquatics of the east end. No part of Glasgow can boast of one-tenth of the interest of the Green on a Saturday afternoon, when its fields are dotted with cricketers, when the footballs describe their parabolic curves in the air, and when the flashing oars gleam in the sunlight as a hundred boats dart hither and thither on the river.

MARYHILL BARRACKS, 1876
Groome's Gazetteer

Before there was a reliable police force, unrest could only be calmed by the use of military force. In this respect Glasgow was no different from other places. Thus through the seventeenth, eighteenth and nineteenth centuries army units were stationed in the city. The first barracks was built in the Gallowgate in 1795 and could accommodate 1,000 men. But by the middle of the next century it had fallen into neglect and a new barracks was built at Maryhill. It was completed in 1872. Until the end of the nineteenth century it was the garrison for several regiments and after the First World War it was the permanent depot of the Highland Light Infantry. It is now a housing scheme.

The infantry barracks are to the SE, and consist of three blocks two storeys in height for the married men, and four three-storey blocks for single soldiers, accommodation being provided for 824 men – about 90 married and 734 unmarried – and 38 officers in the officers' quarters. The infantry parade is in front to the N. The cavalry and artillery barracks are to the W of the infantry parade ground and consist of seven blocks – two for married men and five for the single men and for stables. There is accommodation for altogether 302 men – 32 married – and 12 officers; cavalry, 148 men and six officers; royal artillery, 154 men and 6 officers. The stables have room for 104 horses and 10 officers' horses belonging to the cavalry, and for 96 horses and 9 officers' horses belonging to the artillery, while a separate building accommodates 14 sick horses, and provides cover for 8 field guns. The cavalry and artillery parade ground lies to the N of their barracks.

SCHOOL FOR COOKERY, 1876
The Baillie

The Glasgow School of Cookery opened its doors in Bath Street to the public in 1876. Early prospectuses advertised demonstration lessons and practice lessons. The scope of these lessons were class-related, with superior cookery (becoming high-class cookery), plain cookery (becoming plain household cookery) and cookery for the working-classes. The driving force behind the School was Grace Paterson (1843–1925), who was born in Glasgow in an upper-middle class family. She appears to have been a forceful personality who was described as a feminist and suffragette. As the following extract from a satirical journal demonstrates, not everyone took the new venture seriously.

Superior Cookery – Tickets, 25s per doz. – Potage Ecossais
This superior soup is prepared as follows: Choose a few pounds of beef – thick, juicy, nutritious. Next procure a selection of esculent roots, bulbous and otherwise, together with herbaceous plants as may be in season. Now boil several pints of condensed vapour, placing the beef in the pot while the water is cold, in order to prevent the formation of an albuminous envelope. About an hour before serving throw in the vegetables, previously reduced to atoms by the operation of a mincing knife. Serve hot, in Wedgewood ware, with a ladle argent. When the temperature is below zero this will be found a most excellent and comfortable dish.

Plain Cookery – Tickets, 21s per doz. – Scotch Soup
Take some pounds of beef, fat rather than lean. Buy some carrots, turnips and onions, together with some parsley, if you can get it. Now boil the beef, and throw in the vegetables, nicely minced, an hour before serving. For cold weather no better dish could be prepared.

Cookery for the Working Classes – Tickets, 3s per doz. – Broth
Buy some hochs, also tippence worth o' neeps, sibos, carrots, and ingans. Pit the beef intae the pan wi' cauld water. Bile for an 'oor, then in wi' the vegetables. When the guidman comes in at one, serve het. Eh, lassies, there's naething like a drap o' guid kail on a cauld day.

DOON THE WATTER, 1880
J.J. Bell

For generations of Glaswegians holidays meant a trip 'doon the watter'. Initially, as J.J. Bell intimates, this was no great voyage, Dumbarton being the furthest flung port of call. Later, adventurous travellers went as far as the Isle of Arran, which for many was regarded as being as exotic as the Bahamas.

The Glasgow Fair Holidays began on a Thursday in July and ended on the second Monday following; but few city clerks, who worked from eight-thirty or nine till six, with an interval for dinner (but none for coffee, cigarette or tea), and shop assistants, whose day was even longer, got more than a week as an antidote to 51 weeks of an unairy and often gas-fumey existence. The heads of business might take ten days, but some took less; to the responsible man of affairs the idea of a month's absence from duty – were it ever suggested – would have seemed worthy of a lunatic.

The bicycle was then a lofty thing, spectacular and unpractical, with thin solid tyres, on which one rode jarringly in the tightest of breeches, with no place for impedimenta. Transport was all but confined to the trains and steamers, the horse-drawn vehicle used by one-day excursionists, or by adventurous souls who would penetrate beyond the outposts of the railway into the fastness of, for instance, Sutherland.

Golf was not everybody's game – far from it. In Hillhead small boys, including myself, turned to gape at a man carrying clubs. A woman with clubs we never saw. To our house came only one person who ever mentioned golf, though he mentioned it much. I remember that he played at Troon – always Troon. My father respected him as a lawyer, yet judged him to be a little daft. At any rate, golf was then a holiday consideration of the select. I am writing of the West, but even St Andrews, where we spent our holidays in 1880 or 1881, was small and quiet compared with what it is today, and its solitary course was adequate.

It is safe to say that Glasgow generally was satisfied to make holiday within a radius of fifty miles of the city, and mainly on the shores of the Firth of Clyde. As youngsters we knew one or two families who were annually taken inland, and we pitied them, for to us, as to most boys and girls, the countryside appeared as a place in which there was nothing to see and little more to do.

As for 'Doon the Watter', I cherish a theory that originally it did not imply a voyage beyond Dumbarton, if as far, though it came to include the adventure to the Isle of Arran. Possibly the older generation, or some of its members, of fifty years ago, continued to say 'Doon the Watter' without a smile, but I do not recollect hearing it, save on a jocular note.

Glasgow people generally did not worry about getting 'relaxed', or bother about being 'braced', and so the sheltered shores and heads of the lochs had their goodly shares of summer visitors. My earliest recollection of this kind belongs to Clynder – which many moderns would call 'fuggy' in mid-summer – on the Gareloch, then, as now, an anchorage for ships out of commission. The vivid part of the memory has, in fact, to do with one of the ships, a steamer, a big and beautiful one, with graceful clipper bow, tall masts, and two scarlet funnels, which lay moored off the pier. Once my father rowed me out to her, and the caretaker invited us on board, and showed us over her – a tremendous experience for a small boy. She was the *Scotia*, last of the famous paddle-wheel Cunarders, and therefore historic. Eventually they took away her paddles, gave her a propeller, and she continued to be useful as a cable ship. Clynder, too, is associated with chicken-pox, which we children all developed there, having taken it thither from Sunday school – alas, my poor parents!

The Isle of Arran attracted then, as it attracts now, but, more than any other place on the Firth, it expected to be loved for itself alone. There was a certain sense of adventure in the voyage beyond the Cumbraes and Bute, or even from Ardrossan in the old *Brodick Castle*, with her pair of black and white funnels set close together, and a certain romance in the island's isolation and wildness, also the wonder of freedom, which did not apply to places on the inner Firth. But for those delights there was a price, however cheerfully it might be paid.

Fascination was the word for it. Glasgow people accustomed to abundant space and every comfort packed themselves gladly into cottages in a way that is best described by the sanitary inspector's word 'overcrowding'. The cottages were without water supply; the rooms were small, the ceilings low, the windows sometimes so tiny that the ventilation was almost negligible; and after a stewing hot night one had a real need of all the fresh air the hills and glens and sea could give. In such a night, unable to sleep, I lit a candle in order to read and, lo, the wall-paper was swarming with wood-lice! But was I 'scunnered' at Arran? A thousand times no!

Yet I have since wondered how my mother tholed it. Seven of a family, maybe a visitor or two, the father bringing another at the week-end, and all the difficulties of catering at the head of a glen, maids raging at the small open fire, every pint of water to be carried in from a spring – not much of a holiday for her. Perhaps she was leal to Arran, as well as faithful to her motherhood, for as a girl she had tasted of its delights, without the responsibilities.

KENNEDY JONES, *c.* 1885
Neil Munro

Born in Glasgow, 'K.J.' (1865–1921) as he was known, was educated at the High School before embarking at sixteen on a career in journalism. He worked as a reporter for several local papers before moving south, where he fell under the influence of Alfred Harmsworth. Always entrepreneurial, he returned to Glasgow in 1895 and acquired the Daily Record. *Though not titularly its editor, 'K.J.' determined its style and content, increasing sales from 100,000 to half a million within three years of its launch. Here he is recalled by the journalist and novelist Neil Munro (1864–1930), author of the sublime Para Handy tales.*

In the middle 'eighties a young Glasgow lad, living with his parents in Crown Street, Gorbals, started on a Press career, which terminated in London about the year 1921, when he retired, reputedly a millionaire.

He had begun as acting editor of a boys' paper, and so made certain of having his own contributions accepted. He finished as a partner of the late Lord Northcliffe, whom he was largely instrumental in launching into daily journalism.

In his retirement he occupied his time by keeping a stud of racing horses, and, as a director of Waring and Gillow, took an active interest in Mr. Donald Matheson's preliminary schemes for what was to be the grandest hotel in Scotland, possibly Britain – Gleneagles. But the war intervened; all work on Gleneagles was suspended for some years, and he did not live to see it finished. His last work was to write a volume dealing with his own part in the development of the 'new journalism'.

For a certain number of years the destiny of *The Times* itself had been to no little extent in the hands of Mr. Kennedy Jones, the lad from Gorbals.

The first time I met Kennedy Jones was on a Monday night in the stalls of the Princess's Theatre, Glasgow, where I had gone to write a notice of *The Shaughraun*, as played by Hubert O'Grady's touring company. There was a sparse audience, which doubtless accounted for Mr. O'Grady's bad temper that night.

Sitting next to me was a remarkably precocious young fellow I had never seen before, or heard of, who took an early opportunity to let me know he was editor of a new weekly called *The Detective*, which I had not yet seen. It appeared that *The Detective* specialised in short stories of crime and its nemesis, mainly written by himself, and in guinea competitions.

The previous week he had offered a guinea for the best short contribution dealing with the stage, and written by a professional actor. The guinea had been won by an actor in Hubert O'Grady's company, to whom he was going to present it personally at the end of the performance.

I accepted an invitation to go behind the scenes with him to witness this important ceremony, and we found the successful and highly delighted prize-winner alone in a dressing-room washing off his grease-paint. The presentation was hardly finished and the actor still in his under-pants when a stage hand came into the room with Mr. O'Grady's compliments and the information that we must leave immediately, as visitors in the dressing-rooms were strictly prohibited. Young Mr. Jones had no plausible *locus standi*, but I thought to establish one by sending a messenger back to O'Grady explaining that we represented the Press.

In the messenger's absence the young actor explained that the insult was directed exclusively at himself, as there was a violent feud between him and O'Grady. Two minutes later O'Grady came into the dressing-room, profoundly apologetic. He was in a state of *deshabille*, without coat or waistcoat; one suspender inadequately holding up his breeches; his unbuttoned shirt revealing the hairiest of chests; and his face all streaked with paint.

'I didn't undershtand ye were pressmen, boys,' he said. 'The Press is always welcome. What paper do ye represint?'

'The *Evening News*,' I informed him, quite unaware that a colleague of mine ('Lorgnette') that very afternoon had cruelly written of O'Grady's own plays, as apart from Boucicault's, as of no dramatic value.

Fifteen minutes later, Kennedy Jones and I were contumely ejected into Main Street, Gorbals, accompanied by our friend, the young literary actor, who had there and then thrown up his engagement with the *Shaughraun* company. A painful scene, in which Madame O'Grady, also in *deshabille*, joined her husband and helped him to express his sentiments about us where his own pretty extensive vocabulary fell short!

The Detective soon lost the clue to fortune, died soon after, and Kennedy Jones transferred his talents to a more orthodox Glasgow weekly paper, *The Scottish People*, in which he began a sensational story, entitled, *The Golden Cross*. The plot of it had been suggested to him by the editor, Mr. Andrew Dewar Willock, and its publication began in the paper when only the second instalment had been written. To advertise the new serial, tiny placards three inches square, and gummed on the back, were printed off in thousands for distribution by the newsagents.

Very late one night – or, rather, early in the morning – the author of *The Golden Cross*, on his way home to Crown Street over a deserted Jamaica Bridge, bethought him that here was an opportunity to stimulate the sale of good literature. He had with him a pocketful of the little placards exhorting the public to 'Read The Golden Cross, by Kennedy Jones', which he began to moisten in the natural way upon the back, and stick at intervals all along one parapet of the bridge. Unobserved by him, another belated citizen, a baker, was crossing the bridge behind him, and was intensely interested in this new development in publicity – obviously contrary to police regulations.

The stranger overtook 'K.J.' at the south end of the bridge where he was at the moment sticking on his final placard; watching him gravely for a moment under the lamplight, and then asked, 'Are you by any chance Kennedy Jones, the author of this story?' Jones admitted that he was.

'I thought so!' said the baker. 'I hope they pay you well for working on the night shift', and having so revealed a fraternal interest in the hardships of the humblest of the working classes, passed on into the darkness.

Each week's instalment of his serial, however, came later and later to the printer's hands, till finally he was being sent for to Green's Billiard Room in Drury Street on the day before going to press that he might come across to the office and provide 'copy' for the following day.

The story ultimately became so hopelessly entangled, and 'K.J.' looked so unlikely to finish it within a year, while still its denouement was undecided, that Mr. Willock, the editor, adopted the drastic and traditional old method of dealing with such circumstances, and wrote the final instalment himself. I forget exactly how he disposed of all the surviving characters, but I have the impression that he drowned the villainous ones in a shipwreck and abruptly married off the hero and heroine. So ended 'K.J.s' career in fiction.

BRIEF LIVES, 1888
Dr J.B. Russell

Appointed Glasgow's second Medical Officer of Health in 1872, Dr Russell made many speeches with titles such as 'Life in One Room' and 'The Children of the City', designed to prick the consciences of the powers-that-be. One paragraph illustrates the point he was trying to make.

Of all the children who die in Glasgow before they complete their fifth year, 32 per cent die in houses of one apartment; and not 2 per cent in houses of five apartments and upwards. There they die, and their little bodies are laid on a table or on the dresser, so as to be somewhat out of the way of their brothers and sisters who play and sleep and eat in their ghastly company. One in every five of all who are born there never see the end of their first year.

A VEXED QUESTION IN SANITATION, 4 AUGUST 1888
The Builder

The phenomenal success of the 1851 Crystal Palace Exhibition in London spurred other European cities to emulate it. Somewhat belatedly, Glasgow entered the fray, but when it did it was with uncommon enthusiasm, with three exhibitions in twenty-three years. The first, in 1888, was held in West End Park. Its aim was 'to promote and foster the sciences and arts, and to stimulate commercial enterprise'. Any profits were to go towards setting up a new art gallery, museum and school of art. Although it was supposedly international in nature, there were very few exhibits from foreign parts, though the Empire was well represented. The Glasgow International Exhibition was opened on 8 May by the Prince of Wales and closed on 10 November, by when it had welcomed 5,748,379 visitors and made a surplus of around £46,000. Not everyone, however, was wholly impressed by the experience . . .

This enterprise has just completed the third month of its appointed career, and of success, in the purely business sense of the term, there has hitherto been no lack. The sum of the attendance has been more than respectable, although the form in which the figures, through the medium of the local press, find their way from time to time to the public is hardly a straightforward or rational one. There is no excuse for ranking mere stall assistants as visitors; yet this is done, and not only so, but each entrance is made to count, and an attendant whose exceptional requirements take him in and out twelve times a day, swells the figures by twelve accordingly. There is not the same strength of exception taken to the mixing up of season ticket-holders and complimentary visitors with those who pay at the turnstiles (the only unerring criterion), but it would certainly be more candid to keep the two tables of figures entirely separate. Ticket-holders for the most past reside, or at least pursue their daily calling, within a short distance of the building; many of them make several visits daily, and in doing so contribute (innocently enough of course) to the swelling of these same somewhat deceptive attendance returns.

Since the opening, on the 8th May, a certain degree of change has been going on amongst the general exhibits, chiefly at the fancy of sundry exhibitors who were unable to open with a full show, or who had afterthoughts as to additions which appeared to them desirable. There has been a gradual process of accretion due to this influence, and there are cases, perhaps, in which it has gone too far. Pottery, earthenware and glass goods have been added to very appreciably, and to the extent, possibly, of somewhat seriously upsetting the general balance or proportion of the Exhibition. These fragile goods are found, not only in set places, but everywhere, and are come upon incessantly by the examiner, at the imminent risk of suggestion iteration in an offensive degree. Many of the specimens are of undoubted excellence of manufacture and of some artistic merit, but many are only moderately endowed with good qualities of any kind. This department of the Exhibition is decidedly overdone, and a ton or two of this class of goods might be carted away, not only with safety, but to the general advantage.

On the other hand, there are sections which would bear some augmentation in the interests of this same balance and proportion. Models from the pattern-rooms of shipbuilding yards are present in a force which more than satiates; but although the Kelvin flows immediately under the north façade of the building, and, by special deepening operations, has been purposely made navigable to a practicable extent, there is nothing on its bosom save a mooring-buoy, a gondola, and two or three craft of the small launch order, only one of these – a new lifeboat deck seat – presenting features at all out of the common. More might have been made of it than this.

The Kelvin itself, however, forms an instructive exhibit, although to one or two of the senses in some sort an objectionable one. Its presence here as an inclosed and thoroughly domestic feature of an institution destined within a brief space to be visited by two or three millions of people, many of them of high initiative rank, may exert an after influence on a still unsolved problem – the prevention of the pollution of rivers. This inconsiderable stream rises in the heart of the Scottish midlands, at a point fully half-way across to the Firth of Forth, thence flowing picturesquely through the valley to which it gives a name, on to the confluence with the Clyde at Glasgow, about half a mile below the Exhibition. It has many polluting factories on its banks, and receives several tributaries subject to similar befouling influences, besides carrying away the sewage of a good many towns and villages – none of a very large extent, however. Up to within a few months ago a considerable portion of western Glasgow drained into it under the grounds of the park, just at the site of the Exhibition, and it still receives the household impurities of those suburbs of Glasgow which fringe the opposite or right bank of the river. Of late years, during the heats and droughts of summer, the Kelvin at this point has emitted a stench past all bearing, quite outdoing the larger-volumed and more fully-diluted Clyde in that respect; but it has been partially relieved by recent deepening and cleansing operations, and it will certainly prove less obnoxious this year. Yet, at this point, even now, it is not a considerable remove above the grade of a very badly outraged stream as regards the sewage and manufacturing refuse still permitted to drain into it. As nearly every visitor will cross and recross it, its condition is bound to attract attention; and, as a kind of impromptu exhibit, in this sense it may help towards the solution of a vexed question in sanitation.

DRINK-SODDEN, 1889
Sir John Hammerton

Born in Alexandria, Dunbartonshire, Sir John Hammerton (1871–1949) was credited by the Dictionary of National Biography *as 'the most successful creator of large-scale works of reference that Britain has known', i.e,* Harmsworth's Universal Encyclopaedia. *His description of the drunken antics of some Glaswegians is confirmed by others. In the mid-nineteenth century there were pubs in Glasgow and Edinburgh for every 130 people. But they were outdone by the likes of Tranent and Dunbar in East Lothian where, respectively, there were 52 pubs (one for every 76 inhabitants) and 53 (one for every 83 inhabitants). As the historian T.C. Smout has remarked: 'Nowhere else was as sodden as that.'*

In 1889, Glasgow was probably the most drink-sodden city in Great Britain. The Trongate and Argyle Street, and worst of all, the High Street, were scenes of disgusting debauchery. Many of the younger generation thought it manly to get 'paralytic' and 'dead to the world'; at least on Saturday there was a lot of tipsy rowdyism in the genteel promenade in Sauchiehall Street, but nothing to compare with the degrading spectacles of other thoroughfares, where there were drunken brawls at every corner and a high proportion of passers-by were reeling drunk. At the corners of the dark side streets the reek of vomit befouled the evening air, never very salubrious. Jollity was everywhere absent: sheer loathesome, swinish inebriation prevailed.

UNLUCKY WITH SHIPS, *c.* 1890
Catherine Carswell

The daughter of a merchant involved in shipping, Catherine Carswell (1879–1946) grew up in middle-class Glasgow where she attended Park School. Music was her first love but she was eclectic in her artistic tastes and lectured for a spell on art. In 1907 she became drama critic of the Glasgow Herald, *but lost her job when she reviewed D.H. Lawrence's banned novel* The Rainbow. *Following the death of her mother in 1912 she left Glasgow for London. Her first, well-received novel,* Open the Door! *(1920) is transparently autobiographical. Its successor,* The Camomile: an Invention *(1922) was less successful. However, it is for her controversial* Life of Robert Burns *(1930) that she is best remembered. Bardolaters, aggrieved at her portrayal of their hero, heaped abuse on her and even sent her death threats. The following passage is taken from Carswell's autobiography,* Lying Awake (1950).

There are two rivers in the city where I was born. One is a romantically genteel stream with high banks along which nursemaids wheel prams. Upon the other – of which this stream [the Kelvin] is a feeder – the prosperity of the place has been built up. Poems and songs – none of them good – have been written about the stream, none, so far as I know, about the river. Our living was derived from the river, whence my father sent ships and merchandise to the West Indies, but we rarely saw it. We lived – latterly

– on the banks of the stream and in the region to which it gave its name.

We did know the river farther down where it grew salt and turned into the lochs upon which we spent part of our summer holidays, and we saw it farther up. The Clyde in Glasgow itself we scarcely thought about.

Money was a subject I never remember as a topic of conversation at home during my youth. Such things as the rent of our town house or the cost of country lodgings for holidays, or even the prices of clothes, food or household articles never came up in talk. Father, of course, went off on foot each morning (after kissing us all round the breakfast table and being assisted with his coat and hat in the lobby and waved out of sight) to 'make money' for us; and he returned each evening a little tired after having presumably made enough for our needs. He came home also for a midday meal, after which he lay down on the long red-leather-covered sofa where, covered by us with a huge tartan shawl and undisturbed by the continued family life about him he immediately slept. After some twenty minutes he sprang up refreshed and fit for a renewal of his money-making.

The building where these daily efforts were made bore an appropriate resemblance to a money-box – one of those early money-boxes that were known as 'savings banks'. These were of cast metal painted black, square in shape, elaborately corniced with a slot in the roof for the entrance of pennies. It was in West Regent Street, and we entered it only on special occasions. As we drew near to its pseudo-Gothic portals we became silent: as we ascended the wide but dirty stone staircase awe fell upon us. My father was, I believe, a commission agent. He negotiated in particular the shipping and sale of textiles to the West Indies. Some of the ships concerned were built for, and for a time at least owned by, him. One of these, a steamship named the *Claudine*, I launched from its slips on the Clyde when I was perhaps thirteen years old, and we all took part proprietorially in her trial down the river. Another of his ships, the *Collossie* – a sailing vessel named after the village where part of his childhood was spent – my sister Fanny launched. The *Claudine* was wrecked on her first voyage, the *Collossie*, under a diferent name, came to figure in Robert Louis Stevenson's tale *The Wrecker*. It would seem that father was not lucky with ships, and looking back I seem to know now what was then never apparent to me, that he was frequently unlucky in business undertakings, which were much in the nature of commercial gambling. I remember once his bringing home to show us a yard or two of printed cotton – yellow corn stalks in full ear effectively set against a background of turkey red. Some of this, he told us, had been sent 'on spec' to the Sandwich Islands, and it had so pleased the islanders that the more prosperous took to riding about on horseback with streamers of the fabric fluttering from their shoulders. To such a pitch did this emulation in display develop that he had a request for a repeat order of many bales – possibly the hold of the *Claudine* was full of them.

But such exotic hints had little or no connexion in my mind with the making of money by my father. I had a vague idea that consequent upon certain mysterious ceremonies enacted before his large desk, of which he was the sole master, coins in sufficient quantity insinuated themselves through a hole in the office roof. I have said we were awed when we were there. Father in these surroundings became for us a different being – more distant and impressive because of the numerous underlings through whom we had to pass to reach him.

Of the money father made we each had a penny a week in pocket money. Much thought and choice was expended each Saturday on the laying out of this penny that father had made and given us. In those days, a penny seemed to go a very long way. You could buy a wooden box of sherbet for a halfpenny (with a wooden spoon in it to eat from delicately) and the other halfpenny could be laid out in a more permanent possession, such as a rubber balloon, or one of those contraptions at the end of a long string, which by a process of suction could fish up something desirable from the deepest street area, if lowered between the iron bars on pavement level. I have even on occasion fished up another penny, thus increasing my weekly allowance by 100 per cent. At a more advanced age we began to receive a threepenny piece each Saturday and when this was raised to sixpence, maturity was announced.

Coins counted to us, not money. This persists with me even now. With a half-crown to finger in my pocket, I feel far removed from destitution. As a petty trader I take some beating. But money in its larger sense has always remained a mystery, with me as an uncomprehending outsider. It is something that is made in larger or smaller quantities. If I were to pick up piles of stones in his field for a farmer I should demand and value the sixpence paid for each pile. But I cannot see myself as 'earning' money.

With guidance and encouragement I should have made a good counterfeit coiner.

'GLASGOW', 1890
William Topaz McGonagall

Long after his death William McGonagall's position as the world's worst poet remains unchallenged. Born in Edinburgh, which is not something the capital likes to boast about, McGonagall (1830–1902) was of Irish stock. He spent part of his childhood on Orkney before settling in Dundee. Drawn to the boards, he did some acting but it was as a poet, and a woeful one at that, that he was to achieve fame. In 1878 he published his first collection of poetry, which included his 'masterpiece', 'The Railway Bridge of the Silvery Tay'. Cursed with what's been described as a 'calypso-like disregard for metre' and a tin ear for rhyme, he went on his way regardless of the brickbats thrown at him. What can be said of his paean to Glasgow? That it could not have been written by anyone else?

Beautiful city of Glasgow, with your streets so neat and
clean,
Your stately mansions, and beautiful Green!
Likewise your beautiful bridges across the River Clyde,
And on your bonnie banks I would like to reside.

Chorus:
Then away to the West – the beautiful West!
To the fair city of Glasgow that I like the best,
Where the River Clyde rolls on to the sea,
And the lark and blackbird whistle with glee.

'Tis beautiful to see the ships passing to and fro,
Laden with goods for the high and the low;

So let the beautiful city of Glasgow flourish,
And may the inhabitants always find food their bodies to
nourish.

The statue of the Prince of Orange is very grand,
Looking terror to the foe, with a truncheon in his hand,
And well mounted on a noble steed, which stands in the
Trongate,
And holding up its foreleg, I'm sure it looks first-rate.

Then there's the Duke of Wellington's statue in Royal
Exchange Square –
It is a beautiful statue I without fear declare,
Besides inspiring and most magnificent to view,
Because he made the French fly at the battle of Waterloo.

And as for the statue of Sir Walter Scott that stands in
George's Square,
It is a handsome statue – few can with it compare,
And most elegant to be seen,
And close behind it stands the statue of Her Majesty the
Queen.

Then there's the statue of Robert Burns in George Square,
And the treatment he received when living was very unfair;
Now, when he's dead, Scotland's sons for him do mourn,
But, alas! unto them he can never return.

Then as for Kelvin Grove, it is most lovely to be seen
With its beautiful flowers and trees so green.
And a magnificent water-fountain spouting up very high,
Where people can quench their thirst when they feel dry.

Beautiful city of Glasgow, I now conclude my muse,
And to write in praise of thee my pen does not refuse;
And, without fear of contradiction, I will venture to say
You are the second grandest city in Scotland at the present day!

A MINOR EPISODE, *c.* 1892
John Buchan

Perth-born John Buchan (1875–1940) was the son of a Free Church of Scotland minister. He was educated at Hutchesons' Grammar School and between 1892 and 1895 at the University of Glasgow. Thereafter he juggled several careers, in all of which he shone. Today he is best known as a writer of fiction and will forever be associated with The Thirty-nine Steps *(1915), in which he introduced the character of Richard Hannay. Between 1922 and 1936 he wrote a thriller a year. Despite accusations of racism, anti-semitism and snobbishness, his reputation has endured, not least because of the power of his story-telling. In 1935 he was appointed Governor-General of Canada, taking the title Lord Tweedsmuir of Elsfield.*

I never went to school in the conventional sense, for a boarding school was beyond the narrow means of my family, but I had many academies. The first was a dame's school, where I learned to knit, and was expelled for upsetting a broth pot on the kitchen fire. The next was a board school in the same Fife village. Then came the burgh school of the neighbouring town, which meant a daily tramp of six miles. There followed the high school of the same town, a famous institution in which I believe Thomas Carlyle once taught. When we migrated to Glasgow I attended for several years an ancient grammar school on the south side of the river, from which, at the age of seventeen, I passed to Glasgow University.

I found my first real intellectual interest in the Latin and Greek classics. For the next three years I was a most diligent student, mediaeval in my austerity. Things have changed now, but in my day a Scottish university still smacked of the Middle Ages. The undergraduates lived in lodgings in the city and most of them cultivated the Muses on a slender allowance of oatmeal. The session ran from October to April, and every morning I had to walk four miles to the eight o'clock class through a variety of the winter weather with which Glasgow fortifies her children. My road lay through the south side of the city, across the Clyde, and so to the slopes of Gilmorehill. Most of that road is as ugly as anything you can find in Scotland, but to me in the retrospect it was all a changing panorama of romance. There was the weather – fog-like soup, drenching rains, winds that swirled down the cavernous streets, mornings that dawned bright and clear over snow. There was the sight of humanity going to work and the signs of awakening industry. There was the bridge with the river starred with strange lights, the lit shipping at the Broomielaw, and odours which even at their worst spoke of the sea. There was the occasional lift in the London train, which could be caught at a suburban station, and which for a few minutes brought one into the frowst of a third-class carriage full of sleepy travellers from the remote and unvisited realm of England. And at the end there were the gaunt walls of the college often seen in the glow of a West Highland sunrise.

As a student I was wholly obscure. I made few friends; I attended infrequently one or other of the numerous societies, but I never spoke in a debate; and I acquired the corporate spirit only at a rectorial election, when, though a professed Tory, I chose to support the Liberal candidate, Mr Asquith, and almost came by my end at the hands of a red-haired savage, one Robert Horne, who has since been Chancellor of the Exchequer. My summers were spent in blessed idleness, fishing, tramping and bicycling up and down the Lowlands. But my winters were periods of beaver-like toil and monkish seclusion. I returned home early each afternoon and was thereafter at my books until midnight.

STEEL DROPS, *c.* 1895

J.J. Bell

There is nothing particularly modern about quack medicines and ersatz remedies for common complaints. Nor has there ever been a dearth of snake oil salesmen eager to off-load them on to gullible hypochondriacs. J.J. Bell, the author of the pawky novel Wee Macgreegor *(1902), about a small boy and his adventures in Glasgow, also wrote two volumes of memoirs about his early life in Glasgow,* I Remember *(1932) and* Do You Remember? *(1934).*

I forbear to give a list of medicines which, however pleasingly reminiscent to my contemporaries, would probably be as sound and fury, signifying nothing to my younger readers. But I should like to mention Steel Drops, one of the favourite tonics, ere yet the days of hypophosphites and glycerophosphates have dawned. Steel Drops, though the name is suggestive of small shot or ball-bearings, are a yellow-brown ferruginous liquid, and, preparatory to becoming stronger, you let fall so many drops into so much water, three times a day, before (or possibly after) meals. The only drawback to the Drops is that you have to purchase also a glass tube, so that you may imbibe the strength-giving fluid without spoiling your teeth. Of course, you may already have a tube at home, having been a partaker of Steel Drops those many years, though as yet the bloom of health has not become apparent.

One druggist sells a goodly quantity of Flowers of Sulphur, especially in the Spring, for many people still believe in Mr. Squeer's mixture of brimstone and treacle; and other people buy chunks of rock variety, as I believe they yet do, to put in their doggie's water, all with the same touching faith that inspired the old lady to place a bright screw nail in her canary's seed. The only popular disinfectant, I think, apart from carbolic, is Condy's Fluid. Pears' Soap has lately arrived, and in a few years half the population, with an air of originality, will be saying 'Good-morning!' and asking the other half if they have used it. 'Worth a guinea a box' has not yet appeared on the hoardings. There is little, if anything, in the shop that has come from America, apart from Florida Water, in tall slim bottles, with its crude, quaint floral label, as now.

GLASGOW BOYS, 1897

Francis 'Fra' Newbery

Over a period of twenty years at the end of the nineteenth century, a group of young painters based in Glasgow, but working across Scotland, established an international reputation for realism and plein-air painting. Among the most prominent were James Guthrie, John Lavery, Arthur Melville, George Henry and E.A. Hornel. Known collectively as 'the Glasgow Boys', they shared an enthusiasm for naturalistic subject matter and strong, clean, fresh colours, as well as a willingness to range widely from the east coast of Scotland to France, the Mediterranean and the Middle East in search of subjects, settings and inspiration. Another unifying factor was their dislike of the Scottish artistic establishment, embodied in the Edinburgh-based painters who dominated the Royal Scottish Academy. 'Fra' Newberry was Director of the Glasgow School of Art from 1885 to 1917.

It is curious to note how most of the great triumphs of Art have been won in cities, and in cities, too, whose life was oftentimes of the busiest and most complex description. Rome, with its subtle life of political ecclesiasticism, though never of herself producing an artist, yet, by her attraction of men, dominated in the sixteenth century, the Art of the Italian Renaissance; and Paris to-day is the hub of the Art Universe, because of the blood and brains of men, brought from the outermost confines of France. A civic life would seem to knock fire out of me, like the sparks evolved from the contact of flint and steel.

And at this end of the nineteenth century, in the midst of one of the busiest, noisiest, smokiest cities, that, with its like fellows, make up the sum-total of the greatness of Britain's commercial position, there is a movement existing, and a compelling force behind it, whose value we cannot yet rightly appraise or whose influence is not yet bounded, but which, both movement and movers, may yet, perhaps, put Glasgow on the Clyde into the hands of the future historian of Art, on much the same grounds as those on which Bruges, Venice, and Amsterdam find themselves in the book of the life of the world. And in making such a statement and in advancing such a claim, it were well to guard against either exaggeration of language or an extravagant dealing with facts. All work that is being accomplished, and all effort that has reached a certain present finality, are, on account of their nearness to the onlooker, entirely out of perspective, and have oftentimes a worth that is purely fictitious, and an estimate which bears no relation to the real value.

And in this present instance, dealing with this movement now existing an influence in and from the city of Glasgow, it should be borne in mind that neither revolution nor revelation is being attempted, nor are the minds of the workers bent upon much else than that of doing a day's work with the best possible credit to themselves. These Scottish artists desire to be neither prophets nor preachers, nor do they attempt that which Art should ever have left to the pulpit – namely, the task of conversion. Furthermore, it is extremely unlikely that any such result is to follow from their efforts as was the outcome of the discovery of the Van Eycks; nor are their works likely to displace the treasures the Old Masters have left to us. One thing, however, is certain. The Glasgow portraits and landscapes will never have the sky line at future permanent exhibitions; and the future New-Zealander, after visiting the ruins of St Paul's, may possibly propose to himself a pilgrimage to the city of Glasgow, in order to see the pictures produced by the later nineteenth-century artists who worked within her boundaries.

Now, it may safely be taken that most movements, whether artistic or political or under any other heading, are protests against tradition, as then received. Men think about matters, and some of the clearer among them begin to see there is something wrong in, say, a certain state of affairs. Gaining in strength of thought these men protest, and then and there begins the inception of a movement.

About the time the younger Glasgow men were bestirring themselves, the Association of Painters in London, known as the New English Art Club, was making its assault upon the citadel of academicism, and was endeavouring to throw down the walls of that artistic Jericho, into which they and their works were equally forbidden, then, to enter. In Paris the fight against the tradition of the State school and of the strong man who ran the atelier, resulted in the separation from the old ideals of a body of artists who now find room for their pictures on the walls of the Salôn Champ de Mars . . . In Paris the struggle is going on to-day, and will probably continue so long as a complaisant Minister for the Fine Arts finds room for the two opposing bodies in which to exhibit their trophies.

But in Glasgow there was neither fight nor rupture; and for the simple reason that there was neither academicism to battle against, nor an opposition, fitly to be called such, to be overcome. And what is more, men, resident in the West of Scotland, had painted pictures in a good tradition, and had thereby created an interest in Art matters, in more ways than one, helpful to the rise of the new movement. But here comes in the difference between Glasgow and, say, the majority of northern and midland cities of England. The Royal Academy of London controls not only the Metropolis, but issues its dictum and influences the Art tendencies of practically the whole of England. In the provincial cities and towns of England, an artist's success depends, in large measure, upon the annual acceptance or rejection of his works, by the hangers at Burlington House; and he must be a strong man who can evade the test successfully and yet live.

But in Glasgow, on the contrary, there never was, nor at the present moment does there exist, either a controlling power vested in a body of artists, or an indication of opinion arising from a cultured lay community. Artists were, and still are, free to do what they like, as they like, provided always they take the consequences of their own ways and works. The businessman buys what he likes, or is persuaded to like, or because it pleases him; and though the Glasgow artists might possibly wish for a better representation than at present is the case, either in the municipal or in local private galleries, it would be hard to find a city where there are collections of pictures showing greater bravery of purchase.

The very rivalry between the cities of Edinburgh and Glasgow serves the purpose of emphasising the position taken up by the Glasgow men. The Royal Scottish Academy is now richer in the possession of strong recruits, which a more enlightened policy has had the wisdom to enrol from among the Glasgow men; but when the movement spoken of began, some ten or twelve years ago, there was practically no representative from Glasgow upon the Royal Scottish Academy roll, and very little inducement offered the young aspirants working in the West to contribute their products to the walls of its annual Exhibition. As for Burlington House, it may be questioned whether, even at the present moment, there is any large number of Glasgow painters affected in their work, either by its dicta or its desires. Certainly the Exhibitions of the Royal Glasgow Institute of the Fine Arts are noticeable by the absence of the works of living Royal Academicians, a position of matters that should cause a little regret, especially when it be considered who some of these Royal Academicians are. But it may broadly be stated, that in Glasgow a man's success is not dependent upon the judgment passed on his work by the selecting committee of the Royal Academy; and the possibility has been proved of artists working in Glasgow and attaining to a world-wide fame and reputation, without being even regular contributors to the walls of Burlington House. This young body of painters, therefore, working in Glasgow, and now happily – or unhappily – since styled the Glasgow School of Painters, had no cause to complain of their efforts being thwarted, or their aspirations checked by the influence of a power that held possession, and either ruled the market or dictated the taste. The field for their labours was as clear from any cramping or confining influences, as were the very earth and heavens they delighted to depict, and the traditions of a school – which, like bands binding a prisoner, have to be broken before even the blood can quicken the pulses – never even had an existence in the case of the Glasgow men.

1901–1925

FIGHTING WOMEN

THE CITY MAN, 1901
James Hamilton Muir

There was no such person as James Hamilton Muir. He was a composite of three young, mischievous Glaswegians: the artist Muirhead Bone, his brother the journalist James Bone, who later became the London editor of the Manchester Guardian, *and the lawyer Archibald Charteris. Together they produced a perceptive book called* Glasgow in 1901. *Much that they had to say about the city a century and more ago holds true today, such as: 'The best you can say for football is that it has given the working man a topic of conversation.' Even then there were signs that shipbuilding was starting to decline. Poor people drank too much, the university lacked focus, and there was too much drinking in public, and not of the wonderful water which arrived largely untreated from Loch Katrine.*

Glasgow, like most towns given over to industry and commerce, has no leisured class. Some of the inhabitants do, indeed, contend that the class exists and contains thirty-one persons, who are professors at Gilmorehill. But this is an absurd contention, for if you include professors, how are you to treat the officials of the Board of Trade or of the Custom House, or even lieutenants of the police? No, if the class exists in Glasgow it contains only nine-and-twenty persons, and these are not professors at all, but infantry officers stationed at Maryhill Barracks. And this is why the military man, whom, of a summer afternoon, you recognise by his flannels, his straw hat, and his fox-terrier, has an air so wearied and listless. With the other leisured men in the town he may have dined every night since the regiment came to Maryhill; now, on this pleasant day, he is just a little tired of them and would almost give his dog to any new person of the class who could help him to air it. Think of it! Alone of 750,000 people, he of the straw hat and old flannels has no 'job'.

No doubt there are others who are leisured against their will; the business of a professional man, for instance, who is still on the stocks, the waiters at Drury Street who are out of work, the student who, as the decades roll over his head, is turning 'chronic'. But to avoid being stared at, the man of this stamp adopts at the least the habits of the occupied, and then, like the Sergeant at Law –

> Nowhere so besy a man as he ther nas,
> And yet he seemed besier than he was.

The unashamed leisured are the military man and his rare twin brother the Oxford undergraduate in Glasgow for the vacation.

Now, this character of the Glasgow man as one having a job may be read by him who runs. It affects dress, manners, habits, even expression. Thus, existing more for use than ornament, the Glasgow man has small regard for the delicate niceties of dress. He clothes himself for work, and wears tweeds which have an air of being worth their price. If he should bestow pains on his clothes and do their maker infinite credit, depend upon it, the very rarity of his caprice will earn him the title of 'Tailor's Block'. But even the most modest person respects what he has purchased, and thus in our uncertain climate he will wear his trousers turned up and will carry an umbrella, and these two habits are said to be the stigmata of the Glasgow man, revealing his origin even in the Outer Hebrides. Until he has 'arrived' he rarely (except to funerals) wears a tall hat, unless indeed he is a professional man, and then if he is a lawyer it may sit on his head more as a badge of his calling than as a harmonious element in his colour scheme. Very often he hangs it in a cupboard before leaving his office, and should he chance to spend the next day a-golfing, his clerks will play charades with it in his private room. It is of a piece with his character that he refuses in business hours to be seen in the street with a stick in his hand. So to be seen would occasion the oddest surmises among his friends, the chief that he was leaving his office for good at a strangely early hour, or that he was a wedding guest. He might even seem to be a stranger passing through Glasgow on his way to the West Highlands. In Edinburgh, on the other hand, where appearance, not time, is money, a stick is carried even by the junior apprentice delivering a letter.

Further, the Glasgow man walks quickly, without attention to gait or carriage. He swings his body, even his arms, and sometimes walks on his heels as being nearest the ground. But no one takes offence at this. People are all too busy, and if our friend has the air of being bound for an appointment of importance, every Glasgow man would congratulate him on having so good a reason for his haste. Be his gait never so crab-like, no one will chaff him. Why, after all, should one, if the man gets there? In a metropolis where conventions are inherited it may be different, but here where the people who observe the conventions are those who made them, appearances, unless they collide with a reasonable etiquette, matter not one straw.

If now, from clothes and carriage, you pass to faces, your evidence multiplies that the Glasgow man is a man of occupation. The faces are intelligent rather than handsome, alert and intent rather than gay, more conspicuous for character than breeding. Merriment is not common, yet neither is boredom. It is a sedate people that you see, having itself well under control, aware of its aims and pursuing them without swerving. The vagrant eye is not often seen. Our friend knows his town too well to be attracted greatly by what passes in the streets. He has something else to think about. Yet do not imagine that he looks listless or wearied like the military man, and perhaps unhappy into the bargain. He is simply undemonstrative, and having an object and scope for his activity, he depends for his contentment less on his outward impressions than one who has neither.

The typical Glasgow man whom you see in the street uniting all these characteristics in his person is not the merchant prince with sons at Harrow, the professional man, nor the great shipbuilder or engineer, but is a little grey, wiry man in plain clothes and a square felt hat. He has a good-going business, which is the source, if not of a fortune, at least of a competence. He lives in the suburbs, probably in the South Side; his wife is plump and commonplace and cheerful, his daughter quite pretty, his son at college 'coming out for a doctor' and writing decadent verses for the magazine. He himself is the salt of the middle-class with all its virtues and limitations. His face is full of the character which brought him success; shrewdness, resolvedness, tenacity, energy, canniness, steadiness, and sobriety – all these are imprinted upon it indelibly. Withal it is a kindly face and belongs to one who is without pretension and deserves the epithet which his friends give him, of a 'plain, unassuming man'.

GEORGE SQUARE, 1901
James Hamilton Muir

George Square is to Glasgow what Red Square is to Moscow and St Peter's is to Rome. Situated in the heart of the Merchant City, it is named for George III (1738–1820). Laid out in c.1782, it remained for many years full of filthy water, its banks used for slaughtering horses. Eventually houses were built around its sides and today it is presided over by the City Chambers. It is home to statues of notable worthies, including the first monument ever erected to Walter Scott and one to Robert Burns, which was the first statue to be placed in the Square.

The Londoner who imagines he had turned his back on his city's sins of arrangement finds them repeated in every provincial town he comes to. And so George Square is Trafalgar Square over again – the same central monument, the same weary desert of paving stones, the same feckless designing of the spaces. The absence of the Landseer lions may be counted to it as a negative virtue, but the Scott monument is as dismal, quite, as Nelson's. To set a 'faithful portrait' of a great writer on a pedestal eighty feet above the street level, surely this is a form of strange torture, survived from the Middle Ages. At the head of the great column only a great symbol – a great gesture – is permissible, although an emperor standing guard over his realm might also be a motive sufficiently dignified. But to hoist to this height a man accustomed in life to walk the streets like any other of us, one to whom close observation of his fellows was a real daily need – this offends against all that is just and appropriate. If it be retorted that the column and its figure are the apotheosis of a great writer, why, in the name of art, was the man not purged of his earthly look and transfigured into a great being, high over the land he made renowned? In cold weather, when we are snugly at home, or in the Young Men's Christian

Association Rooms, he is out in the cold and in danger, and this is the sole thought that the Scott monument stirs in us. It is no simple memorial of 'sons to a father', as the Florentine monuments of the Renaissance were. Neither is it a symbol of enduring greatness. It is simply, like Nelson's, a man on the look-out tied to the mast-head. Burns's monument is better, because it is nearer the ground; its clumsy, overgrown, earnest figure is truer to the man. Moreover, there is a faint touch of the appropriate in his standing here, for at a window at the south-east corner of the square his Bonnie Lass of Ballochmyle used to sit and see the folk go by when her poet was dead, and she no longer bonnie. But the square looks best when 'a blast o' Janwar wind blaws hansel in on Robin', and brings with it snow. Then the stupid divisions of granolithic pavement from grass plots are blotted out, and the tramways run through lawns of snow, noiseless as sledges. And James Watt on his statue seems, indeed, a philosopher sunk in meditation, and as the snow settles on his head and lap, deeper and deeper seems his meditation. And Sir John Moore looks still and frozen, very like the hero of the ballad, 'with his martial cloak about him'. The Municipal Buildings, as you view them from the Post Office portico, seem greatly, mysteriously, official, like a facade in Whitehall; the old hotels on the north side are ever so far away, and the statues stand on their white ground like chessmen on their board.

The windows of the General Post Office are the Poor Man's Club. A man is staring from them, and sees not you, but a cottar's roof in Morven, and a girl driving kye home at nightfall. An old mechanic ties up a well-thumbed *Weekly Mail*, and addresses it with a shaking, laborious hand, and drops it among the foreign newspapers, for his son, the engineer, in India.

THE BONE FACTORY, 1901
Edwin Muir

Born the son of a crofter in Orkney, which he thought of as Edenic, Edwin Muir (1887–1959) left the island with his family when he was fourteen. It was the rudest of disruptions and one which left the poet scarred for life. In comparison to Orkney. Glasgow, as he described it in An Autobiography *(1954), was everything his birthplace was not: stinking, dirty, coarse, crime-ridden, unbearable, the sort of place you escape from, not volunteer to go to. In another book,* Scottish Journey *(1935), Muir added to his impressions of Glasgow. It was, he felt, a 'collapsing city', beset by slums, a population close to starvation, sectarianism and a sense of hopelessness.*

The job I took up in Fairport and kept for two years was a job in a bone factory. This was a place where fresh and decaying bones, gathered from all over Scotland, were flung into furnaces and reduced to charcoal. The charcoal was sold to refineries to purify sugar; the grease was filled into drums and dispatched for some purpose which I no longer remember. The bones, decorated with festoons of slowly writhing, fat yellow maggots, lay in the adjoining railway siding, and were shunted into the factory whenever the furnaces were ready for them. Seagulls, flying up from the estuary, were always about these bones, and the trucks, as they lay in the siding, looked as if they were covered in moving snowdrifts. There were sharp complaints from Glasgow whenever the trucks lay too long in the siding, for the seagulls could gobble up half a hundredweight of maggots in no time, and as the bones had to be paid for by their original weight, and the maggots were part of it, this meant a serious loss to the firm. After one of these complaints the foreman, an Irishman, would go out and let off a few shots at the seagulls, who would rise, suddenly darkening the windows. But in a little while they would be back again.

The bones were yellow and greasy, with little rags of decomposed flesh clinging to them. Raw, they had a strong, sour, penetrating smell. But it was nothing to the stench they gave off when they were shovelled along with the maggots into the furnaces. It was a gentle, clinging, sweet stench, suggesting dissolution and hospitals and slaughter-houses, the odour of drains, and the rancid stink of bad, roasting meat. On hot summer days it stood round the factory like a wall of glass. When the east wind blew it was blown over most of the town. Respectable families sat at their high teas in a well of stink. Many people considered that the smell was good for the health.

'KATE CRANSTONISH', *c.* 1905
Neil Munro

Kate Cranston's part in the history of Glasgow is significant and enduring. Born in 1849, she opened a tea-room in Argyle Street in 1878, the city's first. Another followed in nearby Ingram Street. Then, in 1897, she devoted a whole building in Buchanan Street to a tea-room, drawing on the talents of great exponents of 'Glasgow Style' – George Walton and Charles Rennie Mackintosh. In 1903 came the famous Willow Tea Rooms in Sauchiehall Street which were designed by Mackintosh and his wife, Margaret Macdonald. Cranston died in 1934 and, despite a public outcry, the new owner of the Ingram Street tea-room dismantled it completely.

Cranston's in the Argyle Arcade and Queen Street, and Cooper's, for a time had been distilling tiny cups of coffee in their windows. The aroma, extending into the streets, appeared to have an irresistible attraction for the ladies, who began to buy their coffee by the ounce as an excuse for more frequent visits to town and the pleasure of free sampling.

From the gratuitous sample-counter quickly developed a sitting-room where coffee could be amply and leisurely enjoyed at a reasonable tariff, and the strain of shopping in town was relieved enormously. The Cranston family had one time been associated with the Crow Hotel, a famous hostelry which stood on the side of the present Merchant's House in George Square. According to *Who's Who in Glasgow* (1909), Miss Catherine Cranston was born there; the place of her retirement is in its immediate vicinity.

Miss Cranston, clever, far-seeing, artistic to her fingertips, and of a high adventurous spirit, was the first to discern in Glasgow that her sex was positively yearning for some kind of afternoon distraction that had not yet been invented. She mapped out a career for herself and became a pioneer in a lunch-tea movement which in a few years made her name a household word. By general consent it was associated with the ideals and triumphs of the 'Glasgow School' of artists, then entering on international fame.

At the International Exhibition of 1901 in Kelvingrove her Tea-house and Tea-terrace had architectural and decorative innovations which created a sensation even among continental visitors. It meant the funeral knell of ugly and curly 'art nouveau' conventions in domestic decoration, and for the first time introduced a quite original note of surprise and gaiety into the midday 'snack' and its crockery and cutlery.

Miss Cranston's 'Groveries' establishment was, of course, only a temporary affair, which closed at the end of autumn, when the Exhibition itself ended, but by that time any lunch tea-room of hers was assured of permanent popularity. She opened glorious ones in Sauchiehall Street and Buchanan Street, Argyle Street and Ingram Street, designed externally to attract the eye by architectural novelty, yet restrained and elegant.

They were deliberately conceived as houses of light refreshment most obviously for the pleasure of women and run wholly on 'temperance' lines. Even had the cocktail been in fashion at the time, it would have been unprocurable in any of the Cranston's shops, which far more than made up for the absence of alcohol by features peculiar to themselves.

That wonderful woman appeared to have in view her own aesthetic gratification more than the rapid accumulation of a fortune on conventional restaurant lines. She was, herself, unique, vivacious, elegant, always with something of the *fête champêtre* in her costume, and the maids who served her tables took their note from her.

Miss Cranston brought to light the genius of a Glasgow architect, Charles Mackintosh, who died only in recent years and was the inspiring influence of a group of Glasgow artists, men and women, who made her tea-rooms homogeneous in structure, decoration, and furnishing. They were strangely beautiful, the Cranston tea-rooms; women loved them, and 'Kate Cranstonish' became a term with Glasgow people in general to indicate novelties in buildings and decorations not otherwise easy to define.

BAIRD REMEMBERS REITH, 1906
John Logie Baird

By extraordinary coincidence two of the most inspirational and influential figures in the development of television, John Logie

Baird (1888–1946) and John Reith (1889–1971) were Scottish and students contemporaneously at Glasgow Technical College (now the University of Strathclyde). Baird is regarded as the inventor of television while Reith is revered as the founder of the BBC. Reith's time at the College was not a happy one: he remembered it as 'something of a nightmare'. If he had any recollection of Baird there, he made no record of it. Later, in the 1930s, the men's paths crossed again when the BBC decided not to adopt Baird's system, which may well have coloured Baird's view of his fellow Scot.

There were, however, a few exceptions, gentlemen's sons, well off and with real anxiety as to their future. Among these was a tall, well-built youth, the son of the Moderator of the Presbyterian Church, by name, John Reith. I met him for the first time in rather unfavourable circumstances. I was, and still am, very short-sighted and, at the beginning of one of those classes, the Professor asked if those who were short-sighted and wanted front seats, would hand in their names. When I went up to the platform to give him my name, three large impressive students were talking to him. They talked in terms of equality; in fact there was a distinct aroma of patronage. The young gentlemen were of the type we would today call 'heavies', and they boomed with heavy joviality at the poor little Professor, who was distinctly embarrassed and ill-at-ease. I interrupted, timidly, and handed him a piece of paper with my name on it. As I did so, the heaviest and most overpowering of the three 'heavies' turned round and boomed at me. 'Ha! What is the matter with you? Are you deaf or blind?' I simpered something in inaudible embarrassment, and he turned his back on me, and the three 'heavies' walked out of the classroom booming portentously to each other.

This was the first time I saw Reith. I did not see him again for twenty years. Reith did not distinguish himself in examinations; he was worse than I was without the excuse of ill-health, but now we see him as a Cabinet Minister and a national figure while those who soared above him at College are lost in obscurity, little provincial professorlings, draughtsmen, petty departmental chiefs and the like, hewers of wood and drawers of water. The examiners awarded no marks for impressive appearances, no marks for oracular booming voices, no marks for influential relatives. To the examiners an overpowering 'heavy' and a lean rat-faced little cad were all alike.

AT THE PICKSHERS, *c.* 1908
Jim Phelan

Addicted to 'the dream-drift of the road', Irish-born Jim Phelan (1895–1966) was 'a tramp at heart, an opportunist by inclination, a beggar boy by philosophy'. At the age of eleven he left school with little formal education to run wild amidst the 'beggars, slum women, racecourse drifters ... ballad singers, rag-pickers, apple-women, and all the colourful, raucous, roaring denizens' of Dublin's netherworld. An incorrigible, and doubtless unreliable teller of tales, he travelled relentlessly and did whatever it took to survive, in the course of which he was twice sentenced to death and encountered the writers Liam O'Flaherty and H.G. Wells. Eventually, Phelan turned to writing himself and became a regular contributor to radio. In The Name's Phelan *(1948), the first part of his autobiography, he told how, like countless of his fellow countryfolk, he found his way to Glasgow.*

To me Glasgow looked, smelt, and sounded like a dream-town. Now this was a real foreign city at last. I could not understand one word of the speech. Heaven!

After the first couple of hours' wandering. I drifted away from the city centre and the shops. Something like the Combe district in Dublin, I judged the place where I found myself. (Later I learnt to call it the Gallowgate.) From some ragged boys I learnt about lodgings – share of a slum room cost fourpence, and two of the boys lived there. Carefully, almost religiously, I set myself up to imitate their speech.

Years later I knew a wealthy and cultured young Frenchman who, having had the misfortune to slay someone during his first few hours in England, found himself in prison for years. Promptly and of necessity he learnt English – in Dartmoor and similar places.

It was vastly funny to hear him break from the French equivalent of an Oxford accent into, 'I ups and ses to 'im, I ses, "Look 'ere," I ses, "wotcha tike me for?" I ses.' He told me, often, that the English language sounded marvellous to him. That was the way I learnt to speak Scotch, in the Gallowgate.

Sometimes, with other slum boys, I went to beg from the workmen who came from Park Head Forge. One caught glimpses of great flashing fires, heard the thumping of mighty hammers somewhere. Then the crowds of men came out, on their way home.

The begging was very simple. Many of the men would carry home part of their midday meal, uneaten. We stood, in a little crowd, and repeated continually, 'Any bread? Any bread?' The men gave us much more than we could eat.

(Almost I had forgotten! Our chorus was 'Onny br-raid? Onny br-raid?' My own accent was the thickest and most raucous of the group.)

Most of my days were spent in prowling, in the neighbourhood of the docks for preference. But the riverside was not at all like Dublin's. Big warehouses, dead walls, locked gates, hostile men with notebooks, came between the prowler and – whatever it was I looked at. All I remember is a meaningless list of ships and ports.

My companions were far too practical for any such occupation, and again I began to feel over-shy and reserved, something from which I had known blessed freedom for a few weeks. Gradually I came to dislike the boys, discovering them as clumsy, foolish liars *who could not even tell lies*. The end came one evening at the 'pickshers'.

A sailor had given me a shilling, and although penniless except for the solitary coin, I had spent eightpence on taking a boy to the cinema, retaining only the vital fourpence 'stall'.

The pictures cannot have been very enthralling (it was 1908), for the other boy and I talked most of the time. A slum-boy with one leg, a drifter like myself, he lived at my lodgings, had no family as far as I knew. That evening he told about having escaped from a reformatory.

I had read about Glencree near Dublin, knew of reformatories by hearsay only. But after the first few minutes I had picked a hundred holes in the story. These were the silliest lies I had ever heard. And this one-legged boy, fourteen or so, was the leader and most experienced of all. The Gallowgate was beginning to let me down.

The most thrilling part of the escape story ended with the loss of my boy-friend's leg. How, I enquired. Shot off, he explained. He carried a pair of crutches, got about with ease, had no wound or bandage. Yet his leg had been 'shot off' some seven weeks earlier. My Gallowgate dream-world was beginning to fall apart.

Outside the cinema I simply walked away. Although it was evening and I still clutched the fourpence in my trouser pocket, I did not go near the lodging-house, went prowling aimlessly along the river. Tomorrow I would find another stall; I was never going back with that crowd any more. Shot off!

A ROOM AND KITCHEN IN SPRINGBURN, *c.* 1914

Marion Smith

Marion Smith lived in a room-and-kitchen tenement house from 1914 until her marriage in 1927. Her mother had ten children. Her father was a brass worker at a locomotive works. The couple were dedicated to raising their family as well as possible on a very limited income, and instilled in their children strong moral values and a sense of their own worth. Marion was the eldest daughter and shared with her mother the responsibility of looking after the younger children. The kitchen here described was typical of countless others.

All my childhood days were in Springburn. Our first house was a single-end, but when another baby put in an appearance, we moved into a room and kitchen in the same close. We had been away from Springburn for a spell through Dad chasing work again, to the Carron Ironworks. The First World War had started and there was now no shortage of work, so we came to, where else, Springburn.

Our house had a coal fire in a stove, which had to be blackened with a paste mixed up in an old saucer, and then buffed up, and finally shone to a gleaming finish. There was a piece of velvet kept for the purpose. The steel trimmings were shined with emery cloth.

As my father was a brass moulder, the mantelpiece, above the stove, was gleaming with brass ornaments, all made in the works. This was one of the perks of the trade. Everybody made things in the works. We had brass iron stands, brass candlesticks, a little brass anvil, a watch stand, which was in the form of an angel's head with outstretched wings. Your pocket watch was taken off and hung there when you went to bed, presumably watched over by an angel. Other brass items I remember – a shoehorn in the shape of a lady's leg, very daring! A small brass stool with a slot in it, which said, 'Our wee girl is no fool, she puts her pennies in a stool.' We had a solid brass poker, and on the hearth, a solid brass stool intricately patterned, about eighteen inches high. It was called a toddy stool, and was supposed to hold the kettle of hot water at your side, to make your hot toddy with whisky and sugar and lemon. This despite my dad being a teetotaller!

There was linoleum on the floor, which was polished, and a small hearth rug in front of the fireplace. The kitchen chairs were wooden, and the kitchen table was covered with a sort of oilcloth so that it would be wiped with a damp cloth. At each corner of the table there was a cornerpiece with a horseshoe on it bearing the words, 'Good luck'. This held the oilcloth in place and presumably blessed us with good luck whenever we sat at the table.

There was an inbuilt coal bunker and a wooden dresser alongside. Just imagine coal being tipped into a bunker in the middle of the living room! There was a black iron sink with a single brass swan-neck cold water tap. Cupboards for pots were underneath the sink, and the cupboard for food was alongside at right angles. This was always referred to as the 'press'. There was a set-in bed at right angles to the fireplace.

Above the wooden dresser, opposite to the fireplace was a set of electroplated dish covers, which hung on hooks in a row. These ranged from a huge one, suitable for a baronial feast in some place like Balmoral Castle, all the way down in size to a small one. There were four of them, never, ever used. But they were a wedding present. The shelves above, two shelves, held a blue and white dinner service, a wedding present from the firm my mum worked for, hardly ever used, and a tea set, which my mother was proud of; it had pansies on it, hand painted, my mother told us. This was only ever washed then put back on the shelf. Also there, in the centre, a brass jelly pan, and an ornamental brass kettle. On the wall in the room there were two great big photos, oh about eighteen inches by two feet. Lovely portraits, one of my mother, one of my father, taken after their wedding day.

We had gas lighting, quite new then. Inverted gas mantles, 'Veritas' make, and a glass shade. We also had a paraffin lamp. My dad was the only one allowed to touch it, trim the wick, and fill it. It was on a stand and quite elegant, another wedding present.

SUFFRAGETTES AT WAR, 1914
Helen Crawfurd

Originally from the Gorbals, Helen Crawfurd (1877–1954) grew up in East Anglia. However, as a teenager she moved back to Glasgow, where in due course she married a Church of Scotland minister. She became active in the women's suffrage movement at the turn of the century but a decade or so later she switched support to the more radical Woman's Social and Political Union (WSPU). In 1912, she broke the windows of the Ministry for Education, for which she spent a month behind bars. A year later she was twice arrested in Glasgow when Emmeline Pankhurst was speaking. She was again jailed for a month and went on a five-day hunger strike. She left the WSPU in 1914 over its support for the war and joined the Independent Labour Party.

The body of the Hall had a large part of it filled with Socialists and anti-war adherents. The organ was pealing out patriotic songs which were countered by revolutionary songs from the body of the Hall. Many shop stewards, who were fighting in the workshops against the dilution of Labour by women at undercut wages, were also there to hear what the speakers had to say. The question of equal pay for equal work was not discussed but merely propaganda on the patriotic duty of women to go into the factories and produce munitions. Soon the audience became restive, and the singing and shouting rose to a deafening height. The Lord Provost Dunlop said if the uproar didn't stop he would let the munition workers loose on them. The women's patriotic fervour had been lashed to fever heat and they came down into the body of the Hall and up into the gallery and began an attack upon the men, some only with their hands, others with sticks. It was a most disgraceful scene. The fight was an unequal one. The finest men refused to return the blows rained on them, while others gave as good as they got. I was disgusted at Christabel Pankhurst and Mrs Drummond for being a party to such work. To me it was lowering to the dignity of women. I had not taken part in it but sat quietly watching till I could endure it no longer. I got up and walked down the centre passage of the hall, mounted the Reporter's table and protested, saying: 'Shame on you Christabel Pankhurst to get these women to do your dirty work. It is an insult to womanhood.' One of the platform party lifted a carafe of water to throw over me, but Flora Drummond prevented them, saying: 'She is not responsible!!'

BEARDED LIKE A MAN, 1914
Patrick MacGill

It has been estimated that around 300,000 refugees migrated to Britain during the Great Irish Famine of the mid-nineteenth century. Of those around a third arrived in Scotland. The influx of Irish continued well into the twentieth century, with the majority settling in the west central belt, Glasgow and Lanarkshire especially. Patrick MacGill came from dirt-poor Donegal, where he left school at the age of eleven, working for hiring fairs and farms before getting a job on the Glasgow–Greenock railway line. He made his name with a slim volume of verse and for a spell was a journalist. Known as the 'Navvy Poet', he is best known for his book, Children of the Dead End *(1914). In its foreword he wrote: 'When asking a little allowance for the pen of the novelist it must be said that nearly all of the incidents of the book have come under the observation of the writer.'*

I got a job on the railway and obtained lodgings in a dismal and crooked street, which was a den of disfigured children and a hothouse of precocious passion, in the south side of Glasgow. The landlady was an Irishwoman, bearded like a man, and the mother of several children. When indoors, she spent most of her time feeding one child, while swearing like a carter at all the others. We slept in one room, mother, children and myself, and all through the night the children yelled like cats in the moonshine. The house was alive with vermin. The landlady's husband was a sailor who went out on ships to foreign parts and always returned drunk from his voyages. When at home he remained drunk all the time, and when he left again he was as drunk as he could hold. I had no easy job to put up with him at first, and in the end we quarrelled and fought. He accused me of being too intimate with his wife when he was away from home. I told him that my taste was not utterly so bad, for indeed I had no inclination towards any woman, let alone the hairy and unkempt person who was my landlady. I struck out at him on the stair head. Three flights of stair led from the house down to the ground floor. I threw the sailor down the last flight bodily and headlong; he threw me down the middle flight. Following the last throw he would not face up again, and I had won the fight. Afterwards the woman came to her husband's aid. She scratched my face with her fingers and tore at my hair, clawing like an angry cat. I did not like to strike her back so I left her there with her drunken sailor and went out to the streets. Having no money I slept until morning beside a capstan on Glasgow quay.

RENT STRIKE, 1915
John Maclean

In 1915, in the middle of the First World War, many wives in Glasgow whose husbands were serving as soldiers found their rents were escalating. In the words of Helen Crawfurd, who had been raised by middle-class parents in the Gorbals, the 'fight was essentially a women's fight'. Through careful organisation and swift action, a campaign was mounted, supported by the shop stewards' movement and including the likes of John Maclean (1879–1923), who opposed the war on the grounds that it fuelled capitalism. After six months, the government capitulated and passed the Rent Restriction Act.

Through the tireless energy of Mr [Andrew] McBride, Secretary of the Labour Party's Housing Committee, and ardent supporter of the Women's Housing Committee, an agitation was started in the early summer against rent increases in the munition areas of Glasgow and district. Evening and mid-day work-gate meetings soon stimulated the active workers in all the large shipyards and engineering shops.

Emboldened, the organisers by demonstration and deputation tried to commit the Town Council to action against the increases. As it acts as the Executive Committee of the propertied class the Council shirked the responsibility of curbing the greed and rapacity of the factors and house-owners.

Enraged, the workers agitated more and more until the Government intervened by the appointment of a Commission of Inquiry. This was the signal for all the factors in the city to give notices of increase of rent. They anticipated that this united front would influence the Commissioner (as it did), and that the Government wold compromise the situation by allowing half the demands to be made legal . . .

Encouraged by the universal working-class support, and irritated by the operation of the infamous Munitions Act, the Clyde workers were ready to strike. This several yards did when 18 of their comrades appeared before Sheriff Lee. Beardmore's workers at Dalmuir sent a big deputation to tell the Sheriff that if he gave an adverse decision they would at once down tools. We have been favoured with a report of the proceedings in the Sheriff's room from the principal spokesman. It is intensely interesting as described by one of the spokesmen. In the circumstances the Sheriff wisely decided against the factor's demand for an increase. This was the first victory for working-class solidarity. We state the cause of triumph in these terms advisedly, for it really was due to joint action and not to the justice of the case (and there could be no juster) that success came to our side.

The strike having taken place, the workers were bent on letting the Government know that they would come again unless it restored rents to their pre-war level. It now transpires that a Rent Bill will be passed, forcing all factors of houses rented at £21 and under (£30 in London), to reduce the rents to the level prevailing immediately prior to the outbreak of the Great Slaughter Competition.

It should be noted that the rent strike on the Clyde is the first step towards the Political Strike, so frequently resorted to on the

Continent in times past. We rest assured that our comrades in the various works will incessantly urge this aspect on their shopmates, and so prepare the ground for the next great countermove of our class in the raging class warfare.

Readers ought to know that three years ago a report was issued of an investigation into the living conditions of about a hundred families in working-class wards in Glasgow. The investigators found that one out of every three families had to live under starvation conditions, on the assumption that every penny was put to the utmost use. The same conditions prevail to-day, with the infant mortality now deplored by wealthy ladies who themselves refuse to bear youngsters enough to fill up the gaps of war, and who consequently are anxious to keep up the balance of population by amateurish attempts to save the kiddies who, by misfortune or mistake, happen to enter this devilish world. In the circumstances it would be preposterous, as well as impolitic from a capitalist standpoint, to hold back anything from wages. We well know that an attempt will at first be made to limit deductions to those earning £2 and more per week. When once the 'principle' has been established, the process will be gradually applied to all workers by the same piecemeal method as Lord Derby intends to use to force conscription.

It is up to the workers to be ready, and resist with a might never exerted before . . . Every determined fight binds the workers together more and more and so prepares for the final conflict. Every battle lifts the curtain more and more, clears the heads of our class to their robbed and enslaved conditions, and so prepares them for the full development of the class war to the end of establishing Socialism.

A victory at football, draughts, or chess is the result of many moves and counter-moves. We do not lie down and cry when our side loses a goal. No. We buckle up our sleeves and spit on our hands, determined to get two more goals in return, or more. So it is in the game of life. Let us be up and doing all the time, never giving the enemy time to settle down to a peaceful enjoyment of victorious plunder. Prepare, then, for the enemy's counter-stroke to our victory on the rent question!

DOCTORING IN THE GORBALS, 1925
George Gladstone Robertson, M.D.

The connection between poverty and ill-health has long beset Glasgow. Few have documented the conditions as pungently as George Gladstone Robertson. Born in Shanghai, China, Robertson was a son of the manse. After his father's death in 1904, the family returned to Scotland and he was educated at Hutcheson's Grammar School and Glasgow University. Gifted athletically as well as academically, he represented Britain in swimming at the 1920 Olympics at Antwerp. Graduating in 1923, he entered a GP practice in the Gorbals, which was fast falling into decline, having previously been regarded as a place of fashionable elegance. His book, Gorbals Doctor, *published in 1970, six years before his death, makes grim if fascinating reading.*

The tenements in which these people lived, or in many cases, simply existed, were almost universally four storeys high. A great number had been built initially as large houses, but were now divided up into tiny apartments. One of the most squalid blocks was at 197 Centre Street. On each landing a passage went to right and left and four homes were entered from each narrow corridor. A small gas jet beside the stairway provided the only means of lighting this stench-laden cavern and as I climbed the worn steps, usually to answer some calls in the hollow early hours of a long dark winter's night, I would creep through the shadows and hear the sound of snoring, children crying or screaming; the never-ending squabbling between husbands and wives. In this building there was a fifth level of attics, making about thirty-six houses in all. Over two hundred people were crowded together in this miserable and hellish tenement.

The eerie sounds and the flickering shadows of the gas light were only minor obstacles with which I had to contend on my night visits. Men, and sometimes women, too drunk to crawl through their own doorways, lay in the passages. Some I managed to avoid, but more often than not, I would stumble and trip over a sprawling figure to be greeted on some occasions by a stream of oaths from the body I had jerked back into consciousness. This was humanity living at its lowest level and the drunks strewn in untidy heaps, many of them lying in their own vomit, would soon become a shameful symbol of the Gorbals and bring a stigma on Glasgow which the city would find difficult to erase.

In many cases the total possessions of a family would be worth little more than a five-pound note, and sometimes a father, mother and six children would all be living, cramped together, in a single apartment. The birth-rate was high, but so, too, was the incidence of death, especially among the very young. However, despite the squalor and the utter state of hopelessness which stared thousands of people directly in the face, the enlarging of families went on as baby after baby was born into a life surrounded by misery and perpetual torment.

In one three-apartment flat in another part of Centre Street I delivered a woman of her twenty-second child. She was married to her second husband and on the second or third day after the birth of a child she was always up and about and out to work in a greengrocer's shop as if nothing untoward had happened. Even after her twenty-second baby she rose from her bed on the third day and went back to work. In all she had twenty-six pregnancies – there were four miscarriages. To her, childbearing and the ultimate delivery were no joyous and wondrous occasions. They were merely mechanical happenings, bereft of love; duties which she, as a woman, was called upon to perform.

The proportion of late or night calls was always high; not because the baby or child had turned ill at night, but because it was then that the parent became worried or developed a bad conscience over previous neglect during the day. In many cases a husband would arrive home about 11 p.m. after an evening's hard drinking. His wife would immediately set about upbraiding him for wasting his time and neglecting the children. In order to hammer home her feelings she would point to the baby, who, due to the surrounding row, would almost certainly be awake and crying through fright and the pain of teething troubles. This provided a cue for the husband that he would 'bloody soon get her a doctor' and off he would stumble to the nearest phone.

If, in answering the phone, I protested that he should have sent his request earlier or added that he had not yet paid for the last call I had made to his house, I would normally be subjected to a stream of obscenities along with threats of complaints being made to medical executive bodies, the police or the Press – sometimes all three.

CLOSE ENCOUNTERS, *c.* 1925
Edward Gaitens

The McDonnels, whose family fortunes are followed in Dance of the Apprentices, *the 1948 novel by Edward Gaitens (1897–1966), live on the south side of Glasgow. Caught in a melting-pot of social injustice, revolution, war and pacifism, Mrs McDonnel struggles to lift her family and ambitious husband out of slum life. The book's 'apprentices' are inspired by Nietzsche and other European thinkers. In Gaitens' vision, the Gorbals is full of talented people who have few outlets to realise themselves. Sport was one of them, crime another. The close was at the heart of community, a space at once public and private, looking, as Gaitens so brilliantly put it, 'like tunnels cut through solid cliffs of masonry'.*

The close known as 150 South Wellington Street was like thousands of other Glasgow slum closes, a short, narrow walled-in passage leading up to three landings and through to a grassless earthen or broken-bricked backcourt, with its small, mean communal washhouse and open, insanitary midden. In such backcourts the women of the tenements, after taking their weekly turn in the washhouse, hang out the family washing and take it in dried with sunshine or strong seawind and half-dirtied with industrial smoke and grime. They are the only playground of many thousands of the city's children, where the youngsters play football and children's games, climb on the midden and washhouse roofs and escape death or injury from the perilous traffic of the streets.

They look like tunnels cut through solid cliffs of masonry, these closes, and in the slums are decorated in the crudest style. Halfway up their walls are painted a stone or chocolate colour which is separated from whitewash by a stencilled border of another shade. There are often great holes in the walls of these closes, left unplastered or, if filled in, left unpainted and presenting unsightly daubs or crudely plastered cement. As the walls are for long periods unrefreshed with new paint, the old paint cracks and peels and the dingy whitewash flakes and falls before factors will spend money on property renovation. Many tenement dwellers live indifferent to all this ugliness and those with some spirit, who are angered by it all, lose heart in their long, unequal struggle against the tight-fistedness of factors, and live in and die in homes too narrow for fuller life, from which it seems there is no escape. These closes, badly lit, with their dangerous broken-stepped stairs, often filthy and malodorous, smelling of catspiss and drunkards' spew, have been for generations of Glaswegians the favourite, and for thousands, the only courting-place, and many hurried, unhappy marriages have originated there. 'Stonin' at the close' or 'closemooth' is a social habit of tenement dwellers and at all hours lone individuals lounge, staring vacantly.

1926–1950

CANOODLING

BUILT BY THE PICTS? *c.* 1926
Clifford Hanley

Tenements were not unique to Glasgow but they have come to define it. Much that has been written about them has been negative but there were, as Clifford 'Cliff' Hanley (1922–99) reminds us, much that was good about them too. For a start they were solidly built and, for children at least, offered a ready-made playground which, with imagination, could be adapted to accommodate countless scenarios . . .

It is so ludicrous to imagine anybody actually building the things that I have always assumed that Glasgow's tenements have just always been there. Nobody could have put them up deliberately. When I first read about the ancient Picts running about in woad and scaring the life out of Caesar's legions, I took it for granted that they did their running about through the closes and back courts of Gallowgate where I was born.

The tenements are built extravagantly of good sandstone, so that they have out-lasted all those generations of Picts and are still there, and there doesn't seem anything anybody can do about them. It's true that in George Street and over in Govan, on the south side of the Clyde, some of them have started falling down spontaneously during the past ten years, but this is probably because people left them and they got lonely, and not through any constitutional weakness.

Most of them run to four storeys, built in rectangles to enclose the back courts. The back courts are divided by brick walls and brick-built wash-houses built for climbing over. It was on one of these that I made my first acquaintance with the terror that lurks in the big city. I would be four years old at the time, a perilous age in Glasgow because in order to live a full rich life at four, you have to attach yourself to the bigger fry and they can always run faster and jump higher than you can. So I was at the tail end of the line one night on the run along the top of the back court wall in Gallowgate and on to the high wash-houses of Cubie Street, and I was good and far behind when I arrived at one of the obstacles of the course.

There was a turn in the wall, and in order to finish the run you had to dreep to the ground, stand on a dustbin to get astride the next bit of wall and then home to the roofs. The instant I lowered myself to dreep I knew it was too far. It was too dark to see the ground below, but I had heard enough about people breaking both legs. I had heard practically nothing else, in fact, from the time I could walk. But by this time I was hanging by my fingers and I couldn't climb back up either. I shouted, but nothing happened, so I screamed, and I had a good vibrant scream in those days. A Glasgow back court on a dark Tuesday night is the loneliest place in the world.

Some time later my sister Johanne, sitting in the house a hundred yards away and two storeys up, recognised the screams and bolted out to save me. She had to prise my fingers off the top of the wall before she could pick me down.

Danger and death were always familiar acquaintances. A few weeks later the boy downstairs, Tommy Mulholland, was playing on his rocking-horse on the first floor landing when the whole thing overturned and carried him down a flight in a oner. It never seemed to cure him of riding facing the stairs, though it may seem odd that he was riding a rocking-horse on the landing at all.

The explanation is that the close in Glasgow is not just a hole in a building but a way of life. The close leads directly from the street to the back court, and the staircase to the flats above starts in the middle of it; and there is always something going on – somebody is always washing it or writing on the walls or hiding in it or giving a yell to test the echo.

After they wash it, the women give the stone flags a finish of wet pipeclay that dries bold and white and shows every footprint. Then, round the edges, they add a freehand border design drawn in pipeclay; sometimes a running loop like blanket-stitch, sometimes more tortuous key patterns, always mathematically accurate. It's a symptom of the unquenchable folk memory, or something from long-buried Celtic eternity and fertility symbols.

'I BELONG TO GLASGOW', 1927
Will Fyffe

The nearest thing the city has to its own anthem, 'I Belong to Glasgow' was the signature song of the hugely popular music-hall entertainer Will Fyffe. Fyffe always insisted he got the inspiration for it after he encountered a drunk at Glasgow Central Station. Apparently, the drunk was 'genial and demonstrative', as such characters often are, and 'laying off about Karl Marx and John Barleycorn with equal enthusiasm', which may not be quite as common. Engaging him in conversation, Fyffe asked him: 'Do you belong to Glasgow?', to which the fellow replied: 'At the moment, Glasgow belongs to me.' Thus was born the song which is still often heard in the wee small hours in the environs of Central Station and elsewhere. Fyffe, who was born in Dundee in 1885, died in 1947 and is buried in Glasgow.

Chorus:
I belong to Glasgow
Dear old Glasgow town
Well what's the matter with Glasgow
For it's goin' roon' and roon'
I'm only a common old working chap
As anyone here can see
But when I get a couple of drinks on a Saturday
Glasgow belongs to me.

Me and a few o' my cronies
One or two pals o' my ain
We went into a hotel and we did very well
Then we came out once again
Then we went in tae another
And that's the reason I'm fu'
We had six deoch and dorus and then sang a chorus
Listen, I'll sing it to you.

There's nothing in being teetotal
And saving a shilling or two
If your money you spend you got nothing to lend
Well that's all the better for you
There's nae harm in taking a droppie
It ends all your trouble and strife
It gives you a feeling that when you get home
You don't give a hang for your wife.

SPRINGBURN SINNERS, *c.* 1929
Molly Weir

Molly Weir (1910–2004) was for a spell a ubiquitous presence on television. Perky, petite and pretty, she exuded energy. Born in Springburn, she got into acting through amateur dramatics. She is perhaps best remembered for her role as Hazel the McWitch in the BBC series Rentaghost *(1977–84). During the 1970s and 1980s she became famous for a series of rose-tinted memoirs, including* Shoes Were for Sunday *(1970) and* Best Foot Forward *(1972). She was the sister of stravaiger and broadcaster, Tom Weir (1914–2006), who was rarely seen without his bobble hat.*

As well as the big Church, where we went to Sunday School, and Bible Class, and had our church parades of Girl Guides and the Boys' Brigade, we had the excitement of tent missions coming to Springburn to convert us. We didn't know we were being converted from heathenish ways, we just enjoyed the sight of a huge tent being erected on the piece of waste ground at the end of Gourlay Street, and we begged to be allowed to help to hand out the little leaflets telling all that Jock Troup would be preaching and saving souls that night and all week from 7.30 p.m. As soon as our tea was swallowed, we raced back to get front seats, and the adults crowded in at our backs, greatly entranced to be having hellfire preached at them inside a tent. Jock was great value, and we all imitated him afterwards, not in any spirit of derision, but in profound admiration. He could make the flames of hell so real, we felt them licking round our feet, and the prospect of heaven so alluring we often stood up to be saved several times during the week, just to see him fall on his knees in thankfulness at having plucked so many brands from the burning. His hymns were different from those in Sunday School and had a sort of music-hall ring to them which we all enjoyed.

One obviously designed to appeal to our Scottish sense of economy went:

> 'Nothing to pay, no, nothing to pay,
> Straight is the gate, and narrow the way,
> Look unto Jesus, start right away,
> From Springburn to glory, and nothing to pay.'

We particularly liked 'Springburn' coming into the hymn, not realising that he just substituted whatever district he happened to be visiting, and we felt he had composed this hymn specially for Springburn sinners.

A CRATE OF APPLES, 1930
Maurice Lindsay

Maurice Lindsay (1918–2009) was the author of more than fifty books. He was also a broadcaster – he presented the first Scottish arts television programme, Counterpoint *– a poet of note, and Director of the Scottish Civic Trust. Born in Glasgow in a private nursing home, his family was well-to-do; his father was the Scottish manager of a UK insurance company while his mother was 'a gentle creature'. In* Thank You For Having Me *(1983), he painted a vivid and affectionate portrait of middle-class Glasgow life in the 1920s and 1930s, when the city was 'already sinking into decline, but somehow mustering enough self-confidence, in what was perhaps by then already non-achievement, still to think of itself as "great"!'*

With the family growing up a bigger house was needed. In 1930 we moved to 32 Athole Gardens, an enclosed, hilly U-shaped crescent built in the high Victorian manner of the 1870s round a private fenced common central garden containing a grass tennis court. Early in the summer the pink flambeaux of a horse chestnut tree illuminated the front of our house, its flares of light reflecting on the window-panes. From my high-up back bedroom window, I could see across the roofscape at the back of the house a horizon distantly fretted by shipyard cranes.

Although by the early thirties the City's grey and red sandstone buildings had long been darkened by coal-fired industrial and domestic smoke and the dense yellow fogs that licked them every winter, the decay and dilapidation of the post-Second-World-War years had not yet set in. For one thing, the city's wide range of decorated nineteenth-century railings still stood intact. The hasty tearing-down of those practical fringes of Victorian fancy on the orders of Lord Beaverbrook during the 1939 war to be recycled for purposes for which they proved totally unsuitable and could not be used, freely admitted blowing street rubbish and a creeping decline the railings had held trimly at bay. There was no awareness of any concept of conservation in those days, though most of the new buildings put up in the decade before the 1939 war still spoke with a modified version of the Victorian amalgam of earlier styles.

It was not just the buildings in our district that gave it a sense of entity. There was still a sense of community about Hillhead. The Byres Road shopkeepers knew us all by name, and we them. There was Wilkie, the grocer, who sent round a crate of apples at Christmas in appreciation of our custom; the thirties equivalent, I suppose, of such later devices as selling loss-leaders or giving away trading stamps. The three – or was it four? – Misses Horn kept the dairy, with the cow at one time in a byre behind the shop, though I cannot recall this. They had hands as blue as the Dutch wall-tiles of their shop, due, I used to think, to so much scrubbing, though their hands were not as raw as those of the daughter of Andrews, the fishmonger, whose fingers were forever lifting moist fillets off chipped block ice. Comfortably rounded Mr and Mrs Todd, the fruiters, added their contribution to the Christmas scene with a gift of tangerines to all their 'regulars'. Tully, the ironmonger, and Bell of the toyshop featured less prominently, being on the more occasionally visited periphery of my childish world of things. Most exotic of all was Henderson's stable, from which issued forth the musty-smelling horse-drawn cabs that conveyed us to children's parties. The cabs had faded yellowish-green seats and were driven by cabbies wearing greenish bowler hats. They stood slapping their arms and blowing in their glove-ends to keep warm which they waited for their winter 'fares' to materialise from the streets. In time, those cabs gave place to cumbersome-looking limousines which used the same shelter. Cabs and limousines have long since gone, their base now an Underground station.

My mother devoted much time to the ordering of household chores. Our cooks and our parlour-maids usually came from the Highlands, and, like most domestics in these days, spoke Gaelic. To hear them talk in a language incomprehensible to me was my first experience of the Scottish dichotomy. That a dichotomy existed even in the smaller world of the Gael became apparent when frequently they would argue in English, oblivious of my presence, about the meaning or correct pronunciation of a Gaelic word as spoken in Skye, rather than as it was pronounced in Stornoway. From time to time my mother wrote out a daily chart of duties for each of the domestics. For the parlour-maid it went like: Mondays, clean the dining-room silver and polish the glasses; Tuesday, tidy out the kitchen and pantry cupboards; Wednesday, brush and dust the dining-room and parlour; Thursday, brush and dust the drawing-room, the hall stairs and hall landings – and so on. Cook was supplied with the week's menus and instructions on the economics of house-keeping.

There was, of course, in reality a succession of cooks and parlour-maids who came and went for reasons usually unclear to us children. Usually there were mysterious allies, denizens of female warmth in their shining kitchens, where the fire in the cooking-range made the copper jellypans on the shelves of the dresser glint and glimmer; allies surreptitiously chatable-to when the regime of the nursery occasionally slackened. One Lowland cook of exceptional plainness, for whom Gaelic was simply 'a wheen o' blethers', ended unfinished every promising confabulation by relaxing her bulk and her perennial problem into the depth of a chair, gasping: 'Goad! If only ah could get a man!'

A RAZOR ATTACK ON MOSLEY, 1931
Harold Nicolson

In the 1930s Glasgow, like other beleaguered cities in the UK, was not immune to the appeal of fascism but there were always those prepared to oppose it, sometimes violently. Harold Nicolson (1886–1968), who is today best known for his voluminous diaries, was married to poet, novelist and gardener Vita Sackville-West. Well-connected and socially (and sexually) gregarious, he inhabited many milieux and enjoyed all of them. In 1931 he was a supporter of Sir Oswald ('Tom') Mosley's New Party and the unsuitable editor of its journal, Action. *By 1932, however, he had distanced himself from the Mosleyites, writing: 'The difficulty with the New Party is that it is no longer new and no longer a party . . . Now I feel that the New Party as such has become too much identified with Hitlerism.'*

The papers are full of a razor attack made on Tom at Glasgow. On getting to the office I find Peter [Howard, international rugby player, journalist and New Party candidate] back from there. He tells me that the meeting was rather a success. 20,000 people. The speech was got across all right by loud-speakers. During the meeting a note was passed up: 'Be careful when you go – the Reds have got their razors.' When all the questions had been asked and answered, Tom faced the crowd: called out, 'now, boys': stepped from the platform and advanced towards the little group of communists who had created the disturbance. They turned and fled. Tom passed through the crowd. The communists formed behind and attacked them from the rear. A stone was thrown and hit Tom lightly on the head. A man attacked him with a life-preserver but was seized in time. Peter Howard was thrown and rose to knock a man down. They escaped to their cars.

NOT EVEN A SCOTTISH SLUM, 1934
Lewis Grassic Gibbon

Lewis Grassic Gibbon was the pseudonym of James Leslie Mitchell (1901–35), 'my distant cousin'. The son of a farmer, he was born in Aberdeenshire. He worked as a journalist with the Scottish Farmer. *When he lost his job he joined the Royal Army Service Corps and served in the Middle East and elsewhere. From 1928 until his premature death he wrote as one possessed: biography, history, travelogue, polemic, criticism and fiction. In 1932, he published* Sunset Song, *the first part of the trilogy,* A Scots Quair. *A friend of Hugh MacDiarmid, he collaborated with him on* Scottish Scene *(1934) from which the following extract is taken.*

Glasgow is one of the few places in Scotland which defy personification. To imagine Edinburgh as a disappointed spinster, with a hare-lip and inhibitions, is at least to approximate as closely to the truth as to imagine the Prime Mover as a Levantine Semite. So with Dundee, a frowsy fisher-wife addicted to gin and infanticide, Aberdeen a thin-lipped peasant-woman who has borne eleven and buried nine. But no Scottish image of personification may display, even distortedly, the essential Glasgow. One might even go further afield, to the tortured imaginings of the Asiatic mind, to find her likeness – many-armed Siva with the waistlet of skulls, of Xipe of Ancient America, whose priest skinned the victim alive, and then clad himself in the victim's skull . . . But one doubts anthropomorphic representation at all. The monster of Loch Ness is probably the lost soul of Glasgow, in scale and horns, disporting itself in the Highlands after evacuating finally and completely its mother corpse.

One cannot blame it. My distant cousin, Mr. Leslie Mitchell, once described Glasgow in one of his novels as 'the vomit of a cataleptic commercialism'. But it is more than that. It may be a corpse, but the maggot-swarm upon it is fiercely alive. One cannot watch and hear the long beat of traffic down Sauchiehall, or see it eddy and spume where St. Vincent Street and Renfield Street cross, without realising what excellent grounds the old-fashioned anthropologist appeared to have for believing that man was by nature a brutish savage, a herd-beast delighting in vocal discordance and orgiastic aural abandon.

Loch Lomond lies quite near to Glasgow. Nice Glaswegians motor out there and admire the scenery and calculate its horse-power and drink whisky and chaff one another in genteelly Anglicised Glaswegianisms. After a hasty look at

Glasgow the investigator would do well to disguise himself as one of like kind, drive down to Loch Lomondside and stare across its waters at the sailing clouds that crown the Ben, at the flooding of colours changing and darkling and miraculously lighting up and down those misty slopes, where night comes over long mountain leagues that know only of the startled pheasants, silences so deep you can hear the moon come up, mornings so greyly coloured they seem stolen from Norse myth. This is the proper land and stance from which to look at Glasgow, to divest oneself of horror or shame or admiration or – very real – fear, and ask: Why? Why did men ever ally themselves to become enslaved to a thing so obscene and so foul when there was *this* awaiting them here – hills and the splendours of freedom and silence, the clean splendours of hunger and woe and dread in the winds and rains and famine-times of the earth, hunting and love and the call of the moon? Nothing endured by the primitives who once roamed those hills – nothing of woe or terror – approximated in degree or kind to that life that festers in the courts and wynds and alleys of Camlachie, Govan, the Gorbals.

In Glasgow there are over a hundred and fifty thousand human beings living in conditions as the most bitterly pressed primitive in Tierra del Fuego never visioned. They live five or six to the single room . . . And this requires a mental jerk to realise the quality of that room. It is not a room in a large and airy building; it is not a single-roomed hut on the verge of a hill; it is not a cave driven into free rock, in the sound of the sea-birds, as that old Azilian cave in Argyll: it is a room that is part of some great sloven of tenement – the tenement itself in a line or grouping with hundreds of its fellows, its windows grimed with the unceasing wash and drift of coal-dust, its stairs narrow and befouled and steep, its evening breath like that which might issue from the mouth of a lung-diseased beast. The hundred and fifty thousand eat and sleep and copulate and conceive and crawl into childhood in waste jungles of stench and disease and hopelessness, subhumans as definitely as the Morlocks of Wells – and without even the consolation of feeding on their oppressors' flesh.

A hundred and fifty thousand . . . and all very like you or me or my investigator sitting appalled on the banks of Loch Lomond (where he and his true love will never meet again). And they live on food of the quality of offal, ill-cooked, ill-eaten with speedily-diseased teeth for the tending of which they can afford no fees; they work – if they have work – in factories or foundries or the roaring reek of the Docks toilsome and dreary and unimaginative hours – hour on hour, day on day, frittering away tissues of their bodies and the spirit-stuff of their souls; they are workless – great numbers of them – doomed to long days of staring vacuity, of shoelessness, of shivering hidings in this and that mean runway where the landlords' agents come, of mean and desperate beggings at Labour Exchanges and Public Assistance Committees; their voices are the voices of men and women robbed of manhood and womanhood . . .

It is coming on dark, as they say in the Scotland that is not Glasgow. And out of the beast of the Gorbals arises that foul breath as of a dying beast.

You turn from Glasgow Green with a determination to inspect this Gorbals on your own. It is incredibly un-Scottish. It is lovably and abominably and hideously un-Scottish. It is not even a Scottish slum. Stout men in beards and ringlets and unseemly attire lounge and strut with pointed shoes: Ruth and Naomi go by with downcast Eastern faces, the Lascar rubs shoulder with the Syrian, Harry Lauder is a Baal unkeened to the midnight stars. In the air the stench is of a different quality to Govan's or Camlachie's – a better quality. It is haunted by an ancient ghost of goodness and grossness, sun-warmed and ripened under alien suns. It is the most saving slum in Glasgow, and the most abandoned. Emerging from it, the investigator suddenly realises why he sought it in such haste from Glasgow Green: it was in order that he might assure himself there were really and actually other races on the earth apart from Scots!

YOU SAY 'POLIS'; I SAY 'POLICE', 1934
Educational Institute of Scotland

It has long been said that Scottish children speak two languages, one in the playground, the other in the classroom, which this report on 'Glasgow Speech' by one of Scotland's teaching unions seems to confirm.

In most cases Glasgow pupils enter the schools with one language only, the Central Scottish Dialect, and they proceed to learn to write Standard English. As the result of education the vernacular is gradually eliminated from written work, but it persists in colloquial use.

The Central Scottish Dialect is the medium of expression naturally employed by the Glasgow child who may interrogate the teacher during a Dictation lesson with such a question as, 'Whit cums efter, "after"?' In the playground children who try to speak Standard English are generally laughed at, whilst in the class-room a lapse into the mother-tongue is greeted with hilarity. Thus, the boy who during the dinner-interval maliciously created a stampede of his classmates by the cry of 'Polis', that same afternoon cause much amusement in the school-room by reading, 'Sir Robert Peel founded the *Polis* Force'.

NAMING THE YARDS, 1935
George Blake

The Clyde and shipbuilding are umbilically linked. The latter dates to the introduction of steam-powered ship propulsion at the beginning of the nineteenth century when the deepening of the river made it possible for ocean-going ships to reach right into the heart of the city. There followed an impressive stream of technical innovations. New materials – iron, then steel – were greedily embraced and major engineering improvements, yielding greater speed and significant fuel economies, were introduced. By 1900 the Clyde had secured pole position in world shipbuilding, producing about half a million tons of shipping annually, approximately a third of world output, occasionally exceeding the combined German and US totals. After the First World War, however, decline was slow but inevitable and by the time George Blake (1893–1961) published his novel, The Shipbuilders, *in 1935 yard closures, unemployment and empty order books were increasingly the norm and the end of launches of great ships like the* Estramadura *was nigh.*

It was in a sense a procession that he witnessed, the high tragic pageant of the Clyde. Yard after yard passed by, the berths empty, grass growing about the sinking keel-blocks. He remembered how, in the brave days, there would be scores of ships ready for the launching along this reach, their sterns hanging over the tide, and how the men at work on them on high-stagings would turn from the job and tug off their caps and cheer the new ship setting out to sea. And now only the giant dumb poles and groups of men workless, watching in silence the mocking-passage of the vessel. It was bitter to know that they knew – that almost every man among them was an artist in one of the arts that go to the building of a ship; that every feature of the *Estramadura* would come under an expert and loving scrutiny, that her passing would remind them of the joy of work, and tell them how many of them would never work again. It appalled Leslie Pagan that not a cheer came from those watching groups.

It was a tragedy beyond economics. It was not that so many homes lacked bread and butter. It was that a tradition, a skill, a glory, a passion, was visibly in decay, and all the acquired and inherited loveliness of artistry rotting along the banks of the stream.

Into himself he counted and named the yards they passed. The number and variety stirred him to wonder, now that he had ceased to take them for granted. His mental eye moving backwards up the river, he saw the historic place of Govan, Henderson's of Meadowside at the mouth of the Kelvin, and the long stretch of Fairfield on the southern bank opposite. There came Stephen's of Linthouse next, and Clydeholm facing it across the narrow yellow ditch of the ship-channel. From thence down river the range along the northern bank was almost continuous for miles – Connell, Inglis, Blythswood and the rest: so many that he could hardly remember their order. He was distracted for a moment to professionalism by the lean grey forms of destroyers building for a foreign power in the sheds of a yard that had dramatically deserted Thames for Clyde. Then he lost himself again in the grim majesty of the parade. There came John Brown's, stretching along half a mile of waterfront at Clydebank, the monstrous red hull of Number 534 looming in its abandonment like a monument to the glory departed; as if shipbuilding man had tried to do too much and been defeated by the mightiness of his own conception. Then came, seeming to point the moral, the vast desolation of

Beardmore's at Dalmuir, cradle of the mightiest battleships and now a scrap-heap, empty and silent forever, the great gantry over the basin proclaiming stagnation and an end.

A TREE IN ARGYLE STREET, 1935

James Cowan

Argyle Street is one of Glasgow's oldest and had many fine buildings, most of which have now gone, and not a few trees. By the 1930s, however, it teemed with shoppers and traffic and, as James Cowan records in Glasgow's Treasure Chest *(1951), it had so few trees that one was worthy of remark.*

At the west end of Argyle Street there is a four-storeyed tenement known as Franklin Terrace, which has a narrow strip of garden round the front of it. About the middle of this tenement, at No. 1223 Argyle Street, there stands a very tall ash tree, its highest branches reaching far above the top windows of the tenement. This tree is unusually graceful for an ash, its slender trunk being almost as straight as a ship's mast; and there are no heavy side branches to spoil its symmetry. This slenderness is no doubt owing to the shaded position causing the tree to stretch up to the light. It is quite the most graceful ash I have seen.

Vague sentimental stories are always apt to grow up around any interesting object of which the exact origin is not known, and I found this tree to be no exception; but in conversation with a friend I learned how it came to be there.

A friend of his used to live in the house in front of which the tree stands. A member of this friend's family brought home some primrose roots from the place he had been on holiday, and set them out in the plot. The earth around one of these roots must have contained the ash-tree seed, and when the sapling came up it was allowed to remain. That story may not be so sentimentally interesting as one or two others which exist about the tree, but it has the merit of being the true one.

Not very long ago an adventurous cat made its way up the branches of this tree on a level with the rones of the tenement, and then found it could not come down again. For nearly two days it remained there, mewing piteously, until a telephone message was sent for the fire brigade to come and rescue it. At first the fire brigade authorities demurred at being called upon for such a purpose, but at last it was recognised that nothing short of a fire escape would meet the case, and the very latest and longest was sent out. An exciting 20 minutes then ensued, during which long lines of traffic were held up, east and west, and at last pussy was rescued, to the great satisfaction of the cheering crowd who looked on.

As Franklin Terrace was built about 1850 (it appears for the first time in the Glasgow directory of 1851) and my informant could himself remember the tree in question as quite a large one in 1877, it is probable that its seed was set only a few years after the erection of the tenement. I estimate its height at about 75 feet, and if its age be taken as the same number of years, I think that will not be far from correct. It looks healthy enough to last for another 75 years, if allowed to remain, as I hope it will.

AN ANTI-SOCIAL NEIGHBOUR, *c.* 1935
Agnes Muirhead

With so many people living in close proximity to each other, it is little wonder that friction occasionally occurred, and that residents like Agnes Muirhead took it upon themselves to sort it out . . .

This day, it must have been my half day off. And my mother had been washin' when I came in. I said, 'What's the matter?' 'I'm after puttin' out a washin'. Would you have a look at that?' I said, 'What is it?' She said, 'That's them settin' the papers up the chimneys.' I said, 'What dae ye mean, settin' the papers up the chimneys?' She says, 'That's every time ye put a washin' out here!' I said, 'Oh, is it?' So I cut through tae the wash-house, and I copes this woman at the wash-house door. I said, 'Excuse me, who set the wash-house on fire?' 'Who wants tae know?' I said, 'I do.' 'It's oor wash-house, and if we want tae set it on fire, we'll set it on fire.' I says, 'Just do that. But the next time you put out a washin' ye'll have tae take it in.' 'Why?' she says. I says, 'Tae re-wash it.'

So I went tae the neighbour up the stair and I says tae her, 'Do you get your washin' dirty?' She says, 'Agnes, it's terrible here, you've no idea what we're made tae put up with.' I said, 'Is that a fact?' She says, 'That's right.' I says, 'Right, what day do they do their washin'?' 'A Monday.' I says, 'Right, I'll have a Monday off.' I *did* take a Monday off my work. The washin' went out. It was coal fires at the time. I says tae Katie Tinley, 'You have a bucket o' ashes ready.' She says, 'Right.'

Well, where oor ash pits was, their back was open. So I went out with the ash bins. Smack! Right intae their clothes. They came out! I says, 'Told ye ye would need to take your washin' in, didn't I? And every time my mother's tae do a double washin' you'll dae one along wi' her!' So that stopped that. We put an end tae that.

A COCKTAIL BAR AT IBROX, 1936
Hugh Savage

In the annals of Rangers football club few figures loom larger than William 'Bill' Struth (1875–1956). The club's second manager, his tenure lasted thirty-four years, during which time Rangers won thirty trophies, including a remarkable eighteen league championships. It was the kind of record which inspired awe even in a Celtic supporter such as Hugh Savage.

After a short spell in the workshop I was actually sent to the next job with Sanny [McIntyre]. It was to fit a cocktail bar in the main stand adjacent to the directors' box at Ibrox Park. To more than half of all the boys in Glasgow this would have been a dream come true. But I had always regarded myself as a Celtic supporter so my feelings were somewhat mixed. Nevertheless, when entering the empty stadium, the home of Glasgow Rangers, you could not be anything but impressed by the atmosphere.

It was larger than I expected. The stand was built to provide space and the red terracotta brick gave it strength to match its size. The main entrance was most impressive, with its marble floors and columns, and its marble staircase with blue carpets to the fore. What took me by surprise was the friendly atmosphere.

Everybody from the wee women who worked in the kitchen to the squad of cleaners who came in to clean the whole stadium, they were all genuinely obliging and helpful.

No one objected when me and Sanny took our tea-can and piece and sat on the steps of the stand watching the players train. Of course the highlight was the trial games they played at least once a week with the reserves playing the first team. It was no stroll either. All the players put their maximum effort into the game and when they left the field they were sweating heavily. I used to smile to myself and wonder what all the fanatic Rangers' supporters would say if they knew a 'tim' was watching players like Davie Meiklejohn, Jerry Dawson, George Brown, Jimmy Simpson, Dougie Gray, Bob McPhail out training. All of the above-named were automatic choices for any Scottish team, with Meiklejohn regular captain.

The job took much longer than was envisaged and additional work cropped up. Many other tradesmen were working in the stadium. In those days we continued going till 12 noon on a Saturday. The second week there I was in the new cocktail bar with Sanny McIntyre when Mr Struth the manager approached and handed us both an envelope. We did not know what it contained. When he held it out to me he said, 'Now don't you be giving it away.'

As soon as he disappeared I hurriedly opened the envelope. It was a complimentary ticket for the stand for the match with Aberdeen that same afternoon.

Apparently this had been the practice for a long time and Mr Bill Struth always carried it out himself. The joiner who was there working with us had done some work at Celtic Park and I asked him if this practice prevailed there too. He said to me, 'Not on your life. I was there for two months and not only did I not get a ticket but I never knew anyone who did.'

Mr Bill Struth was a genuine legend in his own time. He had been a professional football player but he had been an athlete and the Rangers' Annual Sports day was probably the most attractive athletic event in the entire sports calendar. In those days there were no professionals in athletics but the quality of the prizes and the treatment of the participants ensured that most world-class athletes welcomed an invitation. I remember seeing the great Sidney Wooderson, slightly built with his straight hair parted in the middle and wearing glasses, leaving the world-class field in his wake as he smashed the mile record. The famous Finnish long-distance runer Pavvo Nurmi appeared at Ibrox and lapped the best in the world.

My most embarrassing experience at Ibrox was one weekday when taking material up to my mate in the stand. A player – I think his name was Bobby Mains – asked me if I would close the door after he had put his car under the stand. I never gave it a thought and after closing it I ran up the stairs to the stand and virtually ran right into Mr Struth, who was standing at the top of the steps. I apologised and made to pass him but he stopped me.

'Excuse me but who told you to close that door?'

'The driver.'

Mr Struth then said very firmly, 'your job here is to fit pipes, not to close doors, so go back to your work'.

As far as I remember he told the player off for bringing his car to Ibrox on a training day because it was an unwritten law that all players had to walk from the rail or bus stations. But he never stopped giving me a complimentary ticket for games . . .

MORE A DUMMY THAN A MUMMY, *c.* 1936
Dirk Bogarde

Room in the family home in London – where his father was employed at The Times *– was cramped so Dirk Bogarde (1921–1999) was sent to stay with his mother's relatives in Glasgow, where he spent three misery-laden but, in hindsight, formative years. It was to Glasgow, perhaps, he owed his love of cinema and his liking of subterfuge. Later, he starred in many movies, from slapstick to art house, including* Doctor in the House, The Servant, Darling, Death in Venice *and* The Night Porter. *He also wrote seven well-received memoirs and several novels. He was knighted in 1991.*

At lunch-time, instead of eating my sodden meat pie with Tom or whoever else was sitting on the dustbin wall, I just stuck my cap in my pocket, pinned a handkerchief in my Blazer pocket so that it flopped over the give-away crest on the badge, opened my collar, stuffed my tie somewhere else, and, hands in pockets, one and sixpence saved from here and there, I strolled happily down the hill from the school into the busy crowds of George Square and let Glasgow and its allure swallow me up. It was as easy as that, and no one bothered to check. At first, naturally, I was terrified. I was sure that I would be spotted and carted back to the amiable but fearsome Dr Steel. However, with no badges or colours showing, I passed for any other boy wandering about the city. I found deceit very refreshing.

Woolworths was my usual haven. Because it was warm and bright and filled with people. Here was Life. Pushing and shoving, smiling and laughing, talking and living. Music played all day. The record counter had a constant supply of melody. To the lingering refrains of 'When The Poppies Bloom Again' I would sit on a high stool eating a Chocolate Fudge Ice Cream and beam happily at the world about me. Guiltless. It was all heady stuff.

Later I grew bolder and went, imagine the bravery!, to the cinema alone. For sixpence, in the middle of the stalls with a packet of peanuts or a Mars Bar, I sat in my element and got two movies, all the Advertising, the Newsreel, the Forthcoming Attractions plus a pink, green and amber lit Organ Recital.

Life was *never* to be dull and drab again. I would always live like this, and the Hell with Effort, Loyalty and 'The Times'.

It would be useful to say at this point that it was the moment my whole future was laid before me. The great silver screen, the glamour, the glory, the guns and the chases. Camera angles, Lighting, Back Projection, Split Screen, Fade and Dissolve flew past my eyes twice a week and vanished like dreams. But I was the Original Audience for which these films were made. The refugee from worry, humdrum life, anxiety or despair. I only wanted to be bewitched, enthralled, be-glamoured. The rest of it washed away like silt in a tub. Nothing at all rubbed off at that time. My personal disillusion, even disappointment, was so great, my anger so deep, that I had fixed it clearly that I would try no more. They could come and get me and punish me in whatever way they liked: I had given up. But until they did come to get me, or sent for me, I was going to have as pleasant a time as I possibly could. What on earth was the point of going on any longer? I had tried, and failed again. So be it.

The Paramount was a new, glittering Picture Palace with a deadly reputation. I had heard it spoken of in muted voices in many of the parlours to which I was bidden, or sent, for those Bakings and Teas. It was the meeting place of all the Evil in Glasgow, the Crooks and Thieves and Bookies. Any young girl going there alone, it was said, invariably ended up with a hypodermic in her bottom and a bunk in a boat at the Broomielaw awaiting the next tide down the Clyde for Morocco. Indeed the people Upstairs knew of one girl who, missing her companions, had foolishly gone alone to see Robert Taylor and was never heard of again apart from the fact that an usherette had seen a dark-skinned man helping a young lady to a taxi from the foyer saying that she had had a 'fainting fit'. It made going to the Pictures much more interesting.

In any case I felt secure because of two things: first I was a boy, secondly I always sat in the middle of the stalls where it was lighter, and never in the shadows where, of course, anything might happen. Armed, this day, with my logic, I went to see a special showing of Boris Karloff in *The Mummy*. I had seen it two or three times before, ages ago, but it was still my favourite next to *The Bride of Frankenstein*. I also saw Mr Dodd.

Mr Dodd was almost entirely beige. A beige raincoat, beige face, beige hair and freckles. He sat two or three seats away from me and smiled pleasantly all through the Forthcoming Attractions. And still I didn't know.

During the interval, when the lights went pink and green and the organ rumbled through a selection from something or other, he smiled shyly across the empty seats and I smiled back, and he moved along and came and sat beside me. He asked if I would like an ice-cream, and I said yes, and we ate together in pleasant, companionable silence. He was very polite, quietly spoken and smiled a lot; and when he took my empty ice-cream tub away from me, plus the wooden spoon and stacked it neatly into his own and tidily placed it all under the seat, he patted my leg kindly and whispered with a secret wink that I was, in all probability, playing truant from school, wasn't I? Shattered with surprise that he had so quickly found me out, I lied swiftly and said I was 'off school' with a sprained ankle. That seemed to content him and the programme started again so that there was no need for more conversation.

It was very nice having someone to laugh at the film with, to share fear with, and to enjoy relief with all at the same time. He was very attentive and once, in a particularly creepy part he put his arm protectively round my shoulder, which I thought was very thoughtful of him indeed.

By the time the show was over it was well after six, and I would have to leave my new friend quickly and 'limp' to the station and Bishopbriggs where my aunt would be waiting to hear from me how well the rehearsals for the school play were going. My excuse, true as it happened, for the lateness of my arrival. Mr Dodd was sad, he told me his name and that I was to call him Alec, and made an appointment for us to see the film again at the end of the week. It was to be his treat, he said, and after we would go to Cranstons for tea but that I could still be home in time so as not to worry my aunt.

* * *

Tea at Cranstons was an impressive affair at the worst of times, and this was the best. Quiet, calm, warm, sparkling with silver, white tablecloths, flowers in fluted vases, motherly waitresses in crisp aprons and little caps, and a silver stand of cakes. Mr Dodd knew his way about very well and was pleasant to everyone and anxious that I should eat as much as I could for, he said, he was a Medical Student and he knew just how much 'fuel' the working lad's mind had to have to keep it going. He told me how his mother had saved and scrimped to send him to School and then on to Medical College where he was now studying. The conversation slid back, inevitably, to the film and he astonished me by saying that he knew exactly how mummies were bandaged and how they were embalmed; it was really very easy to do, he said cheerfully, and anyone could make a mummy if they knew how to bandage. I was overcome with curiosity and asked him more and more questions; he tried to demonstrate with his table napkin but it was too small and too thick, so he suggested that since he lived nearby and had all his books and bandages there we should go at once and he could show me in a trice.

I accepted immediately; already telling my aunt the lie about the play. And I still didn't know.

His flat was a rather poky room with a kitchenette in a high block over a tobacconist and sweet shop in Hope Street. It smelled of ether and stale cigarettes and was pretty untidy, for which he apologised, and pulling hurriedly at the unmade bed and taking some dirty plates and a bottle into the sink. There were books everywhere, a typewriter, old shirts, and a gas fire which plopped when he lit it. On the wall were pictures of Rothesay Castle and two men wrestling. He opened a thick book filled with diagrams of bandaging; people were swathed in them, heads, hips, legs, wrists, arms and everything else. It was very comprehensive.

Chattering happily, he pulled a large cardboard box from under the bed and spilled rolls and rolls of blue-wrapped bandages of every size all over the floor. These, he said, were just the trick to turn me into a splendid mummy and if I would just remove my jacket and shirt and vest and sit down in that chair he would turn me into Boris Karloff in the flick of a fly's eyelid.

I dutifully, rather shyly, did as he suggested while he started to unroll yards and yards of filmy gauzes. It was not very long before I was strait-jacketed in strips of thin cotton bandages from the top of my head to my waist, arms securely folded, in the correct position of mummies, across my chest, a small slit left for each eye so that I could hazily see through a vague fringe of white blur, a small hole left for my nostrils so that I could breathe. Otherwise I was trussed like a fowl. Taking down the oval mirror from the mantelpiece he showed me the effect which I found impressive, uncomfortable, and very restricting. I could merely manage a vague motion with my head, which didn't show, and roll my slitty eyes. I could neither see properly, nor even hear for that matter, and I was totally mute.

As he turned from replacing the mirror, and as I stood to indicate that he might unwrap me as soon as possible, I could see that he was speaking, but only a blurred mumble came to my bandaged ears and it was with some rising degree of alarm that I found myself clutched firmly in his arms and dumped on my back in the middle of the brass bed. I tried to struggle and yell out, at least to sit up, but I was totally rigid and the only sound I made was smothered in yards and yards of thick white gauze. Putting his beige face very close to my ear Mr Dodd said that it seemed a pity not to finished the job and make me a full mummy from head to foot, that would complete the Effect.

My shoes and socks were wrenched off and thrown under the bed, then my trousers and to my silent screams of protest, he ripped off my underpants and I was stark naked before his eager, now red-faced, gaze.

Swiftly and with the expert precision of a born embalmer, he rolled me about the bed in a flurry of bandage. I was wrapped like a parcel, rolled this way and that, on my back, on my side, every which way until I was reeling with giddiness and terror. I was wound tightly into a cocoon as a spider rolls a grasshopper. Helpless, inert, more a dummy even than a mummy, I lay rigid as Mr Dodd, his mouth stuck with safety pins, tucked in the loose ends; when this was done, and with great strength he manoeuvred me off the bed, stiff as a telegraph pole, and set me upright on cotton feet to see my reflection in the mirror of his wardrobe door. Peering desperately through the eye slits I could see that he had made a complete and thorough job. Boris Karloff wasn't half as convincing.

Unable to stand by myself I was forced to lean against the serge shoulder of my host whose face was bathed in pleasure. Surely my heart could not beat so quickly with terror and I should still live. It leapt from my chest and now pumped and throbbed in my throat. It stopped entirely when my horrified eyes saw, pathetically through the swaddling rags, my genitals, naked and pink and vulnerable as a sugar mouse.

Mr Dodd placed his mouth to my ear again and said that he thought he had made a very good job of things and hoped I was pleased too, and without waiting for any kind of reaction, which I would not have been able to make in any case, he swung me, like an immense skittle, into an arc of 180 degrees, so that the whole filthy room whirled round my head and I was back down on Mr Dodd's bed; and in Mr Dodd's hands, inches from my face, was a pair of scissors. I tried to faint. I heard him say that in Real Life They Cut That Off – and lay supine waiting for Death. Gently his hands caressed my helpless body, kindly he whispered that he had no intention of doing such a cruel thing for how else, otherwise, would a boy like me be able to masturbate? He said that all boys enjoyed masturbating and that he was much too good to deprive me of the rights. My mind had become a mass of solid jelly, Nothing flickered there apart from deadly terror, shame, and grief at my wickedness. I couldn't rationalise. I closed my eyes and said three or four 'Hail Mary's'.

If I prayed surely, this time, God would hear? The anxious, firm, slippery fingers, caressing and anointing me splintered my whole being into a billion jagged fragments. I was only aware that if they didn't stop something terrible and horrifying would happen.

Which it did. And I knew.

COUPLING, *c.* 1936
Ralph Glasser

The son of immigrant Jews from Russia, Ralph Glasser (1916–2002) grew up in the Gorbals in the years between the two world wars. Taken from school at fourteen he became a barber's soap boy and a presser in a garment factory. After years of night study he won a scholarship to Oxford to which he travelled by bike. 'In pre-war days,' he wrote in Gorbals Boy at Oxford *(1988), 'for a Gorbals man to come up to Oxford was as unthinkable as to meet a raw bushman in a St James's Club – something for which there were no stock responses. In any case, for a member of the boss class, someone from the Gorbals was in effect a bushman, the Gorbals itself as distant, as unknowable, as the Kalahari.' It was a member of the 'boss-class', John Betjeman, who encouraged Glasser to write about his life and upbringing, which he did, beginning with* Growing up in the Gorbals *(1986). Here Glasser describes the effect of living in such close and dense proximity had on people's sex lives.*

Parental approval of 'walking out' seldom extended to canoodling, petting, at home. In theory, canoodling did not take place. Apart from moral prohibitions, most houses, as tenement flats were called, were full to bursting, and privacy was out of the question. A spare room was a rare luxury, possessed by a few better-off families, better off by Gorbals standards – clergymen, skilled artisans – who might live behind Renaissance facades in the tenements in Abbotsford Place on the southern edge of the Gorbals near Eglinton Toll, where Victoria Road and Pollokshaws Road took you to the lower middle class districts of Langside, Shawlands, and on to Newton Mearns.

In most of the houses we knew every space was taken up by beds, mattresses on the floor, a few bare wooden chairs, a battered kitchen table. One or even two of the younger children commonly shared the parental bed, usually a mattress on planks resting on trestles in a curtained alcove in the kitchen.

To enable a coupling to take place in a semblance of privacy behind the curtain, the woman would step out in her shift, snatch a blanket off the bed and wrap the child in it on the floor boards near enough to the cooking range for him to get some radiated warmth from its banked-up fire. Afterwards she parted the curtains and came out naked to lift the unsleeping, finely aware child back into bed, to lie between her and the man lying open-mouthed in post-coital sleep.

For an unmarried girl to live away from home on her own was unthinkable. Even if special circumstances, such as the death of parents, led to her living under someone else's roof as a lodger, she would not be allowed men visitors in her room. As for the few unmarried men who could afford to live on their own in single-ends, one-room tenement flats, no respectable girl, or married woman for that matter, would want to be seen visiting one of them unchaperoned.

That corner of a close beside the ash-pits was a place outside time. Because the celebration did not take place under anyone's roof, moral responsibility could be kept at a distance if need be. The place of that shrine of Venus in the life of the locality was understood by everyone. Fathers knew where to look for their daughters out too late.

A girl impatient to escape from home might go there with her 'feller' and let him 'stamp her card' – get her with child. And then, with luck, persuade him to accept paternity and marry her: a common enough route to matrimony.

No one approved. Few openly disapproved. Fatalistically, all connived.

Residents making their way back through the close to the ash-pits or the clothes line in the back yard, sensing a couple's presence, retreated discreetly and returned later. Lovers seeking a vacant shrine wandered on to the next close, and the next. Some, driven and impatient, gave up the search and stood together in the lavatory on one of the half-landings. But that infringed the code and nearly always led to trouble. In theory each lavatory was shared by people from two floors, about six flats, but in practice by many more. Almost invariably the other lavatory in the close, or some in closes nearby, would be out of action because of blocked pipes or damaged cisterns or flush mechanisms, so there was seldom a moment when every functioning lavatory in a tenement was not in heavy demand, often with a queue stamping their feet waiting to get in. If a couple were making love in one, the anxious souls waiting on the cold stone steps made their feelings plain, firmly but usually not unkindly: 'Och come on! Go an' find yersels a place o' yer ain doon the stairs tae do yer canoodlin' in! Ah'm tellin' ye, if ah don't ge' in there in a minute ah'm gonae shi' ma troosers!'

THE ART OF TAPPING LIFTS, 1939
Alastair Borthwick

For a generation of mainly working-class Glaswegians the city's proximity to countryside and the hills was the perfect way to escape urban tedium and the daily grind. Indeed, many of those who found solace in the mountains were unemployed and had little – if any – money to spare for recreation. On a Friday evening the sight of men laden with rucksacks heading north for the weekend in hope of a lift was common. Once beyond the municipal boundaries the whole of Scotland seemed to open up and there was freedom to roam. In his classic memoir, Always a Little Further *(1939), Alastair Borthwick (1913–2003), who was born in Rutherglen but raised and educated in Glasgow, evokes an era when climbing mountains, which had previously been the preserve of the well off, became a popular pastime with those who hitherto had not had access to them. When Borthwick first happened upon 'the cave' he found three young men in situ, 'squatting round a fire, frying kippers and dangling on a wire over the flames a large black pudding'.*

Thanks to the cave, I came much in contact during the months which followed with the members of that small but persevering class known as the hitch-hikers. Their chief interest, in some cases approaching the proportions of a religion, was climbing;

and hitch-hiking, or the art of tapping lifts, was their method of bringing good mountains within reach of the city.

There are those who take an uncharitable view of the activity, claiming that the man who begs for lifts is no better than the man who begs for pennies, but I prefer to think of the hitch-hiker as the twentieth-century troubadour. Once the troubadour was welcome at any castle, for he earned his keep by song, and song was thought good value for money. So it is with hitch-hiking in its higher forms, as it is practised on the Loch Lomond road today. Words, and not song, are the hitch-hiker's capital. I have met them silent; but as a class they can give the Irish points in dialectic, and they turn a story well. Driving is a boring task. Many a good tale has been told, and many a dull journey enlivened between the Arrochar road-end and Anniesland Cross.

Some of the tales smack of the epic, and not in construction alone, for some hitch-hiking feats verge on the fabulous. For years the record was held by a lad who left Glasgow with half a crown in his pocket and intent to camp in Skye, and tapped a lift on the outskirts of the city which took him to Sligachan Inn, two hundred miles away and not two hundred yards from the spot where he had intended camping; but recently this feat has dwindled into insignificance as the brotherhood has realised the full possibilities of the thumb as mode of transport. In 1936 one Glasgow lad travelled to Paris for three shillings, tapping lifts on both sides of the Channel and making a charming smile bridge the gap created by his ignorance of the French language. His only extra was his cross-Channel fare. And in 1937 two of the Creag Dhu [mountaineer club], finding themselves idle and with time heavily on their hands, tapped lifts to Switzerland and back. The tale goes, too, that they even hitch-hiked up the Matterhorn behind a guide party.

The best story I have heard about this peculiar mode of travelling was told to me one November night at Arrochar by a gentleman rejoicing in the name Choocter. What far-fetched process of corruption and illusion created this nickname I do not know; but Choocter he was, and I never knew him by any other name. He was tall and thin, with a slight stoop. A lock of hair hung down almost over one eye, and his climbing jacket and breeches were patched after the homely manner of all climbing jackets and breeches. His accent was such that any one born beyond the bounds of Glasgow would have found much in his conversation that was obscure. He was as companionable a lad as one would care to meet; and I first fell in with him while he was buying a half a pound of sausages in the butcher's shop at Arrochar. He had travelled up from Glasgow free, of course. I bought what I wanted; and it was while we walked down the road to the Youth Hostel that he told me the story of himself, Wullie, Ginger, and Wee Jock.

It seemed that Choocter and Ginger had been on the point of leaving the Vale of Leven for a few days' climbing in Glencoe, sixty miles away, when they were smitten by a desire to eat chips; and, as all the world knows, there is a shop just before the start of the Loch Lomond road, which has something of a reputation for chips. There they had gone, and there had met the opposition, Wullie and Wee Jock.

'In his kilt,' Choocter added, as if that made it much worse.

'Wullie was just gettin' tore into a poke o' chips,' said Choocter, 'so we pretended we was goin' on ahead. O' course we hid in ahint the first dyke we came to; and in a wee while, by goes Wullie and Wee Jock, in his kilt, stuffin' themselves wi' chips. We waits anither two-three minutes just for to gie them a start, and then sets aff, slow-like.'

For an hour they had walked on, leaving the houses behind them and dropping down the rolling countryside which falls to the south end of Loch Lomond, confidently expecting first rights on any car which passed. But as they approached the loch Choocter glanced behind him, stopped and swore. It was, he saw, going to be a hard night. The fight was on. Diamond was about to cut diamond. For Wee Jock (in his kilt) was a hundred yards behind, emerging cautiously, like a mouse from the wainscot, from behind a hedge. Choocter sighed, and cast about for cover.

The sides were fairly matched; and, an aptitude for guile being strongly developed in all concerned and the means of their journey appealing more to them than its end, compromise at this stage did not occur to them. From that point on, all thoughts of progress seem to have been abandoned, and the journey resolved itself into long waits behind walls and trees, grubbings about in bushes, occupations of darkened barns, and elaborate game of chess in which the only popular move was the knight's. Tactics of a high order were employed. At one stage both parties were even travelling backwards.

The night grew darker, and traffic thinner. Despite piteous thumbings, no car stopped; and as eleven o'clock came and went their hopes dwindled. Even the chance of spending the night at Inverbeg Youth Hostel, a few miles ahead, had disappeared as time and energy were dissipated behind hedges.

'It was cuttin' wur ain throats, mister; it was cuttin' wur ain throats,' said Choocter solemnly.

Stalemate was reached shortly before midnight, when lack of traffic made further attempts useless. Choocter and Ginger gave up for the night somewhere near Luss, where they found a bell-tent left unoccupied at the side of the loch by some trusting soul, and crawled inside, working on the assumption that, as the tent was completely empty, no one would be likely to claim it at that hour of the night.

'We woke early . . . six o'clock,' said Choocter. 'We'd nae blankets, and I was sleeping in a *Glasgow Herald* and a sheet o' broon paper. Ginger woke first. He was in an *Express* but the pages is far ower wee. He wallapped me in the ribs and pointed oot' o' the tent.

'"Look at thon!" he says, fair wild.

'I looks; and there lyin' on the verandy o' a house-boat at the loch-side was Wullie and Wee Jock, in his kilt.'

A nice question of tactics was involved. Wee Jock, having, as has been noted, a kilt as well as a *Glasgow Herald* to keep him warm, was still sound asleep and might be expected to remain so for at least an hour, leaving the road clear for Choocter and Ginger. But the traffic was scarce at that hour of the morning: there are few milk-producing farms north of Luss, and no milk-lorries run to and from the city. The most they could hope for was a stray carrier's van, and even that hope was slender. Besides, if they should fail to tap a lift before Wee Jock awoke, they would leave him with first chance of all lifts for the rest of the day. They decided to lie in hiding until the other two should wake and move on.

The three hours which followed were, according to Choocter, desperate. During two of them, Wullie and Wee Jock slept, the dew of the morning wet on their raincoats, while the sun came up behind Ben Lomond and the island-shadows shortened on the Luss Narrows. The morning mist died in the treetops. And still they slept. It was bright, clear morning, and bitterly cold for those who had little but the daily press to shield them from the chill shadows of the tent. Most galling sight of all was breakfast on the houseboat, which started at eight-thirty. Wee Jock produced a folding stove from his rucksack, and Wullie cooked slowly and deliberately, an operation which nearly broke Choocter's heart, for, as he so delicately put it, he and Ginger had 'nae chuck' and were exceedingly hungry. But in the end they packed and moved off, leaving the others lying on their empty stomachs, contemplating nature.

'We gi'ed them hauf an hoor's start this time, and aff we went. Hauf an hoor. Jings, man, we thought we had them this time, though the wait near kilt us wi' hunger and the cauld. But . . . ach . . . we hudni' gone more nor a mile affore I looks back; and there, jookin' in ahint the last corner, was Wee Jock, in his kilt. Man, it was chronic.'

From nine until noon the running fight continued, first one side gaining the rear, then the other, for the Loch Lomond road is thickly wooded, with cover for an ambushing army. They hid in drains and ditches; they lolled by the lochside in the hope that the others should pass. But when both parties met behind the same hedge, each thinking the other was in the rear, a peace conference was obviously called for. In three hours they had covered only two miles.

They tossed for first lift. Ginger and Choocter won. All four walked on together for an hour until the first car responded to signals, and Wullie and Wee Jock were left in sole possession of the road. It was a good lift, and took Choocter and Ginger over Glen Falloch and beyond to Crianlarich and Tyndrum, where their driver branched off for Oban. They set out to walk the rest.

I should like to be able to record that five minutes later Wullie and Wee Jock drove by in a Rolls Royce and were taken all the way to Glencoe; but well-turned plots happen seldom in real life. The truth of the matter was that the two stragglers were landed at the Tyndrum branch a few minutes later, and all four plodded on again together. After five miles (an unprecedented distance for a hitch-hiker to walk, according to Choocter) an aged but empty car stopped beside them, and its driver waved towards him. He was an apologetic creature.

'I'm sorry to trouble you,' he began, 'but I'm going to Glencoe and want to find a certain hotel there. Kingshouse Inn, it's called. I . . . I wonder if you could tell me where it is?'

Choocter looked at the car. At a pinch it would carry them all. He smiled his most charming smile.

'It's a kinda difficult road to describe,' he began, 'but it wouldn't be takin' me and ma pals far oot o' oor way to show ye. We weren't really thinkin' o' goin' to Glencoe, ye ken, but . . .'

SWASTIKAS IN SAUCHIEHALL STREET, NOVEMBER 1939
The Jewish Echo

The Jewish Echo *was one of several Jewish newspapers in Glasgow. Started in 1928, it closed in 1992. The Mitchell Library holds a complete collection. This short item shows that anti-semitism had its followers everywhere.*

Malicious damage was done to a number of Jewish shops in Glasgow and extensive anti-Jewish propaganda appeared in Jewish-owned property during the black-out at the weekend. About twenty windows or glass panels were cracked and swastikas were scratched with a diamond or metal tool on nearly eighty others.

The discovery of the majority of these destructive acts was made on Monday morning and the police were engaged in pursuing enquiries throughout the day.

Most of the shops affected are situated in Sauchiehall Street, though shops in Argyle Street and Stockwell Street were also damaged. Women's dress shops, furriers and tailors suffered most.

A few of the windows had the words, 'We don't want Jews', printed on the glass, but not all shops affected are Jewish-owned.

A MONGREL AMONG THE DUSTBINS, 1940
Evelyn Waugh

Evelyn Arthur St John Waugh (1903–66) is perhaps best known for his novel Brideshead Revisited *(1945). Among his ancestors was Lord Cockburn, who was his great-great-grandfather. His masterpiece is the trilogy,* Sword of Honour *(1965), from which the following extract is taken, and which drew on his own wartime experiences.*

Glasgow in November 1940 was not literally a *ville lumière*. Fog and crowds gave the black-out a peculiar density. Trimmer, on the afternoon of his arrival, went straight from the train to the station hotel. Here too were fog and crowds. All its lofty halls and corridors were heaped with luggage and thronged by transitory soldiers and sailors. There was a thick, shifting mob at the reception office. To everybody the girl at the counter replied: 'Reserved rooms only. If you come back after eight there might be some cancellations.'

Trimmer struggled to the front, leered and asked: 'Have ye no a wee room for a Scottish laddie?'

'Come back after eight. There may be a cancellation.'

Trimmer gave her a wink and she seemed just perceptibly responsive, but the thrust of other desperate and homeless men made further flirtation impossible.

With his bonnet on the side of his head, his shepherd's crook in his hand and a pair of major's crowns on his shoulders (he had changed them for his lieutenant's stars in the train's lavatory), Trimmer began to saunter through the ground floor. There were men everywhere. Of the few women each was the centre of a noisy little circle of festivity, or else huddled with her man in a gloom of leave-taking. Waiters were few. Everywhere he saw heads turned and faces of anxious entreaty. Here and there a more hopeful party banged the table and impolitely shouted: 'We want service.'

But Trimmer was undismayed. He found it all very jolly after his billet on Mugg and experience had taught him that anyone who really wants a woman, finds one in the end.

He passed on with all the panache of a mongrel among the dustbins, tail waving, ears cocked, nose a-quiver. Here and there in his passage he attempted to insinuate himself into one or other of the heartier groups but without success. At length he came to some steps and the notice: CHATEAU de MADRID. *Restaurant de grand luxe*.

Trimmer had been to this hotel once or twice before but he had never penetrated into what he knew was the expensive quarter. He took his fun where he found it, preferably in crowded places. Tonight would be different. He strolled down the rubber-lined carpet and was at once greeted at the foot of the stairs by a head waiter.

'*Bon soir, monsieur*. Monsieur has engaged his table?'

'I was looking for a friend.'

'How large will monsieur's party be?'

'Two, if there is a party, I'll just sit here and have a drink.'

'*Pardon, monsieur*. It is not allowed to serve drinks here except to those who are dining upstairs.'

The two men looked at one another, fraud to fraud. They had both knocked about a little. Neither was taken in by the other. For a moment Trimmer was tempted to say: 'Come off it. Where did you get that French accent? The Mile End Road or the Gorbals?'

The waiter was tempted to say: 'This isn't your sort of place, chum. Hop it.'

In the event Trimmer said: 'I shall certainly dine here if my friend turns up. You might give me a look at the menu while I have my cocktail.'

And the head waiter said: '*Tout de suite, monsieur*.'

MOB RULE, JUNE 1940
Joe Pieri

The Second World War was a defining event for Italo-Scots. The heightening of pre-existing tensions and prejudices following the declaration of war with Italy in 1940 led to anti-Italian riots across Scotland and in particular in Edinburgh and Glasgow, which had the largest Italian communities. The first Italians to reach Glasgow arrived at the end of the nineteenth century and the beginning of the twentieth, often from Barga in northern Tuscany and Picinisco in Lazio. Most of the immigrants sold fish and chips and ice-cream and were prominent in the restaurant trade, as many still are. It was Winston Churchill who commanded that all Italian males should be apprehended and interned, prior to being deported to Canada aboard the Arandora Star, *which was torpedoed by a German U-boat shortly after it set off. Of the 446 who were drowned, twenty-nine came from Glasgow.*

A muted roar made itself heard from the street below, rising to a crescendo of shouting voices directly under my window. I went over and peered out through the curtains. A crowd of about a hundred shouting and gesticulating people, pushing in front of them a handcart loaded with stones and bricks, were gathering in front of the shop. 'There's a Tally place ... do it in!', came the shout; then to the accompaniment of yells and cheers, a barrage of missiles came flying through the air, smashing the glass frontage of the shop. A dozen or so of the mob, armed with sticks and batons, cleared away the jagged edges of the broken windows and jumped through the shop beyond. Through a curiously detached and dreamlike mental haze I could hear the sound of smashing and curses from below, and peering fearfully through the lace curtains, I watched as the contents of the looted shop were distributed to the milling crowd. That night there were few, if any, Italian shops left untouched by the gangs of hooligans, and although no physical harm was done to anyone, years of hard work was destroyed by unrestrained bands of louts who roamed the streets of Glasgow wrecking and looting in the name of patriotism. As far as I know, not a finger was lifted by the police in an attempt to stop the looting of Italian shops in Glasgow that night.

THE CLYDEBANK BLITZ, 13 MARCH 1941
The Glasgow Herald

The shipbuilding town of Clydebank, near Glasgow, was devastated by two Luftwaffe raids. Hundreds of people died and thousands of houses were destroyed. Production of ships and munitions for the Allies made the town a target. Though one of the aims of the raids had been to reduce morale and prompt calls for an end to the war, it had quite the opposite effect and there were many reports of people reacting heroically, stoically and humourfully in the aftermath of what has been described as 'the most cataclysmic event' in war-time Scotland.

After being entombed in the wreckage of a bombed tenement in the Glasgow area since last Thursday night, two men, one of them a War Reserve Policeman, were rescued alive yesterday.

The policeman, weakened by his severe ordeal, died in the early evening, some five hours after he had been released from the mass of debris. The other man, discovered in the course of the evening – almost eight hours after the raid – now lies in the Glasgow Western Infirmary in a serious condition.

Hopes were raised last night that a girl might be found alive, and rescuers were working with all speed to trace her. At a late hour, however, their efforts had been unrewarded.

The two men concerned in the remarkable rescues, whose endurance aroused the admiration of the rescue workers, were Frederick Clark (32), War Reserve Policeman, and John Cormack (22).

Cormack was found lying in a bed, where he was resting when the tenement was bombed. A big beam lay across him, and only his face and arms were visible. His arms were folded across his breast.

The rescue workers who discovered him were astonished when he feebly waved his hand to them through the debris. Quickly they cleared the way to him.

'Could you go a cup of tea?' Dr Mackay, who had been summoned to the scene, asked Cormack while he was still a prisoner in the wreckage. 'Aye, Ah fine could,' was the reply.

'I gave him a cup of tea and some brandy, and put a cigarette in his mouth,' said the doctor. Cormack was quite warm. Apparently, he had been in bed when the tenement collapsed, and this saved him from dying of cold.

'He was able to help us get him out, and explained how a beam was protecting him. He also told us there was a young girl, somewhere near, and that she had spoken to him about a day before.'

Describing the discovery of Cormack, Jack Couglin, a Dublin-born man, who was one of the rescue squad, said – 'I had a hunch that there was somebody else still alive in the wreckage in the same corner where we had found the other man earlier in the day. I went on working at that spot, and there, when I lifted up some boards, I saw a man lying below. He looked like a statue, lying on the bed with his arms folded. But in a moment I found he was alive. We called other rescue workers to the spot, and very soon managed to release the man.'

Mr D. Barr, who had been bombed from his home in the same street, and was on his way to salvage some of his belongings, was passing when he heard someone shout, 'A man alive! Get a doctor and an ambulance quickly!'

Mr Barr ran at once to the surgery of Dr Mackay near-by. The doctor went at once to the bombed tenement and stood by in shirt sleeves as the workers extricated Cormack. As soon as he could reach him he went to his aid.

When Clark was rescued he was still able to speak. As he was removed on a stretcher to a waiting ambulance, he told his rescuers – 'I'm all right.' Before he was taken to the Western Infirmary Clark was able to drink a cup of tea and eat a biscuit.

Demolition and rescue workers who have been working side by side since last week's blitz, and with decreasing hope of removing trapped victims alive, were astonished yesterday afternoon to hear a moan come from the debris. They had just removed a body when they were startled by the sound.

With the utmost speed they excavated a tunnel through the mess of the twisted wreckage as a woman hastened to the scene from a near-by clinic.

Dr Annie Thomson, of an Outdoor Medical Services Clinic, was the first person to reach the imprisoned man. She crawled through the improvised tunnel, no more than 18 inches wide, and administered an injection. "That wasn't so bad, was it?" she asked the man, still pinned beneath the debris. She was surprised when she found that he was able to reply. 'No,' he said.

As the rescuers worked feverishly and grimly to release him, jacking up wreckage to free his feet, they discovered that a chest of drawers had apparently fallen over Clark's body, thus protecting him from the mass of stone and timber that had crashed above him. He was lying at full length on top of a fallen door in a passageway many feet below street level.

The successful and unexpected rescue effort was described by Mr Norman Manson, a joiner, who was in charge of the rescue squad. 'We had,' he said, 'to smash in a floor and crawl underneath to locate the trapped constable. I estimate that we had to remove seven tons of wreckage before we were able to break a way through to him.'

The rescue operations were in two distinct stages. When the tunnel was driven through to reach Clark it was discovered that he could not be freed until a weight of stone pinning a leg beneath a chest of drawers had been removed.

It was seen that to remove this stone would cause a downfall of more wreckage, and it was decided to dig another passage in the foundation ground of the building below where Clark was lying. While this was being done, warm blankets and hot-water bottles were placed around Clark, who was also given stimulants.

As the under-tunnelling proceeded, Clark's leg dropped clear, while the chest of drawers holding up the wreckage above remained in position, and eventually, after three hours' work, the rescuers were able to free the imprisoned man.

Colleagues at the police headquarters where Clark was stationed said that he was actually on night shift last week, but had left the station for his night off when the raid occurred. He was lodging with a Mr and Mrs Docherty, who, with their two daughters, are believed to be still trapped in the partially wrecked building.

AN OLD-STYLE AMPUTATION, *c.* 1944
R.D. Laing

Born in Glasgow in 1927, R.D. Laing's background was working-class. His father was apprenticed at fourteen in a shipyard and after World War One found employment with the Corporation of Glasgow as an electrical engineer. Laing himself graduated in medicine from Glasgow University in 1951 and went on to practise psychiatry. His principal and controversial thesis, expounded in The Divided Self *(1960) and other books, was that psychiatrists should not attempt to cure or ameliorate the symptoms of mental illness – a term he repudiated – but rather should encourage patients to view themselves as going through an enriching process. In* Wisdom, Madness & Folly *(1985), his autobiography, he wrote: 'As a young psychiatrist in general hospitals and psychiatric hospitals, I administered locked wards and ordered drugs, injections, padded cells and straitjackets, electric shocks, deep insulin comas and the rest. I was uneasy about lobotomies but not sure why. Usually all this treatment was against the will of its recipients.' Laing died in 1989.*

The first surgical operation I attended, at the Glasgow Royal Infirmary, was very atypical of the surgery in this day and age. It was a mid-thigh amputation on an old, seasoned and pickled sea-salt who was beginning to develop gangrene due to advanced arteriosclerosis. His heart and lungs were not in good shape. It was thought he would not stand a chance with a general anaesthetic, so it was decided to try out a procedure that had been reported from Australia: ice-pack anaesthesia. The surgeon ordered his left leg, which was the one due to be amputated, to be packed in ice the night before and for him to be given a bottle of whisky before the night staff went off. The operation was to be performed first thing in the morning.

At the first cut of the knife he went wild, screaming, yelling and cursing. It was evident that the ice-pack had not had its desired effect and, it turned out, the nurse on night-duty who had given him a bottle of whisky had no idea what a bottle of whisky meant in the real world and had given him the contents of a four-ounce hospital bottle, which he had downed in one gulp. It did not touch him at all.

Anyway, it was too late to turn back. He had to be held down and I saw an old-style amputation. The whole thing.

However shocking such things are, I could 'take' them. Life has to go on. Every gamble does not come off. It is no one's fault really. The next patient is already on the table. There is no time to cry over spilt blood . . .

At the end of our first year as medical students, we paid a traditional visit to the Royal Gartnavel Mental Hospital, Glasgow.

This was the first time I had been in a mental hospital. Over a hundred students assembled in the main hall and the Superintendent, Dr Angus MacNiven, from a stage platform, gave a short talk about the hospital and psychiatry and introduced and talked with four or five patients. These were the first psychiatric patients I had ever set eyes upon.

I came in late. There were two men on the stage sitting on chairs having a chat. One of them, in impeccable dress, with a cheerful flower in his buttonhole, sat with composure and assurance, talked fluently with the other man, who had his legs twisted around each other, grimaced, stammered, fidgeted, all but picked his nose, and wriggled around in his chair.

It was not until the interview ended, when the patient got up, gave a bow and left the stage that I realised that Dr MacNiven was the man I had taken to be the patient. Years later, after medical school, six months in a neurosurgical unit and two years as a psychiatrist in the British Army, he was very amused when, now a registrar on his staff, I told him the story.

This was a very decent interview. It sounded like two old friends chatting about the hospital, the changes they had seen. The patient had been in the hospital longer than MacNiven, had been there in the time of D.K. Henderson, later Professor of Psychiatry at Edinburgh University and co-author of a book that became the standard text in British psychiatry. The patient claimed to have been mentioned in despatches, as it were, in that book for calling D.K. Henderson 'the Kaiser', which was cited as an example of paranoid delusion. After a lifetime of social catastrophes in states of manic excitement he had settled in a room in Gentlemen's West Wing, the paying part of the hospital, where most of the time he lived quietly in a state of indefatigable good humour.

RIVETING STUFF, 1946
V.S. Pritchett

Riveting was one of the most skilled jobs in the shipyards and the best riveters were highly prized and generally well-paid. V.S. Pritchett (1900–97) was a novelist, critic, short story writer and memoirist, who was always interested in what people did to earn a living. The following is extracted from Build the Ships, *published by HMSO.*

The riveter is a member of the 'black squad' – a gang of four who turn up to the job with the misleading nonchalance of a family of jugglers. They are the riveter, the holder-up, the heater, and a boy. A speechless quartet, or almost speechless: 'Where's that boy?' is about their only sentence. The 'black squad' can set up shop anywhere and begin performing their hot-chestnut act. You see one swung over the ship's side. He stands on his plank waiting with the pneumatic instrument in his gloved hands. On the other side of the plate, inside the ship, is the heater with his smoking brazier – a blue coke haze is always rising over the ship: he plucks a rivet out of the fire with his tongs, a 'boy' (nowadays it is often a girl in dungarees) catches the rivet in another pair of tongs and steps quickly with it to the holder-up, who puts it through the proper holes at the junction of the plates. As the pink nub of the rivet comes through, the pneumatic striker comes down on it, roaring out blows at the rate of about 700 hits a minute, and squeezes it flat.

One of the curiosities of the ship's side – it is also one of those accidental beauties of line which are sought by modern artists – is the white chalk mark which the rivet counter ticks across each rivet, showing how many the riveter has done in the shift. One sees half a dozen plates cross-hatched in this way by the errant human touch, and a list of figures like a darts score is totted up beside them. Paid by the hundred, the riveter is keeping his accounts. He will average up to thirty-seven in an hour.

THE LOWEST OF THE LOW ON THE *GLASGOW HERALD*, 1946

Peregrine Worsthorne

The Glasgow Herald *– now called the* Herald *– is the longest-running extant daily national newspaper in the world.* The Times, *for example, is two years younger. As such, it has a fabled history and has employed many distinguished journalists and writers. One such was George MacDonald Fraser, author of the bestselling Flashman novels, who in the 1960s was its deputy editor. Peregrine Worsthorne's sojourn with the paper was, as he relates, less stellar. In the 1940s, when Worsthorne joined it, it was edited by Sir William B. Robieson, who regularly denounced the policy of appeasing Hitler. His shift ended at 2.00 a.m. when, in order to return to his bedsit in Kew Terrace, he had to run the gauntlet of drunks and prostitutes in Sauchiehall Street. On more than one occasion the tram in which he was travelling had to be stopped and the police called. As he recalled in his autobiography,* Tricks of Memory *(1993), such encounters with the city's low life amused his colleagues and endeared him to them. 'Instead of being resented as a privileged English high-flyer I was soon taken pity on as a persecuted species in need of protection.' On leaving Glasgow*

Worsthorne had spells at The Times *and the* Daily Telegraph *and from 1986 to 1989 was editor of the* Sunday Telegraph.

Every detail of that interview is embedded in the memory. At no other time in my life have I ever so completely got hold of the wrong end of the stick. As I understood it Sir William [Robieson, editor of the *Glasgow Herald*] was offering me the deputy editorship of his paper. This quite took my breath away. There I was without any journalistic experience or even ambition being offered this lofty position on a plate. True, the salary mentioned was pretty measly, only £6 a week. But one couldn't have everything – a top job and a high salary. Needless to say, I accepted with alacrity and promised to come north without delay.

In the event the post turned out to be sub-editor, not deputy editor, and apprentice sub-editor at that, the lowest of the low. In keeping with my imagined status – but not my actual salary – I had booked myself in at the Central Hotel, Glasgow's grandest, which was only a stone's throw from the *Herald* office in Buchanan Street, where I presented myself at the appointed time, 6.00 p.m. on Monday. Finding the main door on Buchanan Street shut I went round to the back of the building, where there was a squalid entrance guarded by a very surly porter sitting behind a glass panel. 'I am the new deputy editor, could you please show me to my office,' I said politely, only to receive a response which, although incomprehensible, so thick was the accent, did not sound in the least friendly or welcoming, let alone respectful. When eventually I found the sub-editor's room the full extent of my misunderstanding was immediately apparent. My job, as was swiftly made clear, was to make the tea for the other sub-editors. After about three months of doing nothing much more than this, I was put in charge of sub-editing the *Radio Times*, which meant marking up the hours of the programme for the printer; the livestock prices and then, after about six months, the most humdrum news stories – fires, burglaries and so on. At first I thought there must be some mistake and that at any moment Sir William Robieson would summon me to higher things. But months and then two years went by and the summons never came. The great man would occasionally wish me a good morning, but that was all. Of writing opportunities there were none; not even really of rewriting since none of the big stories ever came my way or not until the very end of two years. What I did not know at the time, and only learned later, was that I was a guinea-pig being used in an experiment.

THE QUEST FOR WOODBINES, 1948

Mary Rose Liverani

Mary Rose Liverani grew up in Govan in the 1950s in a large but poor family which – in the days when the Clyde was as red as a field of poppies – was politically vocal and active. They emigrated to Australia when she was thirteen. 'As a kid I found everything really exciting,' she said. 'People used to crowd into our house, everybody was talking politics and my sister and I used to sit under the table and listen.' Her book, The Winter Sparrows *(1976), is her fond remembrance of times past, not the least of which was her mother's constant demand for Wills's Woodbine cigarettes, nicknamed 'Gaspers' because smokers new to the habit found them difficult to inhale.*

I longed for a country where there were no pawnshops and where tobacco companies were doomed to grind out forever and a day nothing but Wills's Woodbines. Turkish Pasha were the only cigarettes freely available in the post-war cigarette market in Scotland. My mother loathed them and refused to smoke them.

'Woodbines, I must have my Woodbines,' she would tell me, counting out the coppers into my reluctant grip. 'Go and get Woodbines and don't come back without them.'

'But where shall I find them?' I would wail despairingly. 'Everybody wants them and there aren't any around. And they don't give them to wee people any way.'

'Get out, get out,' my mother would yell at me, throwing the door open and leaping at me with her right arm raised in a violent gesture, 'get out that bloody door and look for these cigarettes. If ye come back without them I'll lay ye in your own blood.'

Wills's Woodbines were advertised on every imaginable available space in Glasgow, but the little green and gold boxes themselves were never on display. Why the firm sought to stimulate demand for its product when the supply never approached being adequate was one of the seven wonders of my world. Another was why my mother didn't adapt herself to Pashas that she could have smoked night and day in perpetual motion instead of suffering long smokeless hours for a few minutes spiced with the unique savour of Wills's fretted amber. They must be wicked, that firm, I thought, to make people long for their cigarettes and then make only a few.

And so, oscillating between recognition and impotent fury, I would set off on my near-daily odyssey through Glasgow to hunt out minuscule hoards of Woodbines from newsagents, and cafes and small corner shops through Plantation and Govan and Elder Park and sometimes over the river to Anderston. My first stop was always at the papershop of the two spinsters, the Misses Alexander, Sara and Susan. 'The cinnamon sticks', I called them, because their tall, skeletal structures were generally covered by drab brown frocks, unrelieved by buttons or belts. Never once did these women sell me the Woodbines and they never would, I knew, for they believed that I smoked them myself. Still, it was part of the ritual to ask them. Then I could add them to my list of places attempted, of dangers faced in the quest for Woodbines. As usual they smiled thinly and said in a prissy duet:

'No Woodbines today, only Pasha and Turf.'

I hesitated. Turf was sometimes acceptable to my mother depending on how desperate or amenable she was. There was no doubt today, however, that she was in a pretty bad mood. My father had lost time again this week and there would be no overtime at the weekend to make up for it. So I nodded curtly to the two miserly women and went out. What a waste. They had all these Woodbines stashed away under the counter, I was sure of it. They didn't smoke anyway. Probably had lungs like punctured bladders and couldn't draw enough breath.

In the cafes and corner shops I wasted no time.

'Got any Woodbines?'

'No Woodbines.'

'Got any Woodbines?'

'None.'

'Got any Woodbines by chance?'

'By no chance.'

Outside the newspaper shops, however, I always hung around till two or three people had gone inside and then while they were waiting or absorbing the newsagent's attention, I could quickly scan the latest editions of the comics.

'Here you, are ye wanting tae buy these comics?'

'No, I was wondering if you had any Woodbines?'

'Fine well, ye know I havenae any, you cheeky thing. You asked me yesterday. Next time I catch ye going through these comics I'll make ye pay for them.'

A small packet of Woodbines was always worth a pat on the head and other fleeting expressions of gratitude from my mother. I never took any lasting delight in these, however, for circumstances forced upon her two roles: she was the grateful princess who acclaimed the hero returning with tokens of mighty deeds but she was also the villainous king, the princess's father, who insisted on still more and more quests and combats. The endless peregrinations around the city, prompted by the need for either cigarettes or money, fell to me as the eldest because my mother was continually immobolised by pregnancies that she rushed into to avoid cancer of the breast in old age. A Catholic doctor, observing that my mother had successfully practised birth control for three years after her first two pregnancies, warned her that she might thereby bring damage upon her breasts, such as they were, and so for the next six years her womb laboured almost without rest. This relentless procreating ceased only after a Presbyterian doctor hinted at disastrous consequences for the womb, should the routine continue undisturbed. From then on, contraception became the order of the night.

HORSING AROUND, *c.* 1948
Jack House

Who but the Tollcross-born journalist Jack House (1906–91) would have as his lifelong ambition to play the hind legs of a horse in a pantomime? The Queen's Theatre was to pantomime what Lords is to cricket. Situated near Glasgow Green, the Queen's was known in an earlier incarnation as the People's

Palace, where folk from the east end went to let off steam. Its performances were described as 'not for the faint-hearted'. Many scripts were written by Frank Droy, husband of the below-mentioned Doris, in broad, and bawdy, Glaswegian, which audiences lapped up. The Queen's was destroyed by fire in 1952.

I had a great affection for the Queen's Theatre, for it was there that I achieved one of my great ambitions. I appeared as the hind legs of a horse in the pantomime. I can't for the life of me remember the name of the pantomime, but it was the one in which Doris Droy appeared as a woman carter who had taken over her husband's job during the war. Naturally, she had to have a horse with her. The horse was played by a married couple named Carr and Vonnie (Vonnie was Mrs Carr). They appeared on Scottish music-hall stages for many years, but now Vonnie is dead and Jimmy Carr has retired.

The management of the Queen's agreed that I should appear as the hind legs (Vonnie's part) for one performance only. So I went along to the Gallowgate to rehearse. You may not realise it, but pantomime horses are customarily performed by either acrobats or tap-dancers. Carr and Vonnie were tap-dancers, and the whole routine was built on tap-dancing. I am neither an acrobat nor a tap-dancer, and the routine had to be simplified extremely for me. Fortunately, when you are appearing as the hind legs of a pantomime horse, you can see the front legs through a sort of window in the soft under-belly of the horse. The theory is that whatever the front legs are doing you will do the same.

We rehearsed for a whole afternoon. I found that the front legs wore a heavy belt so that, as the hind legs, I bent over and grasped this belt. That kept us in cohesion. Mr Carr said to me: 'See that bit where we fall down on the stage? For heaven's sake don't get the body of the horse twisted. If you do, you won't be able to get up on your feet again, and I'll have to drag you off.'

I promised to do my best, but I can tell you that I felt very worried and excited as I got into the horse's costume in the wings. The entire cast of the Queen's Theatre pantomime were there to see me make my debut. Came the cue, and on we trotted. All went well. We fell down but the body wasn't twisted. We got up again and finished by carrying Doris Droy off on my back.

Then we took off the top part of the costume and went on to the stage to take our bow and show that we were really men all the time.

THE CITIZENS' THEATRE, 1948
James Bridie

Based in the heart of the Gorbals, the Citizens' Theatre – the 'Citz' as it is familiarly known – was established in 1945. After its initial success it lost its way for a while. Directors came and went like football managers and audiences evaporated. This all changed in 1969 when Giles Havergal rode from Edinburgh to its rescue. Ably abetted by designer Philip Price, Havergal staged as his first production an all-male Hamlet. *Later he was joined as director by Philip Prowse and Robert David Macdonald and the Citz's reputation burgeoned both nationally and internationally. Here playwright James Bridie (1888–1951), the pen-name of O.H. Mavor, whose original idea it was, recalls its formative years.*

After Artemus Ward's hero had languished in prison for several years, a happy thought struck him. He opened the window and got out. Starting a theatre is as easy as that.

For years and years those of us who wanted a resident theatre in Glasgow had dug tunnels with rusty screwnails, had tamed mice and taught them to carry messages, had tried to saw through iron bars with dog-biscuits, had written our biographies on our shirts with blood, had implored the immortal gods – all to little or no purpose. Then six of us suddenly sat round a table and found it was quite easy. We asked a few other people for a little money and began.

We took the little Athenaeum for a thirty weeks' season and looked around for a producer. We were given a guarantee by C.E.M.A. [Council for the Encouragement of Music and the Arts] to meet what we thought was an inevitable loss. It was war time. Actors were hard to come by and so was material. The theatre had a comfortable auditorium, but few other modern amenities. But two boards and a passion were enough. We broke even in our first year and made a four-figure profit in our second. We did twenty plays and took two of them through Scotland to places ill-supplied with Drama. We hit a remarkably high standard of acting and production and chose no catchpenny plays.

When I say 'we' all did this, I mean that Mr Eric Capon did it, with the exception of three productions by Miss Jennifer Sounes. Mr and Mrs McCrone, Miss Savile and Mr Gorrie looked after the business side and our Secretaries kept our finances straight. A loyal and clever company worked hard and their efforts were supplemented by such distinguished visitors as Ernest Milton, Jay Laurier, Morland Graham and James Woodburn.

Then Harry McKelvie offered us the Princess's on most generous terms and we crossed the river. Mr Matthew Forsyth, who had a long and distinguished career as an actor, a producer and a manager, took the wheel from Eric Capon and we began on a much bigger scale.

The same people who told us that it was hopeless to start a theatre in the midst of a war and that, anyhow, the Athenaeum was no good, were vocal once more. Nobody would cross the river to the Gorbals to see highbrow plays. Highbrows, apparently, inhabit exclusively the northern bank. Well, highbrow or lowbrow, North, South, East or West, they have come.

To those who have come, we have presented plays that would not, for the most part, be seen otherwise in Scotland. We have rehearsed them with the same time and care and mounted them with the same elaboration as if we had been in holy Shaftesbury Avenue itself. We have provided the most comfortable theatre in Glasgow for our audience. We have kept open for eleven months of the year. We have taken the risk of presenting a higher proportion of new plays than any repertory theatre outside of London has ever dared to do; and most of these plays have been by Scots.

We have taken another risk by keeping our prices down to the minimum. We, as a strictly non-profit-making company, are relieved of entertainment tax and we have handed every penny of it we could spare back to the audience. If we ever return to the days when the customer demands his money's worth, it may interest some of us to consider how much the half crown we pay for a seat is spent directly on providing entertainment and how much goes to gentlemen who are in the business purely for their health and who neither act, dance nor sing. In the Citizens'

Theatre the proportion spent on entertainment is something like two and threepence. I understand that this is not so in the cinema.

While I am boasting about the Citizens' Theatre, I may go a little further and say something about its reputation. A reputation is a hard thing to assess. There is no human activity that produces such a diversity of opinion, informed or otherwise, as the theatre. Two experienced theatre-goers may see the same play. One may be entranced by everything he sees and hears, while the other is irritated and bored. The whole thing is mixed with illusion and emotion. But, out of this welter, a good reputation or a bad reputation arises and, when it does, there is no mistake about it. Almost within the last few months rumour has fixed us as the best repertory theatre in Britain.

That is enough boasting. Whether we have deserved this reputation or not we shall try to do so in future. We have only begun, though it is something to have made a beginning. If the Scottish Theatre ever comes into being, I hope that we shall be a lively, efficient, experienced part of it and that we shall have some credit for producing, even at this early stage, a superior sort of article, honest in purpose and sound in workmanship.

1951–1975

HELLO, DALI

A TALE OF TWO CITIES, 1951
Moray McLaren

The rivalry between Glasgow and Edinburgh is similar to that of sparring boxers; punches may be landed but they are not designed to injure. In the not-so-distant past a visitor might have remarked that in the former, people – invariably men – tend to wear blue collars while in the latter they always wear white. In Glasgow, moreover, it was more usual for working people to get their hands dirty. This was not so in Edinburgh, where ink was the only stain likely to adhere to exposed parts. Moray McLaren (1910–71), who was born in Edinburgh, wrote perceptively on his native heath. He worked in journalism and was the BBC's first Programme Director for Scotland. During the Second World War he was attached to the Foreign Office as head of the Polish Region in Political Intelligence.

It is only forty miles from Edinburgh to Glasgow. Either by road or by one of the frequent trains it will not take you much more than an hour to travel between the two cities. You can do this several times a day if you feel so inclined; and a number of businessmen live in Edinburgh and go to their work in Glasgow. There are even some who do the reverse, sleeping in Glasgow and working in Edinburgh. There are also people whose work is evenly divided between the two and who have homes in each city.

The forty-mile belt that connects the two chief towns of Scotland passes through an on the whole dull landscape, undivided by hills, minor watersheds or rivers or any recognisable natural breaks. Scattered indeterminately upon its length are small towns and villages, most of them of nineteenth-century industrial or mining growth. There is not very much difference between them; for they are all products of the Glasgow–Edinburgh belt, and not of either city. Near Glasgow they become a little more conglomerate and grim. Nearer Edinburgh they lie about more starkly and individually scattered. It is difficult to tell, however, where the eastern Scotland influence ends and the western begins. Nor is it likely that anyone, save the most curious, has tried to discover. The journey by road or rail is too quick and too dull to merit much investigation or even attention.

And yet, the journey having been made, and having arrived in Glasgow from Edinburgh or in the Capital of Scotland from the great city of the West, one does not need to be curious or unusually observant to notice that one has passed from one world into another. All within the small country of Scotland and merely by travelling an easy forty miles. The differences between these two worlds are those of character, of East and West, of climate and appearance, but most of all of character.

The character of Edinburgh and the character of Glasgow, so vivid, so complementary to each other, are in their roots as Scottish as the characters of the Highlands and the Lowlands. For nearly a century and a half they have been as important in the general pattern of the character of Scotland as even the Highlands and the Lowlands were. It is impossible to know the Scotland of today without savouring the difference between the quality of Edinburgh and of Glasgow – and this is not because they are the two largest and most important towns in Scotland: it is because the difference between them is of the essence of Scotland.

THE DALI STORY, 1952
T.J. Honeyman

Spending money on art always has a tendency to bring frothing philistines to the fore. So it was no surprise when Glasgow Corporation decided to use public money to purchase Salvador Dali's surrealist Christ of Saint John of the Cross *that critics began to howl. Tom Honeyman (1891–1971), Director of*

Kelvingrove Art Gallery, pressed ahead regardless and persuaded the powers-that-be that this was an opportunity not to be missed. And so it has proved. Dali's wonderful painting is one of many jewels that belongs to the people of Glasgow. Honeyman's reputation and charm were such that he was able to attract several major gifts to the city's galleries and museums, including the peerless collection of Sir William Burrell (1861–1958). Ironically, and sadly, Honeyman had to leave his post in 1954 after he lost the support of his political master, the new chairman of the Glasgow Corporation Art Committee.

Of course we expected criticism, but not quite the concentrated bitterness or irresponsibility on the matter of the purchase price, £8,200. The decision reached by the Corporation was not lightly taken. Glasgow wanted the picture and Glasgow had to pay the price, which, after considerable negotiation, was fixed at the lowest figure acceptable to the artist – the catalogue price had been £12,000. I remember that about the same time a small picture – in an imperfect state – *Christ and the Woman taken in Adultery* by Peter Brueghel was sold in auction for £11,025. Commenting on this Denys Sutton, then art critic of the *Financial Times* and now editor of *The Apollo* magazine, said 'Its price, though high, bears greater relation to its value than the £8,200 paid by Glasgow for a painting by Salvador Dali.' I still wonder who and what determines that. His and similar criticism led me to retort:

'Some years ago a leading gallery in this country paid something like £12,000 for a "genuine" Old Master. It has now been discovered that the "Old Master" is still alive, and the picture now reposes in a basement as a "curio". At least we *know* who painted Dali's picture. Recently a collector paid an even larger sum for another "Old Master" which is a triumph of the art of the restorer. The "hand" of the master is buried in the velvet glove of contemporary pigments. Paint and canvas begin to undergo the perishing processes within a short time after the completion of a painting. By that token we should be able to enjoy "pure" Dali for a much longer time than some other expensive works.'

We also reproduced in the *Art Review* the pre-Raphaelite picture *Christ in the House of His Parents* or *The Carpenter's*

Shop by Sir John Millais which, not so many years previously, was bought for £10,500. It is in the Tate Gallery. The vicious contemporary criticism, including a piece by Charles Dickens, was also reprinted with a final comment from William Armstrong.

To the artists, including Augustus John, who deprecated this 'wilful extravagance' and deplored such a 'mad price' for a work by a living painter, we said something like this:

'Extraordinary! Why do they not rejoice that, for once, the artist rather than the collector or dealer or their descendants reaps benefit from his labour? Salvador Dali is a man with an international reputation. His "news value" is at least as great as that of Picasso and Matisse and he considers this painting of Christ to be his masterpiece.'

A few months later it was reported than an English actor was to receive £40,000 for playing a part in a film.

The events of the art market of the last ten years, related to living painters, make it seem to appear that we had created a precedent.

Stephen Bone of the *Manchester Guardian* in reporting the distribution of works commissioned by the Arts Council said:

'Will any of them reach Glasgow, a city that has just spent many thousands of pounds on a surrealist Crucifixion by Salvador Dali that no art critic could take seriously? After this sensational extravagance it may be felt that Glasgow Corporation is a little ill-placed for receiving gifts from the taxpayer, but this would be a short-sighted view. Glasgow may soon feel the need of good modern paintings in its galleries.'

His was more than a short-sighted view, for no gallery in the country had acquired through its own limited purchase funds more modern works than Glasgow. True, like most of the others, we didn't ride very high in sculpture. In recalling some very ill-informed criticism I am provoked into a bit of boasting to support our defence: or is it defiance? In my time and on my recommendation Glasgow acquired, by purchase, *Blackfriars* by Derain for £150 and a Utrillo for £450. Other French paintings by artists such as Cassat, Courbet, Gauguin, Marquet, Monet, Pissarro, Signac and Sisley came through the Hamilton Trust. They do not reveal the purchase price but I know all were between £1,000 and £4,000 at the most. We bought excellent examples of L.S. Lowry (in 1943 for £42 and in 1944 for

£135). The works of a number of English and Scottish artists, when they were at the beginning of their careers, were acquired for very little expenditure. We like to think that to the ridiculously small sums might be added the value of an official gesture of support. From the Contemporary Art Society we received some good works, but as we were more distant than our English colleagues the first choices seldom came our way. The Arts Council never favoured us by adding works to the collection.

The Art School, staff and students, were with very few exceptions, particularly against the purchase of the Dali. Some of my University friends were convinced we had made a grievous blunder. 'It will be down in the basement in three years' was the prophecy of one of them. A few had no objections to the acquisition of a work by Dali. After all, he was a leader of a particular movement which was part of art history; but why did we not get a typical surrealist painting instead of this 'non-characteristic' example? One exasperated critic was certain we knew very little or nothing about surrealism.

THE DOUR DRINKERS OF GLASGOW, 1952
Hugh MacDiarmid

Were drinkers in Glasgow any more dour than those elsewhere? Arguably. There were certainly more drinkers and more places in which to drink. Nor was there much else to do in them. Until fairly recently drinking in Scotland was a serious business which was pursued single-mindedly. Unlike their English counterparts, Scottish pubs did not offer food and very little in the way of diversion. Hugh MacDiarmid knew of course of what he wrote. A thinker and a drinker, he was never more content than when throwing spanners into works and oil upon troubled waters. It was in Glasgow, for example that he dared make a controversial speech about Robert Burns, dismissing him as a voice from the past. Could it have been the drink talking?

I have never been able, despite repeated efforts, to understand the periodicity of complaints against the Scottish pub which have been made during the past half century. Made, I suspect, not by women or clergymen, either by English visitors or by Scots who, as Sir Walter Scott said, 'unScotched make damned bad Englishmen'. They are usually accompanied by envious comparisons of English inns, which we are told are far more sociable and cater to family parties in a way Scottish pubs do not. For, in the latter, at their most typical, the rule is 'men only' and 'no sitting' – you stand at the counter with your toes in that narrow sawdust-filled trough which serves as a comprehensive combined ash-tray, litter-bin, and cuspidor. So it was when I first began to drink nearly fifty years ago; so it still is for the most part. Certainly nowadays, in addition to the common bars and to the jug (or family) departments to which women, mostly of a shawled, slatternly, and extremely subfusc order, still repair with all the ancient furtiveness, there are bright chromium-fitted saloon bars, cocktail bars, and other modern accessories in the more pretentious places. And even in most of the ordinary bars there is now a fair sprinkling of women not only of the 'lower orders' or elderly at that, but gay young things, merry widows and courtesans. Men (if you can call them that) even take their wives and daughters along with them to these meretricious, de-Scotticised resorts.

Now, I am not a misogynist by any means. I simply believe there is a time and place for everything – and yes, literally, *everything*. And like a high proportion of my country's regular and purposive drinkers I greatly prefer a complete absence of women on occasions of libation. I also prefer a complete absence of music and very little illumination. I am therefore a strong supporter of the lower – or lowest type of 'dive' where drinking is the principal purpose and no one wants to be distracted from that absorbing business by music, women, glaring lights, chromium fittings, too many mirrors unless sufficiently fly-spotted and mildewed, or least of all, any fiddling trivialities of *l'art nouveau*. If there are still plenty of pubs in Glasgow which conform to these requirements and remain frowsy and fusty enough to suit my taste and that of my boon companions, in another respect the old order has changed sadly and I fear irreversibly. Our Scottish climate – not to speak of the soot-laden, catarrh-producing atmosphere of Glasgow in particular – makes us traditionally great spirit-drinkers. That has changed. Most of us cannot afford – or at that rate cannot get – much whisky or, for that matter, any other spirit. There are, of course, desperate characters who drink methylated spirits. I have known – and still know – resolute souls partial to a mixture of boot-blacking and 'meth', and I remember when I was in the Merchant Service during the recent War a few hardy characters who went to the trouble of stealing old compasses off the boats at Greenock (where we had the largest small-boat pool in Europe) in order to extract from them the few drops of spirit (well mixed with crude-oil and verdigris) they contained. But in Glasgow pubs today at least ninety per cent of the drinking is of beer – and mere 'swipes' at that; 'beer' that never saw a hop. I can remember the time when it was the other way about. What beer was consumed was used simply as a 'chaser' to the whisky in precisely the same way as a 'boilermaker' in New York. For of course you can get drunk quicker on whisky plus water than on neat whisky, and whisky and soda is an English monstrosity no true Scot can countenance at all.

There are other sorry changes in even the lowest-down pubs which in general hold to the grim tradition of the true Scottish 'boozer'. The question of hours, for example. In London one can still drink legally twenty-three hours out of twenty-four. That is because London is a congeries of different boroughs which have different 'permitted hours' so that by switching from one borough at closing time it is easy to find another where 'they' will still be open for an hour or two longer. In Glasgow, moreover, unlike London, there are few facilities for drinking outside the permitted hours. For most people, that is. It will hardly be thought that I am pleading for decreased consumption, but I believe that the same amount of strong drink taken in a leisurely way over a fair number of hours is less harmful than the rush to squeeze in the desired number of drinks in the short time the law allows. Out national poet, Robert Burns, was right when he said: 'Freedom and whisky gang thegither'. What he meant is precisely what my own motto means: 'They do not love liberty who fear licence'. I speak for the large body of my compatriots who uphold this principle and regard respectability and affectations of any kind as our deadliest enemy. There are, of course, clubs and hotels, but the *hoi polloi* have nothing to do with either of these.

Only a few years ago there were also Burns Clubs which took advantage of a loophole in the law and did a roaring trade, especially on Sundays. You did not require to be introduced. You simply paid half-a-crown at the door and automatically became a member for the day. The difficulty – especially for the thirsty stranger within the gates, and indeed for the bulk of the citizens themselves – was to find these places. One heard about them. One heard, indeed, fantastic tales of the alcoholic excess which went on there. But they were exceedingly difficult to find. You had to be 'in the know'. Suddenly they disappeared entirely. I have never been able to discover why. There was nothing in the press – and I could learn nothing over my private grapevine either – about police action having been taken. They must have been very profitable to those who ran them, and a substantial source of revenue to the 'liquor trade' generally. They served a very useful purpose since no one not a resident in a hotel and not a member of a club could otherwise get a drink in Glasgow on Sundays. (It was – and still is – jolly difficult to get a meal even.)

ARMAGEDDON IN GEORGE SQUARE, 1953
George Rosie

In his book Curious Scotland *(2004), the journalist George Rosie (1941–) attempted to answer a number of questions that were haunting him. What became of the sons of Robert Burns? Why do people regularly spit on one particular part of Edinburgh pavement? And, more apocalyptically, what would have happened had an A-Bomb been dropped on George Square in Glasgow? The last-mentioned was in the context of the Cold War, when the world seemed to many to be on the brink of self-destruction. Suffice it to say, Glasgow would have borne the brunt of any nuclear attack on these islands.*

I can never cross George Square without recalling a buff-coloured folder I came across by accident in the Public Record Office in Kew. Official documents are sometimes misleadingly described by journalists as 'chilling' when 'mildly worrying' would be more accurate. But this one was a chiller, without a doubt. Commissioned by the Scottish Office in Edinburgh from the scientists of the Home Office in London, it was an official estimate of what would happen to Glasgow if someone (the Soviets, presumably) detonated an atom bomb over George Square. It had the feeling of worried people trying to come to terms with a real possibility.

There was, I suppose, a lot to worry about in the years of its authorship, 1951 to 1952. The Soviet Union had developed its own atomic weapons. The Chinese People's Army had flooded into North Korea to pursue the war against American-led UN forces that included British troops. The United States was in the grip of what can only be described as paranoia. Two minor Soviet agents – Julius and Ethel Rosenberg – had been condemned to death in 1951 for passing on secrets to the Soviet Union and were later (1953) executed. Atomic devices were regularly tested in the Nevada desert. In May 1951, the Americans tested, in the Pacific, the first hydrogen bomb. It was a triumph of nuclear physics that the Soviets and then the British were to repeat. The 'atomic age' had arrived in earnest.

It was against that background that His Majesty's Government decided to investigate what would happen if a Hiroshima-type atomic device were exploded over the centre of Glasgow. Their calculations are contained in a document marked 'secret' and wordily entitled *Assessment of the Damage and the Numbers of Casualties and Homeless Likely to Result from an Attack on Glasgow with an Atomic Bomb*. The research was carried out between 1951 and 1952 under the direction of E.C. Allen MSc of the Home Scientific Adviser's Branch. The Scottish Home Department and the Department of Health for Scotland (both branches of the Scottish Office) had commissioned it, and the result was approved by the government's Working Party of the Effects of Air Attack. When the document was printed and circulated in January 1953, it carried with it the warning that 'the official in possession of the document will be responsible for its safe custody and when not in use it is to be kept under lock and key'.

What Allen and his colleagues postulated was an explosion at 2,000 feet above ground zero by a 'nominal' nuclear device with the equivalent destructive power of 20,000 tons of TNT (roughly the size of the atomic bomb that destroyed most of Hiroshima in August 1945). Two separate scenarios were explored: one in which the bomb was dropped on Glasgow during the day, the other in which the attack occurred at night. The Home Office men calculated that 932,900 people would be within 2.5 to 3 miles of ground zero during the day, dropping to 854,200 at night. A daytime explosion during the working week was therefore considered to be the greater of the two evils, Glasgow would be about its business. The factories, shops, warehouses, offices, schools, tramcars and streets would be crowded with people. The Home Office team put the number of daytime casualties at 79,700 dead and 25,900 seriously injured, whereas a night-time bomb would yield 59,700 dead and 19,300 seriously injured.

Blast damage to property was also assessed. Up to 3,000 feet from ground zero the effect on stone-built tenements would be 'complete collapse'. At 4,000 feet there would be seventy-five per cent collapse. At 5,000 feet twenty-five per cent collapse. At 1.25 miles all pitched roofs would be destroyed. At 1.5 miles the roof damage would make the building uninhabitable. Beyond 2 miles the damage would be 'superficial'.

Anyone trapped in the rubble of a collapsed Glasgow tenement had little hope of rescue. Lying under two storeys of London or Birmingham brick is one thing. Lying under four or five storeys of Scottish sandstone is something else entirely. This report took this into account and pointed out that the sheer weight of the debris would mean that 'only a small proportion of the trapped and injured were likely to be saved'. The Glasgow tenement's only – and literally – saving grace was that its thick stone walls offered greater protection against gamma radiation.

The report conceded that official thinking about the consequences of nuclear attack until then had been distinctly Anglocentric. 'Previous studies of atomic attack on British cities made by the Working Party have been based on the assumption that the bulk of the people live in small terraced or semi-detached brick houses. This assumption clearly could not be applied to either Glasgow or Edinburgh.' Glasgow was extraordinarily vulnerable, with special problems. The report concluded: 'These special problems result mainly from the density of population in Glasgow, which is greater than that of any British city, but also because much of the population is housed in very large blocks of tenements, some of which are 100 or more years old.'

In other words, no city in Britain would have suffered more grievously than Glasgow in the event of a nuclear attack. So, with these facts and figures at their fingertips, what did the British government do? Ten years later it gave Holy Loch to the US navy as a forward base for its nuclear-armed and nuclear-powered submarines. Soon after it made two more of the Clyde's sea lochs – Loch Long and the Gare Loch – into the base for the Royal Navy's new nuclear submarine fleet. Both bases were prime targets for the Soviet Union's nuclear missiles and bombs. Both lay (and in the Royal Navy's case still lie) fewer than thirty miles from George Square and the heart of Glasgow.

LEARNING ABOUT COLOURS, 1953
Alan Spence

Glasgow is a divided city in many ways but the most obvious is religion. It is embodied in two football clubs, Rangers and Celtic. The former are the standard bearers of native Scottish Protestants who in the late nineteenth century feared an influx of Irish Catholic immigrants who gave their support to the latter. Each side is as distinctive as night and day. Rangers wear blue while Celtic favour green. But as Alan Spence (1947–) recalls, things are more complicated than that.

The earliest holiday I remember was for the Coronation. Every child received a tin of sweets with the Queen's portrait on the lid. I went with my mother to visit my aunt, one of the first people in the area, perhaps in the whole of Glasgow, to have a television set. The set was tiny, with a nine-inch screen, and the house was full of neighbours, crowding round to watch. Afterwards, in the back court, somebody gave a party for all the local children, with crisps and ice-lollies and paper hats, party-games and songs and jokes. It was a great, great day. God save the Queen!

The Queen was a Protestant. My uncle had told me that. My uncle was in the Orange Lodge, and had undertaken my education in such matters. He and my father had already taken me to see Rangers play at Ibrox. I had felt the elation at their victory, the depression at their defeat; I had been initiated. Emotionally now I could feel the connections; the Queen and the Union Jack, being a Protestant and following Rangers; it was all noble and good, all part of some glorious heritage that was mine. And the opposite of all this was Catholic, was darkness, was bad and in some way a threat.

I remember one day my uncle teaching me about colours. I was wearing a blue jersey and he said it was good, was a fine colour.

How about orange, I asked, was that a good colour? The best, he said.

Purple? That was good too.

Red was fine.

Black and white were OK, not good, not bad.

But green was bad. The worst.

I thought of the green park where we went on those summer evenings, and how beautiful it was. But no. It was the colour of Celtic, of the Catholics. They had made it their own, had made it bad.

I was eating further of the tree of knowledge.

My uncle said I was growing into a good Protestant. He said when I was a little older he would get me into the Juvenile Orange Lodge. The thought excited me.

I could march in a parade, perhaps even learn to play flute or drum in a band. But my mother said no. They were all mad she said, just making people hate each other all the more, and for nothing.

Reality was growing more complex and confusing. Nothing, it seemed, was clear cut.

At school I was making progress. The ogre of a teacher was replaced by another, much milder, and I began to flower. From the age of six on, through my whole time at the school, I came top in every exam, won first prize every year. Teachers made much of me. My drawings and handwriting were often on display. I was granted little privileges, like being sent on errands, minutes of glorious freedom from the class. I developed a certain smugness, a pride in my own abilities, a sense that I was special, unique. And to those teachers I suppose I was. Ours was one of the rougher schools in a rough part of the city.

Unemployment was high, there was real poverty, and much small-scale crime. The school itself had some reputation – it was overcrowded, and many of the children were 'problem-cases'.

To the teachers, my little bright spark of intelligence would be something that had to be nurtured and encouraged to grow. One teacher in particular had great hopes for me. She suggested that when I reached the right age, I should try for the scholarship exam for a high school in the city centre. The school was fee-paying, but a small number of bursaries were awarded each year, on the basis of a competitive exam. This teacher encouraged me to read more widely, sometimes gave me extra work, to prepare me. I liked her better than any of the other teachers.

One morning, I was about eight at the time, she came in raging and started to rant at us about the prime minister, Anthony Eden. He had sent bombers to Suez, she said, while at the same time the British government was condemning Russia for invading Hungary. We listened, amazed. These were things we heard about from the world of newspapers, of the radio, but it was beyond all our comprehension. And here was our teacher, turning on its head the way we had come to see things, where the British, which was us, were always in the right. Reality was becoming complex indeed. There was a whole big world out there, full of contradictions.

And how did I fit into it? How was my definition of myself shaping up? Well, I was a Protestant, I knew that. I also knew that I was Scottish. Scotland was my country, Glasgow my city. Sometimes being Scottish meant being British, sometimes British just meant English. But then sometimes Scottish and English were opposed, as in football internationals, as in great battles from the past. My idea of what British meant came originally from war films I had seen. British were soldiers who wore a certain shape of helmet. The other kinds were American, Germans and Japs. British and American were always good, the others were bad. But in Korean War films, the Americans were fighting communists, and my father said my teacher was a communist. It was all too confusing.

RITE OF PASSAGE, *c.* 1953
Tom Gallacher

All workplaces have their rituals, some of which are more tolerable than others. That described here is from Apprentice *(1983), a novel by Tom Gallacher (1932–2001). Born in Alexandria,*

West Dunbartonshire, he trained as a draughtsman and worked at Denny's shipyard in Dumbarton, which experience provided him with much material for his fiction. Apprentice's *narrator, sixteen-year-old Billy Thompson, has attended a Sussex public school and, in the 1950s, has come north to serve his apprenticeship as his successful father did before him.*

Like all closed societies, the world of engineering has its own initiation ceremony. Before he is fully admitted, the apprentice has to be 'greased'. What horrified me was *where* he had to be greased. In the shipyards where I had served my time, there was an adamant preference for the genitals. Since I'd come directly from a minor English public school, that should not have surprised me. And, given the mechanical parallels of piston-rod and regulator-valve, it might even have seemed apt. Nevertheless, I was determined that nobody was going to do *that* to *me*. Thinking of it now, the whole business is fairly amusing, but then, when I was seventeen, the prospect of such abject humiliation was terrifying. For a few months I was successful in avoiding any group of my fellows which wore that menacing, collective smirk and as I got used to the place I persuaded myself that they'd forgotten I hadn't been 'done'. I'd reckoned without the lack of supervision when, during roof repairs, we had to work on the night-shift.

Bent at my lathe in the Light Machine Shop, I realised that Frank, my only reliable friend, was smiling over my head.

I looked around but could see nothing unusual. 'What is it?'

'Nothin'!' But he smiled even more broadly.

The distraction was fatal to the gunmetal valve I was turning. The tool dug under the centre-line and the whole piece rocketed out of the chuck, smashed the machine-lamp and fell with a denouncing clang in the sump. I fished it out and revealed the deep gash in the valve face.

'What shall I do?'

'Whi' everbody else does,' said Frank, unperturbed. 'Dump it in the Dock Burn an' steal another yin fae the store.'

'I'd better wrap it up in something.'

'Wait tae ye finished the shift. The wey you're gaun, there's likely tae be mair.' But again, he was looking behind me and this time I turned quickly enough to see the advance of four or five older apprentices – one of them carrying a large can of axle-tallow.

Frank said, 'Ye cannae dodge it this time Billy. Ye're gonnae get greased.'

'I won't let them.'

'Ye cannae stop them.'

'Will you help me?'

'Naw. But I'll no' help them.'

The long gallery of the machine shop was lit only by the individual machine lights and, since the light on mine had just been shattered, the area around me was practically dark. Frank, who had undergone the business with perfect composure more than six months before, moved away. I gripped the damaged valve tight in my hand and waited. I heard Jock Turnbull's deep laugh and I turned to face that way, but immediately I heard from the opposite direction the creak of the long footboard as someone stepped from the concrete floor onto it. Then they were all on top of me. My wrist was caught and banged against the tail-stock so that the valve dropped again loudly in the sump. I struggled as hard as I could – trying to wrestle my way *under* the machine. They gripped my legs and pulled me back on the footboard. Staring up I saw the repair tarpaulin on the roof flapping against the dark sky before faces and shoulders and arms blotted that out. And I could smell the sickly, thick tallow. My head was pulled up by the hair so that they could start stripping off the one-piece suit of dungarees under which I was wearing shirt and trousers.

PARAFFIN DRESSING, 1956

Alexander McArthur and H. Kingsley Long

If ever a novel can be said to define a place then No Mean City *(1956), co-authored by A. McArthur and H. Kingsley Long, did just that for Glasgow. Though dismissed as turgid and unreadable by literary critics it struck a chord with the wider reading public, who were in turn engrossed and appalled by its portrayal of razor gangs, hooliganism and hard drinking. But as one commentator grudgingly conceded 'it has become the Glasgow novel' and has been constantly in print since its first appearance.*

Its hero, if such he may be called, is Johnnie Stark, 'a product of the Gorbals', who behaves like an animal in the jungle where only the fittest have the chance to survive.

Just across the Clyde from the Gorbals lies Glasgow Green, the city's most frequented park. There, in a triangular patch of the river between King's Street and St Andrew's bridges, is an open-air gymnasium much frequented by the youth of the slums and, occasionally, the battle ground of conflicting gangs.

Johnnie Stark was exercising on the parallel bars. He sank his body until the shoulder blades met and only the elbows and heels were above the bars. Slowly and smoothly he raised himself to rigid, full arms' length. He rose and sank again and again, counting silently until he reached his regulation fifty movements. Then his feet swung free of the bars and he vaulted cleanly to the ground. There were several other young men there of about his own age. They watched him respectfully as he resumed his neat blue jacket. He flung a nod at them and walked away with a little swagger.

Vanity is as much a dominant motive in the slums as outside them. Johnnie had little to be proud of except his strong body and reckless spirit. He spent a lot of his leisure at the Green Gym, and much of his money on clothes. He was not ill-looking and in the Gorbals men and women too are very much judged by their appearance. A good suit of clothes wins a certain respect for the wearer. Johnnie wore 'a whole suit' – that is to say, the coat and trousers were of the same navy blue cloth and had been sold together *as* a suit. His shoes were well polished, a bright 'tony-red'. In the language of the Gorbals, he was 'well put on' and proud of his 'paraffin'. There was actually a paraffin dressing on his sleek black hair, and perhaps there may have been some association of ideas between slumland's passion for smoothed and glistening crops and its general term for a smart appearance.

But Johnnie would never have worried his head about the derivation of words. At school he had not even secured his 'merit certificate', that minimum standard of education which the council had set. His failure to do so meant thirty evenings at night school when, by reason of his age, his normal 'schuling' was at an end. Even a diligent lad can't contrive to learn a great deal in thirty evenings. Johnnie, utterly bored, endured the night school as so much detention and learned nothing at all. He could read the racing papers and the football reports and he could do simple sums and he was satisfied that this was an adequate equipment for all practical purposes.

ARE YE DANCING? 1958
Jack House

To Presbyterians of yore, dancing was tantamount to devil worship. Why Glaswegians paid no heed to such nonsense ought perhaps to be the subject of deeper study. The influx of the Irish – whose feet can never be nailed down when a band begins to play – may have something to do with it. Historians of the city know that Glasgow's love of dancing is by no means recent. On the contrary, it has played an intrinsic part in its development. In the 1950s, while many took to the Great Outdoors an even greater number preferred the Great Indoors. As one keen tango-ist recalled: 'Many young men pass through a phase which has often been described by their parents and friends and sometimes even by themselves as "dancing mad" . . . the search for a mate and dancing go hand in hand.'

Dancing is tremendously popular in Glasgow and there is a higher proportion of dance halls to the population than anywhere else in the British Isles. The standard of dancing was considered, up till 1940, the best in Britain. Experts now say that the standard has deteriorated because of such 'foreign' influences as the arrival of American soldiers and sailors. Although the standard may have deteriorated, the number of dancers is still enormous, and many of the patrons of the big ballrooms attend four or five times a week. In a recent broadcast from Barrowland Dance Hall in the Gallowgate, a girl said that she danced seven nights a week – six nights at Barrowland and Sunday night at a special dance club.

There are more than 30 licensed dance halls in Glasgow and a large number of small halls where dances, as distinct from 'dancing', are held. No dance hall in Glasgow is licensed for the sale of alcohol, and trouble is sometimes caused by young men bringing in bottles secretly and drinking from them in the lavatory. This is sternly discouraged. The occasional fights, followed by police court appearances, on Friday and Saturday nights are most often caused because doorkeepers will not allow 'drunks' to enter.

Dennistoun Palais holds 1,700 dancers and is the biggest dance hall in Glasgow. The Plaza is renowned as the place where family parties go, particularly for twenty-first birthday celebrations. 'Jiving' is not encouraged in any of the big dance halls but one, the Locarno, has experimented in having a special place for 'jivers'.

Many private and club dances are held in Glasgow, in hotels, Masonic halls, community centres and church halls. Less than 30 years ago most churches would not countenance dances, and church youth clubs held what were euphemistically called 'socials'. At some of these the number of dances was restricted to, say, four. But there was no restriction on 'games', so the organisers would include The Grand Old Duke of York, the Eightsome Reel and items of a similar nature as games. Each of the four dances lasted for at least a quarter of an hour. Nowadays church youth clubs are, in the main, unrestricted, and no longer have to call their dances 'socials'.

NORTH AND SOUTH OF THE RIVER, 1958
Jack House

Like most big cities, Glasgow is a patchwork of communities, some more distinct and protective of their identity than others. Jack House (1906–91), one of Glasgow's lustiest psalmists, was well aware of the offence he was likely to cause when, in his book The Heart of Glasgow, *he ran out of space to cover south of the Clyde. Nor, he admitted, had he been able to deal with the 'villages' of Glasgow. 'But what can I do?' he wrote, as if pleading for mercy. And well he might for Glaswegians are forthright in asserting where exactly they come from and why it is a better place to live than elsewhere. Thus you will still find East Enders who talk of the West End as if it were Timbuctoo and vice versa and South Siders who refer to the North Side as if it were beyond Aberdeen. Which, of course, in their minds it is.*

Glasgow may not be the closely-knit city it was in 1901, but there is still a decided difference between the North and South sides of Glasgow – though it may not be as easy to distinguish between a Northerner from a Southerner as it was fifty or more years ago.

Outwardly the inhabitants of both sides of the River Clyde look the same. But most of them say flatly that they would not want to live on the other side of the river. There are numerous cases of South Side families who, for various reasons, have to 'flit' to the North Side, but are soon complaining about their new surroundings and often arranging to go back to the other side of the Clyde. This applies to all classes of Glaswegians. South Siders, in particular, attach some sort of magic to living south of the Clyde. Several South Siders, interviewed when they had returned to the south after a short sojourn in the north, complained about the 'different air' on the north of the Clyde. A middle-class housewife confessed she felt 'unwell' all the time she was living in North Kelvinside. When she returned to Pollokshields, her health improved immediately. A Glasgow journalist, accustomed to living in Ibrox, said that he was 'unsettled' when he had to reside in Hillhead.

The North Siders do not seem to worry so much about the change of air. Few North Siders have had to make the change to the South Side. The North Siders' attitude, however, is well exemplified in the case of the Citizens' Theatre. Most of the entertainment of Glasgow is situated north of the river. The only theatre on the other side is the Citizens'. Many North Siders say they will not go to the Citizens' Theatre because 'it's so far away'. In actual fact, it is just across the Clyde and is well served by bus routes from the north and the west. From the centre of the city – Central Station, for example – the Citizens' Theatre takes less than a minute longer to reach than the King's Theatre, near Charing Cross. And you can get to the Citizens' Theatre more quickly than you can reach the Empress Theatre at St George's Cross. This has been pointed out many times to North Siders, particularly by the management of the Citizens' Theatre, but they still talk about the 'distance' to the theatre, and the 'difficulty' of getting there. South Siders, in the main, *must* cross the river to get their entertainment, and they do not appear to object to this. North Siders make exceptions, by the way, of the Plaza Palais de Danse and Crossmyloof Ice Rink. They never refer to 'difficulties' with getting to these two places.

In Glasgow there is the customary feeling between East Enders and West Enders, but it is by no means as strong as the 'differences' felt by South Siders and North Siders. This is partly because Glasgow originally spread to the East. The move to the West did not take place until nearly half way through the nineteenth century. By that time there were many well-established district communities in the East. The result is that, though, very broadly speaking, the West End is 'well off' and the East End is 'working class', the East Enders do not envy or look up to the Glaswegians of the West. It is in the East End particularly that the vestigial remains of 'village' life are still to be found. Most of the districts of Glasgow that existed up to the First World War retain an independent ambience. In the East End, for example, inhabitants of adjacent districts like Shettleston and Tollcross are annoyed if outsiders mix them up. Two brothers, well known Motor Rally drivers in Britain and on the Continent, expressed their exasperation at being referred to in newspaper reports as 'Andy and Chris Neil of Shettleston'. They pointed out in the strongest terms that they did not come from Shettleston. They came from Tollcross.

BUD NEILL, 1958
Clifford Hanley

Originally from Partick, William 'Bud' Neill (1911–70) moved in infancy with his family to Ayrshire, where he grew up. He first began to draw cartoons while working as a bus driver in Glasgow. In 1944, he started contributing to the Evening Times. *His subject was Glasgow in all its mad and perverse idiosyncrasy. Neill's most famous character, and the one with whom his name is inextricably linked, Lobey Dosser, made his debut in 1949 in the* Evening Times. *A Lobey Dosser in the Glasgow patois is a lodger who, not having the wherewithal to rent a room, must sleep in the 'lobey', i.e. the lobby or hallway. Lobey is the bearded Sheriff of Calton Creek who strives to maintain law and order against the forces of evil, in particular 'Rank Bajin'. There is a bronze statue of Lobey Dosser in Woodlands Road across from the Halt Bar, featuring Lobey and Rank astride El Fideldo, who is to Lobey what Rocinante is to Don Quixote.*

Bud Neill came of a comfortable Ayrshire family, but according to various stories he told me in my cups, he spent the first seven years of his life in Tibet, as a husky dog. Later, when doubts were cast on his ability to pull a sledge, he left Lhasa in a fit of pique, fitted with a two-stroke engine, and crossed the Sahara Desert in a cement-mixer.

'That was before I joined the *Record*,' he explained. 'From the Dalai Lama to the Dalai Record, ha! You didn't know that, boy, did you?'

'I did,' I muttered thickly. 'I was the second dog on the left.'

'That's ma boay!' he shouted.

I met Bud while I was writing an unsuccessful radio series for Stewart and Mathew, the husband-and-wife comedy dancing act who graced the old Dave Willis Half-past-eight shows at the King's Theatre and are stars with the famous Fol-de-Rols. Charlie Stewart was a boyhood friend of Bud Neill, and also incidentally of Eric D. Clarke, another Ayrshire character who came to Glasgow to do his comic artist turn and has been doing it and getting more and more boyish with it for over twenty years. Bud turned up in the King's Arms one afternoon when I was having a drink with my stars and mulling over the murderous notices we were getting in the *Evening News*. The artist was already a kind of cult among all social and intellectual strata in Glasgow.

In fact, he worked as a bus driver, funeral undertaker, and various other things before he started to draw cartoons in earnest and was invited to join the staff of the *Evening Times*. His daily cartoon wasn't a joke in the sense that any other artist of the time was drawing jokes. It was just a bit of Glasgow, often meaningless on the surface, and whoever on the *Evening Times* first thought of taking him on must have had more perception than most newspaper editors, which wouldn't be hard. He was the first evidence of new indigenous Glasgow humour since J.J. Bell and Neil Munro. After the first jolt of incomprehension,

Glaswegians started to tear open the *Evening Times* to gobble the latest Bud Neill titbit, as salty and esoteric and Glasgow as a black puddin' supper. How do you explain the art of a man whose finest product was a squashed drawing of two shapeless things against the background of a square tenement with the caption:

'Haw Jennifer! Ma kirby's fell doon a stank!'

He was tall and thin, in smart careless clothes with a trace of American accent; a face composed of bold planes of bone under a fine dome head with straight thinning hair; he wore gleaming false teeth and rimless glasses, and could have been a successful salesman from a Frank Capra film.

It's true that he can't draw, in the same way that James Thurber can't draw. The recurrent heroine that waddles through his work is a dream, or a nightmare figure, of the shrewd, sentimental, unlettered Glasgow wifie sunk in thick ankles and clasping hands under sprawling bosom designed for wedging over a windowsill for a good hing, and she rises to the level of poetry when her inarticulate hunger for beauty drives her to sigh: 'My, ah like rid herr. Rid herr's rerr.'

'Ach poetry ma bottom,' said Bud when I accused him of it. 'Honestly, now, don't you think that's *good*?' 'Well, it's all right, I suppose. Who knows what's good? Still, if you say it's good there must be something in it – something that in my preternatural ignorance, ha, that's good, something that in my preternatural ignorance I have not as yet detected. Detected, is that right? My vocabulary is somewhat inchoate tonight. I must be sober, or something equally horrible.' He leaned back for a better look and glinted joyfully through his Glenn Miller specs.

A CUPBOARD FOR COAL AND MARMALADE, 1959
John Betjeman

Though he is best known as a poet, John Betjeman (1906–84) was also passionate about architecture and was never happier than when discovering new places and new buildings. He travelled widely throughout Britain and brought to bear the eye of an artist on what he witnessed. He visited Glasgow at the behest of the Daily Telegraph *and he was clearly surprised and inspired by what he saw. Betjeman had been earlier to Edinburgh and could not resist comparing it with its rival. 'While all praise Edinburgh,' he wrote, 'there are few to hymn Glasgow. To visit Glasgow after Edinburgh is rather like meeting a red-faced Lord Mayor after a session with a desiccated and long-lineaged Scottish peer. They are both magnificent in their ways, but so different that there is no comparison.'*

Though this great city is ancient in origin, most of its buildings of note belong to the last century. Alexander ('Greek') Thomson produced in Glasgow a simple architecture, solid and so perfectly proportioned that, though none of his buildings are very big, they command a respect which the least observant cannot help giving them. His Presbyterian churches in St Vincent Street and Queen's Park, his terraces – Great Western Terrace and Moray Place, Strathbungo – display a delicacy of detail and a perfection of proportion which are a Greek answer to St Mungo's Cathedral so many centuries earlier.

All over Glasgow there is distinguished cast iron in lamp posts, fences and balcony railings, in conservatories and railway station roofs. Possibly the best example of the last is the great semicircular roof of Queen Street Station.

And then, at the end of the century, to go with the interest in art which the merchant princes of this vigorous city showed, there are both the collections of pictures in the public galleries and the Glasgow School of Art, by some considered the origin of what is today known as 'contemporary' architecture. The pictures, Italian, Dutch and French Impressionist in the Glasgow Art Gallery, together with the Whistlers in the University, make up what must be our finest collection of paintings outside London.

The Glasgow School of Art (1897–9) designed by Charles Rennie Mackintosh, is in its delicately mannered simplicity one of the most original buildings in Britain. It is as though Scottish Baronial had been translated into stone and wood and glass by Aubrey Beardsley. Glasgow is rightly proud of Mackintosh, and a dress shop in Sauchiehall Street still wisely preserves a room for its brides which Mackintosh originally designed for Glaswegians to drink tea in and eat baps and bannocks.

This is the bright side of a great city. But there can be no city in these islands which has darker spots. Out of a population of over a million, about 400,000 are not satisfactorily housed.

At Anderston Cross, built in the middle of the last century, I visited the worst slums I have ever seen. The stone buildings, four and five storeys high, looked solid enough on their street faces. Enter one of the archways to the courtyards which they enclose, and you will see the squalor.

Small children with no park or green space for miles play in rubbish bins with dead cats and mutilated flowers for toys. Spiral stone stairs, up which prams and bicycles have to be carried, lead to two-storey tenements with one lavatory for four families.

One such tenement I saw housed five children and the parents. The coal and the marmalade and bread were in the same cupboard. There was one sink with a single cold tap. There was a hole in the roof and a hole in the wall, and the only heat was from an old-fashioned kitchen range on which was a gas ring for cooking.

Yet these people, though they complained, were not bitter, and I was told there were 150,000 such houses in Glasgow. The Gorbals is by no means Glasgow's worst district. The Corporation has a slum clearance problem far greater and more complicated than that of any other city. Politics no doubt hamper its being carried out. But Christian charity must overrule political expediency.

'GLASGOW, 1960'
Hugh MacDiarmid

Undeniably a controversial figure, and a professional contrarian, the poet Hugh MacDiarmid (1892–1978) must nevertheless be given credit for attempting to drag Scots out of the kailyard and into the modern world. Born in Langholm, he was an autodidact who read his way through all the books in the local library. He did not wear his learning lightly. Rather he shoved it down his readers' throats with a shovel. He was the enemy of parochialism, the scourge of amateurism and the slayer of mediocrity. For him, Scotland was mired in ignorance, anti-intellectualism and smugness, and was over-interested in sport, especially football, which numbed the brain and made individuals part of the herd. He dreamed that things might be different, that instead of rushing to watch grown men kick a ball Scots would throng to hear what poets such as himself had to say. Such is the stuff of dreams.

Returning to Glasgow after long exile
Nothing seemed to me to have changed its style.
Buses and trams all labelled 'To Ibrox'
Swung past packed tight as they'd hold with folks.
Football match, I concluded, but just to make sure
I asked; and the man looked at me fell dour,
Then said, 'Where in God's name are *you* frae, sir?
It'll be a record gate, but the cause o' the stir
Is a debate on 'la loi de l'effort converti'
Between Professor MacFadyen and a Spainish pairty.'
I gasped. The newsboys came running along,
'Special! Turkish Poet's Abstruse New Song.
Scottish Authors' Opinions' – and, holy snakes,
I saw the edition sell like hot cakes!

THE ART OF STABBING, *c.* 1962
Jimmy Boyle

In the lore of Glasgow, Jimmy Boyle (1944–) looms large. A convicted murderer, he turned his life around and became a respected author and sculptor. He was born in the Gorbals into a life of crime to which he took with enthusiasm. Shoplifting, vandalism and street-fighting were for him daily occurrences. In his early teens he was sent to a remand home, from which he graduated to borstal and, eventually, Barlinnie Prison, his first experience of which is described below. Dubbed 'Scotland's Most Violent Man', he was convicted for the murder of Babs Rooney and given a life sentence. In 1973 he was one of the first offenders to participate in Barlinnie Prison Special Unit's innovative rehabilitation programme, which garnered as many bouquets as brickbats. His biography, A Sense of Freedom, *was published in 1977 and was later adapted for the screen.*

I was in a single cell which had a chamber pot, table, chair, and bed. There was a heavy steel frame with glass panes in it at the window and a set of thick steel bars. The routine in prisons is very rigidly structured and almost the same in every prison in Scotland. In the morning there is slop out and wash up then breakfast, either in the cell or in a dining hall. Work at 8 a.m. then lunch at noon; after lunch there is an hour's exercise either in the prison yards or round the gallery of the halls if it is raining. Back to work till 4.30 p.m. then evening meal. Lock up at 5 p.m. till the screws go for their tea than slop out at about 6.30 p.m. Those prisoners eligible for recreation are allowed out to the dining halls, which act as the recreation halls for an hour or so, then it is lock up and the screws go away at 9 p.m. The only variation is on Saturdays and Sundays, when the screws go away at 5 p.m. till the following morning, and on both of these days it is lock up most of the time.

The sentence that I was doing was quite big for a guy of my age with no prison sentence before but I wasn't really horrified at it. There was a sort of pride in it as I felt really good to be in beside lots of hard men as I was on the way to being one myself. When we were in cliques it would be all 'facades' and tough talk, but that wasn't what prison was to me. To me at that time prison was just a hazard of the life I was leading. It was all part of the sub-culture for everyone going about trying to impress everyone else.

I was allowed to write one letter a week to my family and all in-going and out-going mail was censored. The screws were very petty and would concentrate on small things just like the prisoners. They would come in and search your cell and person. You could be put on report for hanging pin-ups on the walls. Some of us serving lengthy sentences would bribe one of the painters (prisoners working as painters) to steal some paint for us and we would paint our cells as they were only painted every seven years by the prison and they were filthy. I lost remission for very petty offences. One day I was walking along in single file with over a hundred others when this screw started shouting at me like I was dirt. Maybe I was, but as far as I was concerned so was he; so I thumped him on the jaw and was dragged off him by some other screws and taken to the bottom flat of the hall and thrown into the punishment cell, after having my clothes and shoes taken from me. I knew that if I did anything back there would be more charges so I more or less took what they gave giving token resistance and they left. Much later I was taken to the hospital in the prison and gave the reason for my injuries as having fallen. The following morning I was taken in front of the Governor and the screw described what had happened and I agreed with it and was sentenced to fourteen days. The fact that I had heavy bruising on one side of my face didn't raise the Governor's curiosity.

One day I was pulled out of line for having tight trousers and locked up in the punishment cell. They took the trousers off me to act as evidence, giving me an ill-fitting pair to take their place but I refused to wear them. When the time came for me to go in front of the Governor for a breach of discipline I went in my shirt tail, refusing to dress. He sent me to solitary for seven days but I still refused to wear them. While I was in solitary confinement I was opened up three times each day to slop out my chamber pot and I would walk to the toilet naked. After doing this for some time the door opened and my old trousers were thrown in. When my punishment was completed I was taken in front of the Governor and told that I was being put on Rule 36 for subversive activities. I was informed that Rule 36 is not a punishment but that I was being segregated from the other prisoners as I was a bad influence on them. I was taken to a cell at the far end of the hall above which was the Hanging Cell, and outside the window were the unmarked graves where the condemned men were buried.

* * *

Stabbings amongst prisoners were common occurrences and there was never any great hassle or upheaval over them; the prisoners took them for granted. Prison stabbings are usually well set up events and those carrying them out would take pride in doing a neat job. I did one of these and it was against a guy from my district who had been causing some trouble amongst our group. In things like this the done thing is to make a hit and make it quick because everyone weighs these things up and if they see people getting off with things then they think you are soft. So I set this deal up while walking through the corridor, the main 'hit' place, as the prisoners walk single file through dark corridors. It usually takes about four to do it, with the guy who is making the hit carrying the knife, with two in front of the victim and two behind. The guy walks up, makes the hit, then passes the knife to the guy in front of the victim and this was what I did. Before the screw can notice that someone has been hit the guy is well away, and only the victim is left, the weapon concealed by this time in a pre-arranged place. When getting to work there is a discussion as to whether it was a good hit or not. In this context, you have the art of violence in which the manner of its execution is very much appreciated just as works of art are appreciated in another culture. People in the art world understand what art is all about whereas in my world we think it's a load of balls, a big con; just as people in most sections of society view our cutting and maiming each other as hideous. The fact is that this is how we lived and if someone were to cut my face I wouldn't like it but I would accept it, knowing it was a hazard of the life I was leading. I would be intent on getting back at whoever had done it, but on the whole slashing, stabbing, shooting and death are to be expected amongst those of us who live like this.

'KING BILLY', 1963
Edwin Morgan

Edwin Morgan (1920–2010) was one of twentieth-century Scotland's greatest poets and its first Makar. Born in Glasgow, he lectured in English at the university from 1947 to 1980. As prolific as he was inventive, he combined humour with experimentalism in such poems as 'The Loch Ness Monster's Song'. Glasgow was an endless source of inspiration. 'King Billy' appeared in his collection, A Second Life *(1968).*

Grey over Riddrie the clouds piled up,
dragged their rain through the cemetery trees.
The gates shone cold. Wind rose
flaring the hissing leaves, the branches
swung, heavy, across the lamps.
Gravestones huddled in drizzling shadow,

flickering streetlight scanned the requiescats,
a name and an urn, a date, a dove
picked out, lost, half regained.
What is this dripping wreath, blown from its grave
red, white, blue, and gold
'To Our Leader of Thirty Years Ago' –

Bareheaded, in dark suits, with flutes
and drums, they brought him here, in procession
seriously, King Billy of Brigton, dead,
from Bridgeton Cross: a memory of violence,
brooding days of empty bellies,
billiard smoke and a sour pint,
boots or fists, famous sherrickings,
the word, the scuffle, the flash, the shout,
bloody crumpling in the close,
bricks for papish windows, get
the Conks next time, the Conks ambush
the Billy Boys, the Billy Boys the Conks till
Sillitoe scuffs the razors down the stank –
No, but it isn't the violence they remember
but the legend of a violent man
born poor, gang-leader in the bad times
of idleness and boredom, lost in better days,
a bouncer in a betting club,
a quiet man at last, dying
alone in Bridgeton in a box bed.
So a thousand people stopped the traffic
for the hearse of a folk hero and the flutes
threw 'Onward Christian Soldiers' to the winds
from unironic lips, the mourners kept
in step, and there were some who wept.

Go from the grave. The shrill flutes
are silent, the march dispersed.
Deplore what is to be deplored,
and then find out the rest.

TEETH TO TEETH, 1963
Jack House

Known, not exactly fondly, as 'the English comics' grave', the Empire had the kind of reputation that made performers turn to jelly. Built in Sauchiehall Street towards the end of the nineteenth century, it had a capacity of nearly 1,700. Among those who felt appearing there was akin to the fate of Christians facing lions in the Coliseum were Morecambe and Wise, whose first two appearances were greeted in silence. When on their third they received a smattering of applause, a stage hand told the pair: 'Aye, boys, they're beginning to like you!' The Empire closed in 1963.

The Empire was undoubtedly the best-known Glasgow theatre in London. This was because so many Southern comedians spread the myth that the most dangerous thing you could do in the music-hall business was to appear at the Empire. One even described how he fainted on the stage at the reception he got the first night on Monday. The dangers of the Empire were even chronicled in books by authors who should have known better.

I'm not suggesting that the Empire audiences were angels. They could cut up rough if they didn't like the show on a Friday or a Saturday night, when you might find characters who had been on a pub crawl before they arrived at the second house. In all my visits to the Empire I never once saw an act get the bird. I did, once or twice, see players get a rather cold reception. But I saw much worse at the Pavilion and no English comedian ever said a word against it.

Indeed, if I have a criticism of Empire audiences, I would say it was the other way round in its latter days, when American acts appeared with monotonous regularity. They all received what I can only call mindless applause.

Laurel and Hardy, for example, were at the end of their tether but possibly their reception was an expression of sympathy. Jerry Colona, whose only attribute turned out to be his loud voice, had a rapturous response from the Empire audience. It was more muted for Sophie Tucker, who had seen better days, but even then the night I was there a gentleman in the front row of the stalls stood up as she took her curtain and threw a bouquet of flowers on to the stage. Maybe he had accepted her invitation to come up and see her some time.

I have, of course, been describing shows at the last of the Empires. I was fortunate enough to see the Old Empire, a smaller and more attractive theatre. It had started as the Gaiety Theatre in 1874 and the name was changed to the Empire when the new owners took over. I first went there with my father, 69 years ago. I had taken up conjuring as a hobby and, having read all I could about the art, decided that the greatest magician in the world must be David Devant. The Empire, incidentally, seemed to specialise in conjurers and I should think every top performer in Britain, from the Continent and some top men from the United States, including the great Chung Ling Soo, appeared there.

Not that Chung Ling Soo was American, or even Chinese. He was a Scotsman named Robertson who had emigrated from Aberdeen to the USA. He was tall, not to say majestic, and during his entire act he never uttered a word, which was perhaps just as well. He was killed on stage when performing his famous trick of having a marked bullet fired at him and catching it between his teeth. To this day nobody knows whether it was an accident, murder or suicide.

Of the many American stars who appeared at the Empire, I place one high above the rest. She was Lena Horne and I have never seen or heard any singer quite like her. Teeny-boppers, thank God, didn't exist then or, if they did, they didn't bop in the theatres. Lena Horne was listened to with love and, can I say it, with respect.

In my opinion the finest American comedian to appear at the Empire was the great Jack Benny. I've never seen such immaculate timing in my life. He was assisted by a trio of gigantic Negresses and, as they galumphed about the stage, all Jack Benny had to do was to look at the audience and lift an eyebrow and the audience roared.

One last memory of the Empire before it disappeared forever more. We were alerted that a new English comedian who had been doing well in the Provinces was to get his big chance in the Scottish Palladium, otherwise the Empire. I was asked to meet a top theatre man from London who had come up specially to see how the famous (or infamous) Glasgow audience would treat him.

I met the entrepreneur at the Empire for the first show on Monday. The place was half empty and we sat well back from the stage so that Ken Dodd wouldn't recognise anybody. From the moment Ken dashed on, I was for him. I'd never seen such energy on the stage from any performer except acrobats. He just bashed the audience into laughing.

I felt he was the funniest man I had seen for a while and I laughed a lot. The great man from London did not laugh once. At length he delivered wisdom, shaking his head the while. 'He'll never last at that rate,' he said.

Ah, well, we can't all be right. I had a picture taken with Ken, 'teeth to teeth', for I have much the same occlusion as Mr Dodd has. The only marked difference is that his front teeth are insured for some enormous sum. Mine are not. In fact, they're not even mine nowadays.

WHERE IS THE GLASGOW? *c.* 1965
Adam McNaughtan

In the iconoclastic 1960s Glasgow, like many other cities, took a terrible bashing, losing many familiar landmarks. But as Adam McNaughtan laments, it wasn't only buildings that were disappearing, it was a way of life.

Oh where is the Glasgow where Ah used to stey,
The white wally closes done up wi' pipe cley;
Where you knew every neighbour fae first floor to third
An' to keep your door locked was considered absurd.
Dae you know the folk steyin' next door to you?

An' where is the wee shop where Ah used to buy
A quarter o' totties, a tuppenny pie,
A bag o' broken biscuits an' three totty scones,
An' the wumman aye asked, 'How's your maw gettin' on?'
Can your big supermarket gi'e service like that?

An' where is the wean that wance played in the street
Wi' a jaurie, a peerie, a gird wi' a cleek?

Can he still cadgea hudgie or dreep aff a dyke
Or is writin' on wa's noo the wan thing he likes?
Can he tell chickey-mellie fae hunch-cuddy-hunch?

An' where is the fitba' that Ah played an' saw:
The fair shou'der charge an' the pass aff the wa'?
There was nae 4-3-3, there was nae 4-2-4,
An' your mates didnae kiss ye whenever ye scored.
Is the gemme, like big Woodburn, suspended sine die?

An' where is the tramcar that wance did the ton
Up the Great Western Road on the auld Yoker run?
The conductress aye knew how to deal wi' a nyaff:
'If ye're gaun then get oan; if ye're no, then get aff!'
Are there ony like her on the buses the day?

An' where is the chip-shop that Ah knew sae well,
The wee corner cafe where they used to sell
Hot peas an' brae an' MacCallums an' pokes,
An' ye knew they were Tallies the minute they spoke:
Dae ye want-a-da raspberry ower your ice-cream?

Oh where is the Glasgow that Ah used to know,
Big Wullie, wee Shooey, the steamie, the Co.,
The shilpet wee bauchle, the glaiket big dreep,
The ba' on the slates an' your gas in a peep?
If you scrape the veneer aff, are these things still there?

SUNDAY BLUES, 1963–65
Kenneth White

Who can forget those Sundays of yore when dreichness entered the soul and Scotland shut down for the day? Glasgow was no different, as Kenneth White (1936–) recalls. Born in Glasgow, he gained a double first in French and German at the university. There followed many years as an 'intellectual nomad', immersing himself in other places and cultures, eventually settling in France, where he is feted and where he held a chair at the Sorbonne. The following extract is taken from Travels in the Drifting Dawn *(1989) and covers the 1960s when White, along with William Burroughs (1914–97), Alexander Trocchi (1925–84) and others, participated as 'a non-secret agent' in Glasgow in what was called Project Sigma.*

Sunday afternoon.

One of those holy, obnoxious Sundays such as there are fifty-two a year in this god-forsaken place, and to while away the weary time (big, dutiful clocks all over the cancerous landscape), I go for a walk along the docks, coming down Byres Road, then along Dumbarton Road, then, Argyle Street, taking the Kelvinhaugh way down to the river, arriving at Kelvinhaugh Ferry. I cross the river on the ferry, then re-cross, and then re-cross again (the river quiet, the sky a soft grey, the ships berthed in great tranquillity) till the ferryman says to me:

'Are ye enjoyin' yersel?'

Crossing and re-crossing the old Clud on the ferry that grey afternoon, watching the river-flow and the gulls. After ten or so crossings and re-crossings, I move away along Queen's Dock.

There the smell is strange, and yet vaguely familiar. Whisky – thousands of barrels lined there along the quay filled with sour-mash bourbon whisky from Kentucky, USA, with, further on, a load of rye from Indiana. All those barrels, and drunken gulls swooping and yelling over them.

Here and there, too, along the docks, sitting on piles of rope or timber, wee men with bunnets and coloured mufflers reading pink newspapers.

Glasgow. Glasgow.

* * *

Night at Charing Cross, standing at the foot of Hill Street there, wondering where to go and what to do. I see a plaque on a railing:

Rudolph Steiner Centre
Inquiries Welcome

So I decide to go and make inquiries. I push open the gate, enter the gas-lit close, climb to the first floor, see no Rudolph Steiner Centre, continue up to the second floor, and there I see two doors, still no Rudolph Steiner Centre, but on a wall next to one of the doors, I see written in thick pencil the word: Otto (German, like Rudolph, I'm getting hot), so I ring the bell, and then, no answer forthcoming, ring the bell again, which brings an old woman to the door:

'Excuse me,' I say, 'I'm looking for the Rudolph Steiner Centre.'

She looks at me as if I'd said I was looking for Rudolph the red-Nosed Reindeer. Then:

'It's not here,' she says. 'It's down the stair. And it's not open on a Sunday.' She says Sunday with a religious knell in her voice.

'I'm sorry for troubling you, then,' I say.

'Oh, it's quite all right,' she says. 'Only it's a *Sunday*, you should have known, and it's late, it's nearly ten o'clock.'

'As late as that,' I say, 'I'm sorry. Good night.'

Ten o'clock. I go back down the stairs. This time I see a small brown plaque on one of the doors. I ring, just in case. No answer.

Ten o'clock. I continue up Hill Street. Quiet up there. Only an occasional television set shining coldly-blue in some of the big windows. As I walk, I look into the basement kitchens: an old man sitting at a table in semi-darkness with a cup of tea before him; in another, there's just a big bushy cat sitting on a table among the crockery, all alone in its glory.

Then, on the pavement before me, chalked in large letters, I see this rhyme:

I am a mole
and live in a hole

Along Hill Street, then down on to Woodlands Road, then finally I'm in Otago Lane North, at the edge of the River Kelvin, just under the flashing advert for Red Hackle Whisky. I stand there in the out-and-in flashing light, and watch its reflection on the dirty old Kelvin. I stand there for a long while, then I begin to do a bit of a dance, all on my oney-o, singing to myself:

Let the Midnight Special shine her light on me.
Let the Midnight Special shine her ever-lovin light on
me . . .

* * *

I continue flinging crazily about the city.

Today, fog and drizzle. A smoky, leaden indistinguishable mass, the river a wide, misty, empty-looking expanse.

Saturday – I've been through the markets of Shipbank Lane. *The Bonanza*, *Paddy's*, *The Popular*, *The Jolly*, *The Cosy*, *The Super* . . . In the lane, on the cobbles running with dirt, a fire is burning.

I go over the bridge into South Portland Street: dark-grey tenements lining a wide, empty roadway: thousands of uniform windows bare or with a dismal rag of curtain – pale faces behind them. Also dark faces. For many Pakistanis live here – witness the *Kashmir Butcher*, the *Pak Store*, the *Ravi Traders*, the *Wali Dairy*.

South Portland Street continues into Abbotsford Place, in the middle of which is a pub called *The Rising Sun* and at the end of which, in Turriff Street, is the *Glasgow Talmud Society*, and the *Glasgow Maccabi Association*.

Other institutions of the area: *The Medical Missionaries*, *The Muslim Mission*, *The Church of Baptised Believers*.

The Gorbals. Ancestral grounds. All the ghosts.

I find myself in Portugal Street.

There's a play park there, a monstrosity of a play park. A pond, full of bricks and old plaster. An underground cavern of brick, on the outside of which, painted with whitewash, you can read: 'Paddy, you mancit bastard. Buddha. Itali.' There are thick poles too, with a conglomeration of dirty, frayed rope festooned around them. The ground is beaten earth, uneven, strewn with bricks and bottles. The whole surrounded by a high wire fence.

The building opposite deserted – all the windows smashed, except three, in which there is a pale light shining.

It's half past two. Time for 'Bright Hour' at the *Medical Missionaries*.

I go into the *Oriental Cafe*, round from Kidston Street. When I was a kid, if I remember rightly, this cafe was called *Joe's*. The Gorbals have been orientalised.

I drink a coffee, eat a chocolate biscuit; and then start walking again – up the Gushetfaulds, then down into Eglinton Street . . . I'm still walking when night falls.

THE ROAD TO WEMBLEY, 1967
William McIlvanney

For football fans, the England-Scotland match at Wembley, which happened every second year, was not to be missed. Some did miss it, though, invariably because – as novelist William McIlvanney (1936–2015) intimates – of over-indulgence en route. Incidentally, in 1967 Scotland beat England, newly crowned as World Cup winners, 3–2, after which the players were dubbed the 'Wembley Wizards'.

The scene is the compartment of a Wembley Football Special from Glasgow. Slumped in one of the window-seats is a man in his 30s. He is ruminatively drunk. Every so often his eyes rake the other passengers. But there's no cause for alarm. He is merely flexing his malice for London.

His mate comes in and sits beside him.

'Aye then.'

'Aye.'

'Whaur i' the rest o' the boays then?' the man at the window asks.

'Faurer up the train. They've flaked oot like. The beer's a' by. It couldny last forever, eh? Only twa dizzen cans.'

'Aye. Right enough.'

The man at the window wipes the misted pane with his hand, peers out.

'Whaur's this we're gawn through onywey?' he asks.

'Crossmyloof.'

'JOHN, YOU'RE IMMORTAL', 25 MAY 1967
Hugh McIlvanney

When Celtic won the European Cup by beating the mighty Inter Milan 2–1 in the final it was the first time this had ever been achieved by a British club. It was seen as a triumph not only for manager Jock Stein and the players, but also vindication of a style of play that depended more on attack than defence, on flair rather than negativity. Remarkably, the Lisbon Lions, as the eleven heroes came to be known, were all born within a 30-mile radius of Glasgow. A few days later Rangers narrowly lost the European Cup Winners' Cup Final to Bayern Munich, further confirmation of Glasgow's pre-eminence in the beautiful game.

Today Lisbon is almost, but not quite, back in Portuguese hands at the end of the most hysterically exuberant occupation any city has ever known. Pockets of Celtic supporters are holding out in unlikely corners, noisily defending their own carnival atmosphere against the returning tide of normality, determined to preserve the moment, to make the party go on and on.

They emerge with a sudden flood of Glasgow accents from taxis or cafes, or let their voices carry with an irresistible aggregate of decibels across hotel lounges. Always, even among the refugees who turn up at the British Embassy bereft of everything but the rumpled clothes they stand in, the talk is of that magical hour-and-a-half under the hot sun on Thursday in the breathtaking, tree-fringed amphitheatre of the national stadium.

At the airport, the impression is of a Dunkirk with happiness. The discomforts of mass evacuation are tolerable when your team have just won the greatest victory yet achieved by a British football club, and completed a clean sweep of the trophies available to them that has never been equalled anywhere in the world.

They even cheered Helenio Herrera and his shattered Inter when the Italians left for Milan yesterday evening. 'Inter, Inter, Inter.' The chant resounded convincingly through the departure lounge, but no one was misled. In that mood, overflowing with conquerors' magnanimity they might have given Scot Symon [the manager of Rangers] a round of applause.

Typically, within a minute the same happily dishevelled groups were singing: 'Ee Aye Addio, Herrera's on the Buroo.' The suggestion that the most highly paid manager in Europe is likely to be queueing at the Labour Exchange is rather wild but the comment emphasised that even the least analytical fan had seen through the hectic excitement of a unique performance to the essential meaning of the event.

Mundo Desportivo of Lisbon put it another way: 'It was inevitable. Sooner or later the Inter of Herrera, the Inter of *catenaccio*, of negative football, of marginal victories, had to pay for their refusal to play entertaining football.' The Portuguese rejoiced over the magnificent style in which Celtic had taken retribution on behalf of the entire game.

A few of us condemned Herrera unequivocally two years ago after Inter had won the European Cup at their own San Siro Stadium by defending with neurotic caution to protect a luckily gained one-goal lead against a Benfica side with only nine fit men. But he continued to receive around £30,000 a year for stifling the flair, imagination, boldness and spontaneity that make football what it is. And he was still held in awe by people who felt that the statistics of his record justified the sterility of his methods.

Now, however, nearly everyone appreciates the dangers of his influence. The twelfth European Cup final showed how shabbily his philosophy compares with the dynamically positive thinking of Jock Stein. Before the match Stein told me: 'Inter will play it defensively. That's their way and it's their business. But we feel we have a duty to play the game our way, and our way is to attack. Win or lose, we want to make the game worth remembering. Just to be involved in an occasion like this is a tremendous honour and we think it puts an obligation on us. We can be as hard and professional as anybody, but I mean it when I say that we don't just want to win this cup. We want to win it playing good football, to make neutrals glad we've done it, glad to remember how we did it.'

The effects of such thinking, and of Stein's genius for giving it practical expression, were there for all the football world to see on Thursday. Of course, he has wonderful players, a team without a serious weakness and with tremendous strengths in vital positions. But when one had eulogised the exhilarating speed and the bewildering variety of skills that destroyed Inter – the unshakable assurance of Clark, the murderously swift overlapping of the full-backs, the creative energy of Auld in midfield, the endlessly astonishing virtuosity of Johnstone, the intelligent and ceaseless running of Chalmers – even with all this, ultimately the element that impressed most profoundly was the massive heart of this Celtic side.

Nothing symbolised it more vividly than the incredible display of Gemmell. He was almost on his knees with fatigue before scoring that minute but somehow his courage forced him to go on dredging up the strength to continue with the exhausting runs along the left wing that did more than any other single factor to demoralise Inter.

Gemmell has the same aggressive pride, the same contempt for any thought of defeat, that emanates from Auld. Before the game Auld cut short a discussion about the possible ill-effects of the heat and the firm ground with a blunt declaration that they would lick the Italians in any conditions.

When he had been rescued from the delirious crowd and was walking back to the dressing rooms after Celtic had overcome all the bad breaks to vindicate his confidence Auld – naked to the waist except for an Inter shirt knotted round his neck like a scarf – suddenly stopped in his tracks and shouted to Ronnie Simpson, who was walking ahead:

'Hey, Ronnie Simpson, what are we? What are we, son?' He stood there sweating, showing his white teeth between parched lips flecked with saliva. Then he answered his own question with a belligerent roar. 'We're the greatest. That's what we are. The greatest.' Simpson came running back and they embraced for a full minute.

In the dressing room, as the other players unashamedly sang their supporters' songs in the showers and drank champagne from the huge Cup ('Have you had a bevy out of this?'), Auld leaned forward to Sean Fallon, the trainer, and asked with mock seriousness: 'Would you say I was the best? Was I your best man?'

'They've all got Stein's heart,' said a Glasgow colleague. 'There's a bit of the big man in all of them.' Certainly the preparation for this final and the winning of it were impregnated with Stein's personality. Whether warning the players against exposing themselves to the sun ("I don't even want you near the windows in your rooms. If there's as much as a freckle on any man's arm he's for home") or joking with reporters beside the hotel swimming pool in Estoril, his was the all-pervading influence.

Despite the extreme tension he must have felt, he never lost the bantering humour that keeps the morale of his expeditions unfailingly high. The impact of the Celtic invasion on the local Catholic churches was a rewarding theme for him. "They're getting some gates since we came. The nine o'clock and ten o'clock Masses were all-ticket. They've had to get extra plates. How do they divide the takings here? Is it fifty-fifty or in favour of the home club?"

It was hard work appearing so relaxed and the effort eventually took its toll on Stein when he made a dive for the dressing rooms a minute before the end of the game, unable to stand any more. When we reached him there, he kept muttering: 'What a performance. What a performance.'

It was left to Bill Shankly, the Scottish manager of Liverpool (and the only English club manager present), to supply the summing-up quote. 'John,' Shankly said with the solemnity of a man to whom football is a religion, 'you're immortal.'

An elderly Portuguese official cornered Stein and delivered ecstatic praise of Celtic's adventurous approach. 'This attacking play, this is the real meaning of football. This is the true game.' Stein slapped him on the shoulder. 'Go on, I could listen to you all night.' Then, turning to the rest of us, 'Fancy anybody saying that about a Scottish team.'

There is good reason to hope that people will say such things about Scottish and English clubs with increasing frequency in the near future. Now that the Continental monopoly of the European Cup has been broken, British football is poised for a period of domination.

Glasgow Rangers can strike the next blow when they meet Bayern Munich in the final of the European Cup for Cup Winners at Nurnberg next Wednesday. Scot Symon has rebuilt his Rangers team with patient thoroughness this season, and their thrilling draw with Celtic at Ibrox three weeks ago confirmed how far they have come. Spurred by their great rivals' achievement, they will not be easily denied.

Continental clubs can expect no respite next season when the powerful challenge from Scotland will be backed by the presence of Manchester United and Tottenham Hotspur in the two major competitions. It seems unlikely that anything short of the personal intervention of De Gaulle can prevent us from being in among the European prizes again.

WEE TAM'S BREAKFAST, 1967
Jack McLean

Decked out in a fedora and the finest, flashiest suit on Ralph Slater's racks, Jack McLean cut a raffish figure as he flâneured around Glasgow's byways and boulevards. Having attended Edinburgh College of Art he spent sundry years at the chalk face. His true métier, though, was journalism. He first surfaced in the 1970s at The Scotsman, *then edited by Arnold Kemp and his deputy, Harry Reid. When the pair of them moved to the then* Glasgow Herald *they took the man now dubbed 'the Urban Voltaire' with them. His subject was Glasgow and its garrulous denizens and seedy dens. It was as if Damon Runyon had been transplanted to the South Side, fag in one hand, a glass of whisky in the other.*

I was twenty-five when I first stayed in a hotel. And I stayed in it courtesy of the National Union of Students, for whom I was an Executive Member with, as my ex-NUS colleagues tartly recall, irresponsibility for everything. I remember though that I managed to persuade a young female student politician to come up to my room. Once there I thought hard. What does one do in a position like this *in a hotel*? I mean there must be something a little more plutocratic in hotels. So I picked up the 'phone and rang the night desk. 'Night Clerk?' I asked, 'Send up a bottle of bourbon!' I pronounced the last as 'BURBAN'. I was entirely unprepared for the answer. 'F*** off,' the night clerk said. I'll bet that never happened to Humphrey Bogart.

The idea of hotels really gets to me though. As a matter of fact I regularly take morning and afternoon coffee in Glasgow's Central Hotel. Considering that you can get three cups of coffee out of a pot for 50p, and can sit in peace and quiet in old leather armchairs and sleep off the lunchtime booze, it is surely just ignorance that causes people to go to bakery chain teashops. In earlier days I was filled with dread that they would know. 'They' were the snooty waiters who I thought would recognise real money when they saw it, and they would recognise me as bloody riff-raff the moment they clapped eyes on me, and have me ejected. Funny how you don't mind the bum's rush out of a scabby wee bar, but the thought of having your collar felt by a hotel flunkey makes the blood run cold.

Actually I got over that a long time ago, ever since I worked in hotels myself, not as a college job you understand, but as a fully paid-up flunkey, all white jacket, bow-tie, and posh accent upstairs, and bevy, oaths, and larceny downstairs. When I lived in London I used to regularly don the one suit I possessed and go and look at the Rich in the Hilton Hotel lounge bar. By then the feeling of dread had almost subsided. But if I had been Wee Tam, and I had experienced his sordid little saga, it would have taken somewhat longer for my embarrassment to fade away.

When Wee Tam was a lad of seventeen, he was apprenticed to a firm of insurance brokers. This was in the days when you could get a clerical job without having a PhD, and Tam was being groomed, at his tender age, for stardom. Accordingly, he was sent up from Glasgow with two elder colleagues, and they all booked into the Station Hotel in Aberdeen. Not only was this the first time that Tam had been in a hotel, but it was the first time he'd drunk a bottle of wine with his dinner, followed by brandy and liqueurs, and whisky in the hotel lounge. It was therefore a befuddled Tam who fell into his bed that night. It was a hot summer night, and Tam began to sweat horribly. He hauled off the quilt, then a blanket, then two more, and, to cut it short, Tam finally wrenched off his pyjamas, and lay there naked on top of an equally naked mattress.

Tam had ordered a cup of tea and a *Glasgow Herald* for 7.30 the next morning. It was now 7.30 and Tam did not hear the chambermaid's knock on the door. It is a peculiarity of British hotels that the staff want you out of the room as quickly as possible, and indeed would greatly prefer you to give them a cheque and then spend the night somewhere else and not mess up the beds. The chambermaid of course walked in on young Tam, who being only seventeen was, shall we say, not only naked but er . . . rigid. 'Your tea and paper, Sir,' said the chambermaid. Almost immediately realising his predicament Tam emitted a scream and, hurling the bedsheets about him like Ava Gardner in the movies, he promptly upset tea all over the bed. 'Dinnae worry, Sir,' said the chambermaid patronisingly. 'Ye'd be surprised what we see every day in hotels.'

Now if you add an early morning occurrence like that to a hangover you can understand that Wee Tam was not as perky as he might have been as he hurried downstairs, already late for his breakfast with his two superiors. It was bright in the breakfast room, with the crisp white tablecloths glaring in the sunlight. Tam's bosses looked ruddy and fresh, in contrast to Tam's uneasy pallor. 'How do you feel this morning Tom?' asked one of them, to which Tam replied that he felt fine. The two were insufferable that morning, rubbing their hands together jocularly, slapping their palms, talking loudly, clanking teaspoons against a cup, which by the sound of it to Tam's ears may well have been the bell that deafened Quasimodo. The waitress appeared at the table and Tam was handed the menu. 'Remember,' said the manager cheerily, 'The Company is paying for this, Tom. Get a good breakfast inside you. Have the lot.'

Tam looked at the breakfast menu. He never had breakfast at all at home. And he had never seen such things for breakfast before. He had read P.G. Wodehouse though and he knew all about country house breakfasts – fried kidneys and bacon and kedgeree and all that. So Tam looked at the breakfast menu and ordered breakfast. He ordered fruit juice and porridge with cream. There was a line under that and Tam went on to the next section, demanding kippers. He ordered bacon and eggs from the section below, and added scrambled eggs. He took toast and marmalade and a pot of tea, and finally asked for toasted bannocks. The two men looked at him strangely as they ordered their fruit juice and cornflakes.

The waitress brought the porridge and the ordeal began. Tam managed to stagger down the lumpy gruel, and started on the kippers. Bone after bone came in every mouthful. It was like eating a box of dressing pins. Eventually he finished and within seconds two thin rashers of pink bacon appeared on a plate, the grey fat quivering as he touched it with his fork. Two yellow yolks winked obscenely up at him. By now his colleagues were beginning to drum their fingers on the table. By now, too, the other customers were looking over at this amazing boy.

The scrambled eggs came next, a pale yellow mound set in a little puddle of water, like urine round a street lamp. Tam's arm ached with lifting the fork to his mouth. The breakfast room was totally silent, every eye in the place fixed on Tam. The toast and the marmalade was like a torture designed by Edgar Allan Poe. At each mouthful the pendulum swung closer till Tam could feel his flesh creep. Another mouthful. Tam couldn't tell if he'd swallowed it or not. He could imagine his entire intestinal tract, his throat, his gullet, his tonsils, packed with food. He began to envisage himself as an oddly shaped Michelin man crammed with cream buns and kippers and pale eggs. A plate of bannocks, glistening with butter, floated on to the table-mat in front of him. Tam poured out another cup of tea. Just as he raised the tea-cup to his lips, out of the corner of his eye, Tam could see the little windows of the swing doors through which the waitresses came with the food. Both windows were filled with the amazed faces of the kitchen staff. Suddenly their expressions changed and their faces became suffused with laughter. Tam couldn't hear their mirth through the glass. But he could see in the centre of one of the windows, a finger pointing at him, a finger belonging to the figure obviously saying something to the other chefs and waitresses. With a chill going down his spine, Tam recognised the figure as the chambermaid of the naked encounter.

The next thing he remembers is that there was a sudden explosion as his superiors backed instantly out of their chairs. He remembers that he was standing up himself. A great jet of half-digested breakfast was thundering across the table. Tam was sick over the table, himself and over the Area Manager. It was some years later that Tam ventured into hotels again.

WHEN THE CLYDE SWAM WITH SERPENTS, 1967

Alan Sharp

Ostensibly a review of C.A. Oakley's The Second City, *novelist and screenwriter Alan Sharp (1934–2013) here takes the opportunity to memorialise the Glasgow he remembered from the perspective of a native of Greenock. The author of two highly praised novels –* A Green Tree in Gedde *(1964) and* The Wind Shifts *(1967) – he went on to write the screenplays of several films, including* Ulzana's Raid *(1972) and* Night Moves *(1975). Serial killer Peter Manuel (1931–58) is believed to have been responsible for at least eight murders, seven of which he was found guilty of and hanged.*

There are different ways of writing about places. Mr Oakley in his book about Glasgow has chosen to inform and illustrate; and leave evocations to the memories of his readers ... For me Glasgow is still the Metropolis, the place one went to escape the provinces. It's where first things happened. First heavy date, first foreign films, first contact with those denizens of the moral underworld, homosexuals and prostitutes. As the 7.10 rolled over the bridge into the Central and the Clyde swam with serpents of oily neon it was a world of Kafka and Raymond Chandler and Holden Caulfield that we entered, one in which it all might suddenly happen. That it rarely did is why you find a great many people from the outlying towns who decry Glasgow a 'dump' or a 'hole'. There was always a time when they ventured there and returned empty-handed.

The essence of Glasgow has always lain for me in its humour and its devotion to the national sport ... There is in Glaswegian wit a black, sour quality, of whose genuine mordancy 'sick' jokes are but an effete reflection. There is, for instance, a real texture about the quip that Peter Manuel could have pleaded insanity because 'when they picked him up he had a Third Lanark season ticket in his pocket'. Or the woman, children around her coat-tails, following her staggering raucous husband home from the pub and as she passed the Citizen's Theatre and its emerging patrons cocked a head towards her spouse and said: 'Drama.'

With football it's the same ... It is on the barren slopes of Hampden that much of Glasgow manhood has had its character formed, moulding that lyrical pessimism which is the hallmark of the West Coast Scottish imagination ... In Glasgow, as in all industrial societies, there is the week and there is the weekend. Life accumulates a tension, a log-jam of energy from Monday to Friday and erupts on Saturday. Sunday is shot through with a remorse and melancholy that finds external image in the flavour of the Sabbath; the quiet streets, the slant of empty sunlight and the slow drift of hymn-praise from the congregations battened down in the hold of God.

A SUPER YO-YO, 1968
Pearl Jephcott

Built in the north-east of the city, the eight Red Road tower blocks were intended to address a housing crisis, and to a certain extent they did. But as Pearl Jephcott (1900–80), a pioneer of social research at Glasgow University in the 1960s, makes clear, their height introduced problems planners had not foreseen. There were some compensations. On the upper floors you could see the Campsie Fells to Ben Lomond and the Arrochar Alps, then west past the Erskine Bridge and out to Goat Fell on the Isle of Arran, continuing south over Glasgow and east towards Edinburgh. The highest floors of the blocks were reserved for communal drying, which was grand if the lifts were working. The last of the flats were demolished in 2015.

Complete breakdown due to an external cause such as an electricity failure or a strike is one of the hazards that faces the lift user. Glasgow's 1968 hurricane cut off the electricity in certain blocks. At Red Road some families had the alarming experience of walking down to the ground floor, the children terrified because unfamiliar shadows were cast by a candle. A few months later a strike of maintenance men meant that, in a number of cases, one of the block's two lifts was out of action for up to three weeks. One mother told how she had to lug a pram and toddler up 18 flights; on another estate a man walked up and down to a 17th floor four times in one day; in another case an invalid had stumbled down 9 flights, unaided but for her two sticks. The lifts also vary in their basic reliability, in the efficiency of the firm's servicing, and in the caretaker's ability to deal with the minor troubles he is authorised to handle.

Any block with a high proportion of children is especially vulnerable. There is always a critical stage, the early days of the block's occupation, when both the children of the block and those of the vicinity 'play the lift', using it like a super yo-yo. Trouble also tends to occur when the load is heavy, i.e. when school comes, and during holidays. Another strain is caused by the small child who can only reach the button by jumping, using a stick, etc. One real sinner, in that he holds up the lift, is the milk boy who props its door open with his crate while he collects from perhaps 16 flats. Or on a quiet floor footballers have been known to use the lift cage for a goal!

The necessity to use a lift can have odd repercussions on the tenant's daily life. Somehow one needs to be tidy if going in the lift. Thus it deters people from popping out in their slippers for the odd bit of shopping, or seeing what the kids are up to. Or again, there is the pensioner who, if he has to use the lift, won't bother to take a turn round the estate before the evening sets in. The occasional whiff of fresh air, and the occasional brief spell away from the rest of the household, are useful in terms of health and temper: but they have gone as far as the 'typical' flat-dweller is concerned. That the lift may even dictate the pattern of the tenant's day was shown in the case of the mother who never went out in the afternoon because of the risks of the early evening queues which meant she could not be sure of getting back in time. She was also liable to incur black looks if her pram stopped others from squeezing on to the lift, a matter that did not make for good relationships within the block. The lift's uncertainties had other repercussions. People spoke of the difficulties doctors had in getting to their patients because of lifts not coming, or out of order, and of workmen who went away disgusted with the jobs not done.

'CITY OF RAZORS', 1969
Eddie Linden

Who Is Eddie Linden? *was the title of a book by Sebastian Barker, which was subsequently adapted for the stage. It was a question that had long perplexed many writers, many of whom had been published in Linden's legendary magazine,* Aquarius. *By any standard, his life was remarkable for the Dickensian cruelty that was visited upon him. Of Irish-Scots extraction, he was born in 1935, 'illegitimate', adopted and rejected. He left school at fourteen and abandoned Glasgow to take up a number of menial, low-paying jobs in London. Homosexual, he has had a love–hate relationship with Catholicism. By the time of his eightieth birthday, in 2015, he was one of the few, true surviving bohemians. His poem 'City of Razors' is his less than fulsome salute to the place that made him and very nearly broke him.*

Cobble streets, littered with broken milk bottles,
reeking chimneys and dirty tenement buildings,
walls scrawled with FUCK THE POPE and
  blue-lettered
words GOD BLESS THE RANGERS.
Old woman at the corner, arms folded, babe in pram,
a drunk man's voice from the other pavement,
And out come the Catholics from evening
  confessional;

A woman roars from an upper window
'They're at it again, Maggie!
Five stitches in our Tommie's face, Lizzie!
Eddie's in the Royal wi' a sword in his stomach
and the razor's floating in the River Clyde.'

There is roaring in Hope Street,
They're killing in the Calton,
There's an ambulance in Bridgeton,
And there's a laddie in the Royal.

'CHOLESTEROL', *c.* 1970
Adam McNaughtan

Is there a 'Taste of Scotland'? Or, for that matter, Glasgow? Undoubtedly. We are talking here about saturated fats and a surfeit of sugar. Fruits and vegetables are for sissies. What we like are puddings and pies, with a side salad of chips. Those who know about such things say with authority that the shrivelled size of Glaswegians came from their dismal diet, which led to disease and early death. As the historian Tom Devine has opined: 'It was clearly safer to endure the privations of life in the Western Highlands than a hazardous existence in the perilous conditions of the wynds and alleyways of Glasgow and Dundee.' Be all of that as it may, there are still countless Glaswegians who, like the folksinger Adam McNaughtan, are still to be convinced by the advocates of healthy heating.

Ah've been taking advice on the right things to eat
Since shortly before Ah was born,
From the National dried milk and the cod liver oil
To powdered rhinoceros horn.
In thae days they tellt us to lay aff the starches
The sugar, potatoes an' breid;
Noo they've done a U-turn, tell us breid and potatoes
Will gi'e us the fibre we need
So Ah've made up my mind that the menus designed
By the experts just urnae for me.
Nae trained dietitian nor general practitioner
Dictates what Ah huv for my tea.
Brown bread with a low-fat paste thinly spread on
May be healthier than a meat pie
But who wants to grow old eating St Ivel Gold?
I would rather taste butter and die.

Cholesterol, Cholesterol,
My chance of surviving is small
But Ah'll no get a dose o' Anorexia Nervosa
Cause Ah love my cholesterol.

Now the thing that has brought this affair to a head
Is the 'Good Hearted Glasgow' campaign.
Ah just said 'What's that?' an' the doc had his needle
Sucking blood oot my handiest vein.
Two weeks later they measured my height an' my weight
An' took my blood pressure and all.
The computer said, 'Mate, to survive at your weight
You would need to be seven feet tall.'
But Ah'm no going to take the suggestions they make
About changing the wey that Ah eat:
Cutting out cheese and nae chips if you please,
Nae chocolate, nae ice cream, nae meat.
Oh they tell you to gi'e up these goodies below
And they promise you pie in the sky.

Well, semi-skimmed milk might diminish my bulk
But Ah'll take double cream till I die

Cholesterol, Cholesterol,
My chance of surviving is small
The cream I consume it could lead to my doom
But Ah love my cholesterol.

Now it's a' right for you that smoke 40 a day
Or spend every night in the bar
You can tell the health visitor you'll cut it down
She'll say, 'What a fine fellow you are!'
But when Ah tellt her Ah'd never smoked in my life
And Ah was teetotal to boot
She said, 'Go away! There is nothing to dae.
You've nae vices that you can cut oot.'
Now Ah don't mind them probin' in my haemoglobin
If it's just for a case history
But it puts the health visitor into a tiz
At her duty: to try and save me.
She says 'Fresh fruit and yoghourt's a lovely dessert.
Why don't you give it a try?'
But Ah don't gi'e a hoot for her yoghourt and fruit.
Ah'll have Black Forest gateau and die!

Cholesterol, Cholesterol
My chance of surviving is small
The wey that Ah dine, Ah'm on course for angina
But Ah love my cholesterol!

STAIRWAY 13, 2 JANUARY, 1971
Andy Ewan

The Old Firm derby between Rangers and Celtic was always an occasion of heightened emotion and unbridled passion. In 1971, in front of a crowd of 80,000 at Ibrox, Rangers' ground, the game was goalless as it entered its final phase. In the 89th minute, however, Jimmy Johnstone scored for Celtic. Believing their team was destined to lose, Rangers' fans began to leave. But seconds later Colin Stein equalised for Rangers and their jubilant fans attempted to return to the ground. Andy Ewan was one of many supporters who found himself caught up in what was the worst Scottish sporting tragedy in the twentieth century. In total, sixty-six people died as a result of crushing and asphyxiation.

I was lying face down about four feet from the cold concrete steps, trapped from waist to toe in the massive crush of bodies. It was halfway down Stairway 13 at Ibrox Stadium on 2 January 1971, just before 5 p.m. Immediately around and above me it was strangely silent, with only muffled cries and sobs but higher up, at the top of the Stairway and beyond, I could hear the singing and chanting of happy football supporters. Amazingly, a matter of yards in front of and below my straining body, hundreds of fans were reaching the bottom of the steps and walking casually towards the exit gates, completely unaware of the disaster they had escaped by seconds.

A policeman, shocked and staring, came up the stairs and began to help those of us at the front of the huge pile of bodies. He was able to pull some people out but I was so tightly jammed that he found it impossible to release me so he moved on. All the time I could feel the tremendous weight on my legs increasing as supporters approaching the Stairway from the passages at the top of the terracing continued to press forward, unaware of what was happening below. There was a sudden movement in the bodies above me, I felt my legs being twisted round and was now lying almost face up with my back to the ground. Up until then I had felt a sense of shock and unreality rather than fear but now a stab of panic went through me. I could feel the strain on my back increasing and was seriously concerned about what further movement above me might bring. I was lucky – after a few minutes, the crushing weight on my legs seemed to ease slightly and I called to the policeman again for help. This time he gripped me firmly under the armpits and, with a powerful heave, pulled me clear. He half-walked, half-carried me to the bottom of the Stairway and I collapsed heavily on the lower steps, still unable to grasp fully what had happened. I had only been trapped for about ten minutes or so but it seemed a lifetime since the referee had blown his whistle for final time on that fateful afternoon.

Unless you have experienced it, it is difficult to explain just how helpless and vulnerable you feel when trapped in the middle of a large crowd of people, especially on steep or uneven ground. You are completely at the mercy of hundreds of others, many of whom you cannot even see. You are swept along, unable to influence what is happening and can only concentrate on keeping your arms high, out of the crush and staying on your feet. By the time I reached the top of Stairway 13 I was scared. I had been caught up in big match crowds before but never had I experienced the level of pressure that was now being exerted on everyone around me. All of us were suddenly aware that this time it was worse than usual, that danger genuinely threatened. People were shouting, trying to get others to stop pushing forwards from the back and sides but it was hopeless. As we began to descend the stairs I felt a slight tug on the bottom of my jeans and was horrified to just make out the hand of someone on the ground. He was trying desperately but hopelessly to rise against the mass of people so tightly jammed together it was almost unbelievable that he had been able to fall. Someone else trod on my heel and I immediately pulled my foot out of the shoe, thankful that I was wearing slip-ons instead of my usual lace-ups. My other shoe soon followed as the pressure intensified. People were now really suffering; there were cries for help, agonised gasps for breath and faces with veins and eyes bulging. By this time I was about half of the way down the stairs and intent only on keeping upright and staying alive.

What happened next? Did a crush barrier buckle under the intense pressure or did people further down the steps simply stumble under the huge weight of the fans above them? I don't suppose we will ever know for sure but suddenly I was falling, amidst flailing, heaving fellow supporters, a mass of us collapsing on to people below and in turn, being buried by those above.

I don't remember how long I sat on the steps, as more police and rescuers began to appear. Eventually I got to my feet and realised I had lost my supporter's scarf and both shoes and was starting to ache all over. I went back up the stairs and asked a policeman if I could do anything to help. He took one look at me and told me to go home. Cold, bewildered and probably in shock

I walked slowly out of the ground. I cannot remember much about the next hour or so but someone in a supporters' bus saw me wandering along the icy pavement in my stockinged feet and took me on board. I tried to explain what had happened, that there were dead and dying people lying on Stairway 13 but I don't think anyone took me seriously. Then, as the bus headed for the city centre, reports started to come through on the fans' radios and the previously cheery atmosphere disappeared. I was dropped off near Bridgeton Cross and eventually got a taxi back to my home in Hillhead. By this time the disaster was the main news item, with the death toll rising steadily.

GORBALS MEMORIES, 1972
Glasgow News

The Gorbals is believed to derive its name from the Latin word 'garbale', which is a tithe paid to the Church in the form of grain. The history of the Gorbals stretches back centuries. In the seventeenth century, for instance, it was known for coal mining, and the manufacture of guns and worsted plaid. In the same century it was annexed by Glasgow, despite being a burgh in its own right. Throughout the eighteenth century it was as fashionable in its day as the Merchant City is at present. By the end of the nineteenth century its population had ballooned to over 40,000, mainly due to an influx of immigrants. After the Second World War the tenements in the old Gorbals were largely demolished and the inhabitants were moved to high rises, some more willingly than others ...

Woman – Cleland Street (20 years in Gorbals).
Aye, I'll have to go. I don't want to go but I'll have to go. I've got a good house. (*Would she like to move to a modern flat?*) No, I would not. Just look at those houses over in Crown Street. The rooms are too small – look at all those wee windows. And concrete stairs inside your house! I work as a home help in one of these multi-storeys and they all have these big long corridors from here to (*gestures about 100 yards*), and all these wee doors, it's like a prison. You expect to see the prisoners coming out to empty – you know. Look at that one over the there (*opposite the*

Citizen's) – I don't know what it'll be like when it's finished but just now it's a thousand windows . . .

Newsagent at Centre Street (25 years in the same shop).
Oh, I'll be glad to see it go. Well, it's progress isn't it? (*Do you really think it's progress?*) Well, no, to be honest I don't. The people here dread the high flats. I mean, we have all these planners and they build these schemes and there are no amenities, there are no public toilets and the roads are not wide enough for the traffic – where's the planning in that? Just take around here – there were four schools here at one time, now the last one's closing in June. There were four newsagents in this street and we were all making a living. Now I'm the only one left. There'll be no shop left here at all – the people'll have to go over to the shopping centre at Eglinton Street. They'll be at the mercy of the supermarkets then . . .

Pensioner, Abbotsford Place.
The houses are rotten – too many years on them. Do you know I pay £4 for a couple of rooms here, here's my rent book if you don't believe me. I want an old person's flat in a new block, that would suit me fine. Of course, there were beautiful houses once. I lived in Norfolk St when I was a girl and Abbotsford Place was all doctors then. But there's been nothing done to them for years – I suppose they could be done up but they'd be too big for us. An old person's flat, that's what we're looking for.

Old lady, 44 years in Main St., Gorbals.
(*What do you think of redevelopment?*) I think it's great. But there's some'll miss it. There's some go away from here and then they want back. No, I'll not be going for a while yet. They'll not be pulling down this building for at least six year. They'll maybe be moving me out before that – feet first!

NEVER SIT WITH YOUR BACK TO A DOOR, 1972
T.C. Campbell

Thomas 'T.C.' Campbell led a life of violent crime, as he describes in Indictment: Trial By Fire *(2001). He is best known for the so-called Ice-Cream Wars, which culminated in 1984 in the murders in Ruchazie of five members of the Doyle family. Campbell, along with his co-accused, Joseph Steele, was found guilty but after a long campaign in which both men protested their innocence, the 'Glasgow Two' were released after spending eighteen years in jail. Here Campbell recalls an incident from his blood-spattered youth.*

At seventeen I was tall, with a Van Dyke beard, and everyone assumed I was older so sitting in the pub with Maggie and the troops was not unusual. On this particular occasion, it had been just a few days since someone swinging a sword had lost a few fingers and apparently wasn't too pleased about it.

Drinking bottled beer, large Whitbread or McEwan's Pale Ale, pouring our own, the theory being that the bottles were always handy to have around in case of an unexpected attack. So much for the theory for, in reality, when an attack comes unexpectedly, it's the last thing y'think of. I was just having a sip of a pint when I heard these three loud bangs simultaneous with bright flashes and my bobbing head rattling my teeth off the glass, spilling beer down my chin. Putting the glass down and looking up surprised and puzzled, feeling at my mouth for any damaged teeth or tissue. I could see everybody staring in wide-eyed shock, mouths opening and shutting, flabbergasted, while others made frantic hand signals, mimicking some TV show, *What's My Line*, or something.

'What? Three guesses?' said I. 'Eh? Hammer?' Aye, right first time they nodded frantically indicating BIG hammer, pointing at the door behind me. Turning round as I put my hand to my head, seeing the exit door still swinging and feeling the bloody mush of my new hair-do I soon got the picture. Sure enough, I'd been battered over the head with a big Thor type hammer as they later described it. The assailant could only be identified by his bloody bandaged hand. I got a matching set of three nine-stitch zips in my concussed skull and a bloody good lesson about sitting with my back to doors. Everyone who had seen it thought they had witnessed my murder and couldn't believe that I hardly felt it, putting it down to bravado. But I had, quite honestly, believed that it had been the room which shook and not I.

THE MOST FOREIGN TOWN IN BRITAIN, 1973
George Gale

Few journeys have been more often reprised than that taken in 1773 by Samuel Johnson and James Boswell. Two centuries later, English journalists Paul Johnson (1928–) and George Gale (1927–90) set out to emulate the odd couple's 'Highland Jaunt', travelling by car rather than the more rudimentary means of the eighteenth century. Johnson took the part of Boswell while Gale attempted to emulate the other Johnson's sourness. They encountered a city in a state of flux, with many old buildings being torn down and many new, high, ugly ones being put up in their place. 'We drove through most of it,' reflected Johnson, 'on a great concrete bridge, spanning demolished sandstone slums. This grim and beautiful city . . . was nobly conceived in the first fine flush of the industrial revolution, a vast classical artefact carved in stern local stone; now they are nailing upon it a high superstructure of fast roads, as in any large American town of the Middle West. It will soon be nothing more than a visual incident – a flash of urban scenery – on a rapid thrust to the hills and lochs.'

We drove partly around and partly above Glasgow: the huge motorways through the city and across the Clyde were not then quite completed.

'This,' I said to Paul, of Glasgow, 'is the most foreign town in Britain.'

'Yes, and they cleared the slums and put motorways in their places.'

'The tenements of the Gorbals are fine buildings. They look ugly to us because we think of the Gorbals as being ugly. Glasgow's slums are fine architecture. Its council is corrupt. Look at this motorway!'

'Look,' said Paul, 'we're in the middle of the lunch break. Look at all those shabby works buses.'

'They are not works buses. Those are Glasgow Corporation buses. And it is dinner, not lunch.'

* * *

Scottish national newspapers are parochial in the way that English local newspapers are parochial. Scotland possesses a pride in itself which constantly requires replenishment. Scotland, too, is aggressive about its Scottishness in the way that little men, when drunk, sometimes seek fights with bigger and stronger and sometimes sober men. The Glaswegianality of Glasgow is different: Glasgow is a big fellow who has made himself ugly; a handsome man of almost classical features, disfigured by an inherent wildness, a propensity for violence and disaster.

Glasgow is a city built in stone; and although it may be difficult to build modest domestic apartments of stone, it is almost impossible to build ugly buildings in dressed and unpainted red sandstone. Glasgow is built of such stone, which seems to enforce the dignity of decent proportions on the windows and doorways of the great tenement blocks. Their tiled passageways are different. The ugliness or beauty of anything depends partly on what it is and partly on what it looks like: it is what they are much more than what they look like which makes the ugly parts of Glasgow ugly.

They drink heavily and fast in Glasgow, conscious that it is never far from time being called; and nastily, mixing lemon juice with whisky, and pouring their 'heavy' beer or their draught lager on top of the whisky. Belfast is Glasgow's daughter, or twin, city; and Belfast apart, no other city in the kingdom has so much the feel of vehemence. It is the most forcign and potentially the most frightening (which may be saying the same thing). There are plenty of places in Glasgow where it would not strike me as ridiculous to be given the advice the metropolitan magazine *New York* gave to its readers – 'Walk along the curb of a sidewalk and avoid shadowy doorways or building recesses . . . If you think you're being followed and your building is not served by a doorman, keep on walking . . . Have your keys ready when you enter your building . . . Organise tenant or street associations . . . If you are mugged, don't resist . . . Don't hesitate to help someone in distress.' I do not mean to say that Glasgow *is* a dangerous place. I mean that it is a place I could imagine becoming dangerous, like the Chicago I imagine, or the New York which I know and liked. It is Glasgow's capacity to produce such imaginings that makes it the most foreign of towns I feel not lost and abroad in.

GANGS, 1973
Anonymous

Gangs have been a fact of Glasgow life for decades, perhaps centuries. Historians record that the Penny Mob in Townhead may have the claim to be the city's first gang. The period after the First World World is reckoned to be their heyday, when gangs such as the Redskins, the Norman Conks, the Billy Boys and the Antique Mob ran amok and caused grievous bodily harm, usually to themselves and their rivals. What was their point, other than to defend themselves and their territory? Who knows, but they certainly struck terror into otherwise peaceful neighbourhoods. Here a 15-year-old boy explains their appeal. A gemme was someone who was ready to fight whatever the odds, 'even if defeat or physical punishment is inevitable'.

'Most of the Gangs in Glasgow are Gemmies. I think if you are in a Gang you just go for the fun of it. When you are in a Gang it is very easy to get birds whereas if you're not you don't get so many because most of the birds go for boys in Gangs because it makes them feel big. I go about with a Gang called the Possil Uncle; it used to be called the Fleet, then Border Troops, the Rebels and the Possil Pigs. The Maryhill Fleet boys go about with us. Sometimes we go to the Granada dancing or go up to the Milton to fight the Tongs or the Thrush from Kirkintilloch. I get a lot of fun going about with a gang because we smash aw the bam-pots up that try to get fly when they get you by yourself with their mates.'

CONNOLLYMANIA, 1973
Colin MacFarlane

The impact Billy Connolly (1942–), otherwise known as 'The Big Yin', made when he metamorphosed from a folk singer to a stand-up comedian is incalculable. With his flowing locks and beard, he had the appearance of a Glaswegian Merlin. Unlike other comedians of that period, he did not tell jokes. Rather he spun tall stories which grew more ridiculous and surreal the longer they went on. Often they were concerned with bodily functions, drunkenness and religion. He seemed effortlessly to cause offence which, in turn, made him all the more popular. He had worked in the shipyards and, as a consequence, had a bottomless well of anecdotes to draw upon. Regularly touted as one of the greatest comedians ever, he is also a notable actor, starring in many films and television programmes. Here, Colin MacFarlane remembers Connolly shortly before his career went into another orbit.

When I was out seeing Charlotte [his girlfriend] in Carfin one day, she said to me, 'There's a new Glasgow comedian performing at a hotel just up the road. Do you fancy going?'

'Whit's his name?' I asked.

'Billy Connolly.'

An article in the local newspaper said that he was to perform at the Tudor Hotel in Airdrie and that the gig would be recorded for a live album. When we turned up at the hotel the following night, the place was jam-packed and the performance was a sell-out. There was an absolutely incredible atmosphere. Even before Connolly appeared, it was electric and when he arrived on stage he did the most hilarious sketches I had ever heard. One of them, about the Last Supper taking place in the Gallowgate rather than Galilee, had everyone falling about laughing. When I listen to the album, I can distinctly hear my own laugh during a couple of the sketches.

The *Solo Concert* album went on to sell more than a quarter of a million copies. After its release, Connolly's rise to superstardom began in earnest. He even had his own comic strip in the *Sunday Mail* called *The Big Yin* written by him and artist Malcolm McCormick. It was an instant rival to *Oor Wullie* and *The Broons*. In one such strip, Billy's uncle comes down from Uist and is told, 'If ye're jist gonnae sit scrounging bevy, ye can away back where the animals run aboot an' streams run doon the slopes.'

'Ye mean Hampden?'

Connolly's big achievement was to make the Glasgow dialect something that people loved, appreciated and found hilarious not only in Scotland but the world over. Some people, though, were not amused by his strong language and sketches about religion. Connolly recorded a religious-affairs programme for BBC

Scotland in which Moses said things like, 'Nip hame and git yir people . . .' And short jokes like the following did not endear him to Christian fundamentalists: 'Whit are the three most unnecessary things in life? A nun's tits, the Pope's balls and a round of applause for the band.'

Religious zealots such as Baptist minister Pastor Jack Glass started to mount demonstrations outside his shows. Connolly wasn't surprised, and shrugged. 'Ah, well, it's not every day you get a demonstration in your honour', adding that the pastor was 'an ass'.

He had other detractors as well. Tony Blackburn, a Radio 1 DJ at the time of the *Solo Concert*'s release, told his millions of listeners that he couldn't see anything funny about the Glasgow patter merchant. But Connolly's management said that Blackburn slagging off the album was one of the highest recommendations a comedy record could get. Others found Connolly's humour too lavatorial for their liking, while many people in Glasgow believed that their patter was just as good and that Connolly had made it big only because he was lucky and had a pushy manager. He even got poison-pen letters.

Connolly mocked the typical Scottish reaction to success in a joke about the Second Coming: a man rushes down the street to tell his neighbours, 'He's here! He's here! He's come!'

'Who has?'

'Jesus Christ!'

'Aye, Ah kent his faither.'

But Connolly was quite adept at dealing with hecklers during his shows. He'd say things like, 'The last time I saw a mouth like yours, pal, Lester Piggott was sitting behind it', or 'The more I hear of you, the more I believe in birth control.' When one heckler shouted 'IRA!' in Dublin, he replied, to rapturous applause, 'Aye, you're very brave down there in the dark, pal. Try shoutin' that in the middle of Ibrox Park some time.'

Connolly was slightly different from other Scottish comedians around at that time as he had been influenced by the outrageous storytelling of American comics like Lenny Bruce. A story that had a big impact on Connolly was about Lenny Bruce on stage in San Francisco. There were policemen in the audience waiting to arrest him for using obscene language. Bruce got up on the stage and explained to the audience that because the police were there, he'd use alternative words. For example, when he wanted to say a four-letter word that started with C and ended with T, he'd say 'tulip'; when he was going to say a word that started with F and ended with K, he'd say 'daffodil'; and the word that started with B and ended with D would be 'rhododendron'. He checked with the audience to see if they'd got the code – tulip, daffodil, rhododenron. Then he started off, 'There was this Mexican c***s****r . . .'

There is a poster that hangs in the People's Palace museum on Glasgow Green that sums up the city's attitude to its comedians:

'When Connolly was at the peak of his fame, a survey revealed that 74 per cent of the population of Glasgow thought that they could be funnier than Billy Connolly given the chance, while 17 per cent thought they were already funnier than Billy Connolly. The other 9 per cent thought that they were Billy Connolly.'

THE BIGGEST HOUSING SCHEME IN EUROPE, 1975

Cathy McCormack

It was Billy Connolly who described estates like Easterhouse as 'deserts wi' windaes', which was just about right. Except that in deserts it is hot and dry whereas in a place like Easterhouse it was more often cold and damp. The Easterhouse project got under way in 1954. One of Glasgow's four great post-war schemes, it was over-exposed to the elements and lacked basic amenities. Soon it became a byword for deprivation and unsocial behaviour, despite the sterling efforts of residents such as Cathy McCormack.

Greater Easterhouse is made up of fifteen areas and in January 1975, we moved from Cranhill to our own flat in Easthall. It was then the biggest housing scheme in Europe. Just a few years before, in the 1960s, the singer Frankie Vaughan had donated the takings of his show at the Pavilion Theatre in Glasgow to the Easterhouse Project. This was aimed at stopping gang warfare and he helped co-ordinate an arms amnesty. Unfortunately the media circus which followed him gave Easterhouse a bad reputation that still lives with us to this day. People were also further disadvantaged by reputation when it came to job applications. Even so, you had to have a reference to get a house up here and a lady called Helen Ewing recommended we get this house.

What we moved to was basically a concrete bunker. It had a gas fire in the living room and an electric fire on the wall of one bedroom, but no heating in the other rooms or in the hall. There was nothing to keep the heat in or the cold out. But at the start we were delighted to get our own space and there was a garden and we were close to my sister, who lived round the corner. They called me Paintbrush Annie because I was always cleaning and decorating.

The first shock I got was when I stripped the wallpaper off the bedroom and the pattern was on the wall. I couldn't believe it. That was the first indication we got of how damp the house was. It was cold when we moved in and soon after, the mould started. I was continually washing the walls with bleach.

There was a pulley in the kitchen and Sharon [her daughter] had the real McCoy nappies. But if you were boiling nappies you were creating steam and there were no fans to draw out the moisture. In Cranhill at my ma and da's house the living room and the kitchen were back to back with a coal fire. Then came the Clean Air Act. It was passed in 1956 and in the 1960s, Glasgow Corporation ripped out all the coal fires. It certainly stopped the smog – my ma started to see dampness in her bathroom. But my end bathroom was the worst affected and a mustard carpet turned green. Taking away the coal fires started the real dampness epidemic. In their efforts to clean the air outside they polluted the air inside with fungal spores. And in the un-insulated concrete box that I lived in when Sharon was a baby, we were all struggling to fight the dampness and pay sky-high fuel bills.

In our house in Easthall, the toilet was badly affected with mould and so were the wooden window frames. When it was really cold outside we had icicles hanging from inside our bedroom windows. In the summer it wasn't so bad because I had a garden and a verandah but in winter it was a nightmare. 'Oh my God it's coming up Christmas again – look at the state of that room.' I always had a paintbrush in my hand because it was never-ending. I was always complaining to the local housing office about the dampness. That was an amazing experience. You'd fill in a form to complain about the dampness. Usually nothing happened. So you'd go back and complain again. You'd complain and complain until you did get a response. And then somebody from the local housing office would come to investigate the condensation and dampness. They'd say: 'You boil too many kettles. How many baths do you have a week? Oh – I see you have washing up on a pulley . . .' At the end they started talking about me not having enough insulation on my letterbox – that's when I thought we should draw a line under it.

THE ONLY SANE MAN IN GLASGOW, 1975
Matt McGinn

Singer and songwriter Matt McGinn (1928–77) was born in the Gallowgate in the Calton, the eighth of nine children. His formal education ended when he was sent to an approved school at the age of 12. Latterly, however, he attended Ruskin College, Oxford, and taught for a while but he preferred the more nomadic life of a performer. He wrote hundreds of songs, including 'Red Yo-Yo', 'Coorie Doon', 'The Ibrox Disaster' and 'The Wee Kirkcudbright Centipede'. Politically active and vocal, he was forever having scrapes with the authorities, some of which were decidedly surreal, as he described in McGinn of the Calton.

On the third of October nineteen seventy-five the newspapers were full of it.

'Roll up, roll up for the Great Sheriff Court Show, starring at great expense Comedian,' ran *The Scotsman.*

'How the Sheriff learned about the Bees,' headlined the *Daily Record.* The *Daily Express*, which also did a very humorous piece on the Sheriff Court Show, printed a small poster with my face on it, declaring 'Wanted, for Flybillposting'.

The Scottish press and a large part of the English plus Radios Clyde and Forth, Scottish Television and even the pussyfooting BBC Television rose to the occasion and treated the Great Sheriff Court Show as the comic opera farce by which term I described it in Court.

Charged with having displayed posters on sites throughout the city without the permission of the owners of the said sites, I was found not guilty of putting up the posters but guilty of refusing to get them down, and fined thirty pounds.

The posters, fifty-one of which were mentioned, had appeared on walls and hoardings one night almost a year before, advertising two Long Playing records and reading in part 'Matt McGinn's Fantastic New LP, "The Two-Heided Man Strikes Again". (The Big 'Shike) the follow-up to "The Two-Heided Man", (The Big Effen Bee) on sale at Woolworths, Boots and other record shops.'

Now Glasgow was full of such illegal poster advertisements informing the world that certain wares were available to people, such as Datsun cars at so-and-so garage, demonstrations to be held for and against abortion and telling of meetings where one could hear Harry McShane talking about unemployment or Yoko Hami on Karate or Paul Foot on how easy it would be to have a revolution next Tuesday at half-past-two provided it weren't raining. There were literally thousands of them with as many names on them. But these ones with my name on them seemed to be special for some people, and on the basis of them some persons in Glasgow City Chambers decided to pounce.

For those Chambers I have never had a great deal of respect. That well-known character The Clincher, had more respect for them than I. He was a hairdresser from the Maryhill district of the city whom certain officials connected with those chambers had at one time tried to have declared insane.

The doctor at Hawkhead asylum to which he had been referred by one of the magistrates for examination stated that The Clincher was as sane as he himself was, to which The Clincher had retorted, 'Could you give me a written statement to that effect?'

From then on The Clincher, whom I remember seeing standing in the Trongate roaring and bawling about 'The municipal Chamber and those who sit in it', developed the habit of holding up his doctor's letter and shouting, 'I am the only sane man in Glasgow with a certificate to prove it.'

In attacking the people connected with George Square he was expressing the disrespect which most Glaswegians have for these bureaucrats, if we are to judge by the fact that a thirty per cent poll at a municipal election is considered massive, but such attacks merited in their eyes special treatment for The Clincher, and like The Clincher I was to be singled out for extraordinary action.

The other posters might be objectionable but the ones with McGinn's name on them were outright obnoxious.

The telephone rang in my Rutherglen home.

'I would like to speak to Mister Matt McGinn,' a voice said.

'Speaking,' says I.

'This is a Mister Cumming of Glasgow Corporation Planning Department,' said the voice, shocking me with the news that Glasgow had a Planning Department. Until then I had thought that those bloody great concrete jungles and deserts like The Calton and Dalmarnock and Partick had arisen by accident.

'What's your first name?' says I.

'I don't think we'll be on first-name terms,' says the voice.

'What's your first name?' I insisted, finally eliciting the information that it was Andrew.

'Hello Andy,' says I, still thinking I was being phoned regarding an engagement.

'A number of posters have appeared throughout the city,' said the voice, 'advertising records of yours and I am phoning to warn you that if they are not taken down in the next seven days you will be prosecuted under the terms of the Town and Country Planning Act.'

'I never put them up,' says I.

'Your name is on them,' said the voice.

'I've never seen them,' says I, 'but I never put them up.'

'Who did put them up?' asked the voice.

'I don't know,' says I, 'but I've an idea who might have done and I'll pass on your message to them.'

Some days later an official letter arrived from Cumming or Cummings indicating that he had done some considerable homework on these posters and that he or someone else had been spending a great deal of the ratepayer's money in touring the city looking for posters with my name on them, singling them out from a million others and threatening prosecution if I did not have them removed.

From previous experience in political campaigns I knew that pasting posters illegally is a tricky business and the business of taking them down proved every bit as tricky or even more so. Apart from the business of not being caught by the police there is the technical thing which makes taking a poster from a wall or boarding a great deal more difficult than pasting it up.

However, I did not wish to have a clash with the law and after midnight that night, equipped with a paint scraper, I headed for Waterloo Street where I had seen a number of these posters on the front of a disused shop. In my own opinion the posters actually enhanced the appearance of the broken-down building but they were nonetheless illegal. There was even an inscription on the shop front saying 'Bill stickers will be prosecuted', under which someone had written, 'Bill Stickers is Not Guilty'.

So was I not guilty, but desirous of steering clear of the courts I set to with the scraper. I had not managed to remove four square inches of the first poster when a policeman's torch shone on me.

'What have we here?' said the Bobby.

'I'm trying to take down this poster,' says I.

'Have you the permission of the owner of these premises?' says the Bobby.

'No, I'm afraid not,' says I. 'But I have been instructed to get them down by Glasgow Corporation.'

'Get on your way,' says he, 'or I'll arrest you for defacing that wall or even worse.'

1976–2000

DESERTS WI' WINDAES

AN INDIAN SUNDAY, 1977
Hardeep Singh Kohli

Migrants from the Indian sub-continent have been coming to Scotland for centuries and gradually became part of the local community. In the nineteenth century, for example, Indian students came in increasing numbers. However, it was not until the 1920s that many arrived with the intention of staying permanently. In his book, The New Scots: The Story of Asians in Scotland *(1992), Bashir Maan suggests that these early settlers originated in the Punjab. Not the least of their contribution has been cultural, with curry competing with fish and chips to supplant haggis, neeps and tatties as the national dish. Hardeep Singh Kohli (1969–) was born in London. He moved to Glasgow with his parents, who had come to Britain from India in the 1960s, when he was four. A graduate in law from Glasgow University, he is best known as a broadcaster, and for his love of food.*

Sunday was our day to be Indian. After a week of mundane Scottish life, my mother would wrangle her three sons into smart clothes and assault us with a facecloth before tramping us off with our dad to experience the delights of *gurdwara*, the Sikh temple. I never understood why we had to be smartly dressed to visit the temple. If God (who was the omnipotent and omniscient and all other words beginning with *omni-*) judged who we were rather than how we appeared, then why did we need to ensure that our trousers were freshly pressed and our shirts free of ketchup? This philosophical musing of an eight-year-old was often met with the counter-argument of a skelp across the back of the thighs.

Temple was great. The religious component of praying and being holy was simply one of a myriad of activities that took place in what was no more than a rundown, near-derelict house on Nithsdale Drive in the Southside of Glasgow. As kids we mostly ran around at breakneck speed in our ironed trousers and ketchup-free shirts, trying our best to crumple our trousers and mark our shirts with ketchup. *Gurdwara* was where the entire community gathered; it was our parents' single chance to re-engage with Sikhism and Sikh people. It must have been a blessed relief for them to feel relaxed amongst their 'ain folk', for at least one day of the week. When I think about the hard time I used to get as a small brown boy in Glasgow, I forget that my parents had to deal with yet more abuse in a more sinister, less forgiving world.

There were two good things about the *gurdwara*, apart from the fact that about a hundred kids were at liberty to play and laugh and generally have a great time. At the end of the religious service, after the hordes had prayed collectively, the holy men would wander amongst the congregation who were sat cross-legged in the floor, handing out *prasad*. *Prasad* is a truly amazing thing. If you ever needed convincing that the universe has some higher power at its helm, then *prasad* would be the single substance to convert you. It's a semolina- and sugar-based concoction bound together with ghee. It is bereft of nutritional value, but it is hot and sweet and lovely. And it's holy. What more could you want?

After *prasad* the congregation would filter downstairs to enjoy *langar*. I believe the Sikh religion to be the grooviest, most forward-thinking of all the world religions. Obviously, I have a vested interest, but given the fact that as an organised belief system Sikhism is little over 300 years old, one begins to understand the antecedents of its grooviness. It is a young, vibrant religion that is not bogged down with ancient scripture and dogma. Sikhs were able to experience the other great religions of the subcontinent and construct a new belief system that accentuated the positives whilst attempting to eradicate the negatives. And no more is this innovation exemplified than with the beautifully egalitarian concept of *langar*. Every temple is compelled to offer any comer a free hot meal. In India this happens on a daily basis, but when I was growing up in Glasgow, Sunday was the day of the largest communion. You can be the wealthiest man in Punjab or the lowliest cowherd, but together you sit and share the same modest yet delicious meal, cooked in the temple by devotees. This is *langar*.

Our bellies full, we would drive a few miles from the temple into the centre of Glasgow, to the Odeon on Renfield Street. In the seventies and early eighties, cinemas were closed on Sundays, a fact utilised by the Indian community the length and breadth of Britain. For six days of the week, cinemas were bastions of British and American film, but on Sunday the sweeping strings and sensuous sari blouses of Bollywood took over. And it felt like every brown person in Glasgow was there. From three o'clock in the afternoon we had a double bill of beautiful women dancing for handsome moustachioed men; of gun fights and fist fights; of love and betrayal. These films were in Hindi, a language lost on us boys; we barely spoke any Punjabi. But the images were bold and strong and most importantly Indian. And guess what? There was also food involved. Hot mince and pea samosas were handed round and occasionally the cinema would fill with the sound of old men blowing cooling air into their hot triangular snacks. Pakoras would be illicitly eaten with spicy chutney. There would be the inevitable spillage and some fruity Punjabi cursing, involving an adult blaming the nearest innocent kid for their own inability to pour cardamom tea from a thermos whilst balancing an onion bhaji on their knee. It was only some years later that I discovered that eating food in the cinema was banned.

'THE BARGAIN', 1977
Liz Lochhead

The Barrows or, as it is more commonly known, The Barras, is a legendary Glasgow institution. Its origins can be traced to the 1920s, when there was a market in Clyde Street on which cheap goods were displayed on hand-barrows. When this was closed in the 1920s, Mrs Margaret McIvor and her husband, who had hired barrows to traders, bought land in the Calton and invited their former clients to set up shop. It expanded rapidly, selling mainly second-hand clothes. In the 1970s and 1980s, The Barras fell into disrepair and disrepute, but with the formation of the Barrows Enterprise Trust it enjoyed a revival, becoming one of Europe's largest street markets. Liz Lochhead

(1947–), poet and playwright, is a national treasure who from 2011–16 was Scots Makar, Scotland's national poet.

The river in January is fast and high.
You and I
are off to the Barrows.
Gathering police-horses twitch and fret
at the Tron end of London Road and Gallowgate.
The early kick-off we forgot
has us, three-thirty, rubbing the wrong way
against all the ugly losers
getting ready to let fly
where the two rivers meet.
January, and we're
looking back, looking forward
don't know which way

but the boy
with three beautiful Bakelite
Bush radios for sale in Meadow's minimarket is
buttonpopping stationhopping he
doesn't miss a beat sings along it's easy
to every changing tune,

Yes today we're in love aren't we?
with the whole splintering city
its big quick river wintry bridges
its brazen black Victorian heart.
So what if every other tenement
wears its hearth on its gable end?
All I want
is my glad eye to catch
a glint in your flinty Northern face again
just once. Oh I know it's cold
and coming down
and no we never lingered long among
the Shipbank traders.
Paddy's Market underneath the arches
stank too much today
the usual wetdog reek rising
from piles of old damp clothes.

Somebody absolutely steamboats he says on
sweet warm wine
swigging plaincover from a paper bag
squats in a puddle with nothing to sell
but three bent forks a torn
calendar (last year's)
and a broken plastic sandal.
So we hadn't the stomach for it today.
We don't deserve a bargain then!
No connoisseur can afford to be too scrupulous
about keeping his hands clean.
There was no doubt the rare the beautiful
and bugle-beaded the real antique dirt cheap
among the rags and drunks
you could easily take to the cleaners.

At the Barrows everything has its price
no haggling believe me
this boy knows his radios.
Pure Utility
and what that's worth these days.
Suddenly the fifties are fashionable
and anything within a decade of art deco
a rarity you'll pay through the nose for.
The man with the patter and all these curtain lengths
in fibreglass is flabbergasted at the bargain
and says so in so many words.
Jesus, every other
arcade around here's
a 'Fire Surround Boutique' –
and we watch the struggling families;
father carrying hearth home
mother wound up with kids.
All the couples we know fall apart
or have kids.
Oh we've never shouldered much.
We'll stick to small ikons for our home –
as long as they're portable –
a dartboard a peacock feather
a stucco photoframe.

We queue in a blue haze of hot fat
for Danny's Do-Nuts that grit
our teeth with granulated sugar.
I keep
losing you and finding you –
two stalls away you thumb
through a complete set of manuals for
primary teachers in the thirties
I rub my sleeve
on a dusty Chinese saucer
till the gilt shows through.
Oh come on we promised
we'd not let our affection for the slightly cracked
trap us into such expenditure again.
Oh even if it is a bargain
we won't buy.
The stallholder says we'll be the death of her.
She says see January
it's been the doldrums the day.

And it's packing up time
with the dark coming early
and as cold as the river.
At the bus-stop I show you
the beady bag and the maybe rosewood box
with the inlaid butterfly and the broken catch.
You've bought a record by the Shangri-las
a pin-stripe waistcoat that needs a stitch
it just won't get and a book called 'Enquire
Within – Upon Everything'.
The raw cold gets colder.
There doesn't seem to be a lot to say.
I wish we could either mend things
or learn to throw them away.

LATIN OR FRENCH? 1981
Alasdair Gray

In this extract from his novel, Lanark *(1981), Alasdair Gray describes an experience familiar to many Scots of his era. Few children today are offered Latin at school and even French is regarded as increasingly recherché.*

Whitehill Senior Secondary School was a tall gloomy red sandstone building with a playing field at the back and on each side a square playground, one for each sex, enclosed and minimised by walls with spiked railings on top. It had been built like this in the eighteen-eighties but the growth of Glasgow had imposed additions. A structure, outwardly uniform with the old buildings but a warren of crooked stairs and small classrooms within, was stuck to the side at the turn of the century. After the first world war a long wooden annexe was added as temporary accommodation until a new school could be built, and after the second world war, as a further temporary measure, seven prefabricated huts holding two classrooms each were put up on the playing field. On a grey morning some new boys stood in a lost-looking crowd near the entrance gate. In primary school they had been the playground giants. Now they were dwarfs among a mob of people up to eighteen inches taller than themselves. A furtive knot from Riddrie huddled together trying to seem blasé. One said to Thaw, 'What are ye taking, Latin or French?'

'French.'

'I'm taking Latin. Ye need it tae go to university.'

'But Latin's a dead language!' said Thaw. 'My mother wants me to take Latin but I tell her there are more good books in French. And ye can use French tae travel.'

'Aye, mibby, but ye need Latin tae get to university.'

An electric bell screeched and a fat bald man in a black gown appeared on the steps of the main entrance. He stood with his hands deep in his pockets and feet apart, contemplating the buttons of his waistcoat while the older pupils hurried into lines before several entrances. One or two lines kept up a vague chatter and shuffle; he looked sternly at these and they fell silent. He motioned each class to the entrances one after another with a finger of his right hand. Then he beckoned the little group by the gate to the foot of the steps, lined them up, read their names from a list and led them into the building. The gloom of the entrance steeped them, then the dim light of echoing hall, then the cold light of a classroom.

Thaw entered last and found the only seat left was the undesirable one in the front row in front of the teacher, who sat behind a tall desk with his hands clasped on the lid. When everyone was seated he looked from left to right along the rows of faces before him, as if memorising each one, then leaned back and said casually, 'Now we'll divide you into classes. In the first year, of course, the only real division is between those who take Latin and those who take . . . a modern language. At the end of the third year you will have to choose between other subjects: Geography or History, for instance; Science or Art; for by then you will be specialising for your future career. Hands up those who don't know what specialising means. No hands? Good. Your choice today is a simpler one, but its effects reach further. You all know Latin is needed for entrance to university. A number of benevolent people think this unfair and are trying to change it. As far as Glasgow University is concerned they haven't succeeded *yet*.' He smiled an inward-looking smile and leaned back until he seemed to be staring at the ceiling. He said, 'My name's Walkenshaw. I'm senior Classics master. Classics. That's what we call the study of Latin and Greek. Perhaps you've heard the word before? Who hasn't heard of classical music? Put your hands up if you haven't heard of classical music. No hands? Good. Classical music, you see, is the *best* sort of music, music by the best composers. In the same way the study of Classics is the study of the *best*. Are you chewing something?'

Thaw, who had been swallowing nervously, was appalled to find this question fired at himself. Not daring to take his gaze from the teacher's face he stood slowly up and shook his head.

'Answer me.'

'No, sir.'

'Open your mouth. Open it wide. Stick your tongue out.'

Thaw did as he was told. Mr Walkenshaw leaned forward, stared then said mildly, 'Your name?'

'Thaw, sir.'

'That's all right, Thaw. You can sit down. And always tell the truth, Thaw.'

Mr Walkenshaw leaned back and said, 'Classics. Or as we call it at university, the Humanities. I say nothing against the study of modern languages. Naturally half of you will choose French. But Whitehall Senior Secondary School has a tradition, a fine tradition of Classical scholarship, and I hope many of you continue that tradition. To those without enough ambition to go to university and who can't see the use of Latin, I can only repeat the words of Robert Burns: 'Man cannot live by bread alone.' No, and you would be wise to remember it. Now I'm going to read your names again and I want you to shout Modern and Classics according to choice.'

He read the list of names again. Thaw was depressed to hear all the people he knew choose Latin. He chose Latin.

A STRANGLED PEEVISH HICCUP, 1982

Paul Theroux

After eleven years living in London, the American novelist Paul Theroux set out to travel clockwise round the coast and find out what Britain and the British are really like. It was 1982, the summer of the Falklands War and the royal baby. As is the way with day-trippers, Theroux's views were snapshots, but no less valid for that. Of Aberdeen, he wrote: 'The food was disgusting, the hotels overpriced and indifferent, the spit-and-sawdust pubs were full of drunken and bad-tempered men – well, who wouldn't be bad-tempered?' Dundee, he discovered, had well-earned its reputation for dullness, while he barely spent enough time in Edinburgh to blow his nose. Nor did he spend much longer in Glasgow . . .

After my days being menaced by Belfast's ugly face I went by boat and train to Glasgow and found it peaceful, even pretty. It had a bad name. 'Gleska', people said, and mocked the toothless population and spoke of razor fights in the Gorbals, and made haggis jokes. Yet Glasgow was pleasant – not broken but eroded. The slums were gone, the buildings washed of their soot; the city looked dignified – no barricades, no scorchings. Well, I had just struggled ashore from that island of antiquated passions. In Ireland I had felt as though I had been walking blindly into the dark. But Scotland made me hopeful. This sunny day stretched all the way to Oban, where I was headed.

On my way from Glasgow Central to Queen Street Station, I fell in with two postmen. They asked me where I had come from. I told them Ulster. They said, 'Och!'

'It's full of broken windows,' I said.

'Aye. And broken *hids*!' one said.

The other man said, 'We got our Catholics. Ha' ye nae heard of the Rengers and Celtics fitba matches? They play each other a guid sux times a year, but there's nae *always* a riot.'

No alphabet exists for the Glaswegian accent – phonetic symbols are no good either without a glottal stop, a snort, or a wheeze. I met rural-dwelling Scots who told me they could not understand anyone from Glasgow. The Ulster accent took a moment to turn from noise to language: I heard someone speak and then in the echo of the voice there was a meaning. But this did not always happen in Scotland: the echo was meaningless, and in Glasgow it was a strangled peevish hiccup, sudden and untranslatable.

LINGUA GLESCA, 1982
Stanley Baxter

Before visiting Glasgow it is recommended that tourists become acquainted with a few phrases to assist them in their negotiations. The following list of the more obscure Glaswegian words and phrases with approximate definitions in ordinary English may be of some use to non-Scots who visit the great cultural melting-pot on the Clyde. Stanley Baxter (1926–), the renowned comedian, was born in Glasgow, and, ably abetted by journalist Alex Mitchell, produced a series of sketches and books aimed at enlightening the ignorant in the city's patois. Their model, apparently, was the BBC series Parliamo Italiano. *In one justly famous scene Baxter approaches a trader at a local market and asks: 'Zarra marra onna barra, Clara?', which he translates as 'Is that a marrow on your barrow, Clara?'.*

SHURSEL, HULLAWRERR, YURTHERR: Words of greeting.

GOARRA, used in various contexts, as follows –

GOARRAMADRI, an acute thirst has assailed me.

GOARRAFAGOANYE, a request for a cigarette.

GOARRAHELL, used when declining to give the importunate person a cigarette.

Various terms are used by the natives when discussing the vagaries of the weather.

SWAARMRADAY, the temperature has risen.

RASUNZOOT! a miracle has taken place!

SPELTINARAIN, we have returned to normal climatic conditions.

SELLUVAKOLNOO, the temperature has now fallen.

MASPUDZIZFROZE, my feet are extremely cold.

Many Glaswegians seek their holiday pleasures abroad. Foreign doctors might find it advisable to acquaint themselves with some of the terms used in describing the symptoms of various ailments.

MADIALZBEALIN, some skin is no longer adhering to my face.

MACHAMPURZIZBROON, even my dentures are sunburnt.

AVAHEIDANAHOF, the modestly-priced wine is stronger than I thought.

AVASERRKYTE, I am suffering from stomach pains.

AMOFFI PEELIWALLI, the large seafood meal I ate has made me somewhat frail.

ASATOANA DAUDAGLESS, I failed to notice the broken wine bottle before I sat down on the beach.

On their return from a sojourn in mainland Spain or Majorca many Glaswegian natives display their snapshots with pride. Expressions that accompany their photographic exhibition are –

WANNISEE WURPHOTIES? Can I induce you to suffer an hour of extreme boredom?

ERRMAMURRAPAIDLIN, that is a study of my mother seeking a sea-water easement of her painful corns.

WEEFELLA BELLAFELLINWI, a small gentleman who took Bella out in a pedalo which capsized.

RAWEANFLIN SAUNABOOT, the child merrily throwing sand about.

SKELPINFURRAWEAN, father cutting short the child's enjoyment.

MAWYELLINHURHEIDAFF, my mother has inadvertently sat on a bee, wasp or hornet.

Foreign students of our language are surprised to find that it contains words which are apparently of Japanese origin. A common greeting is –

HEHYU or HIYU

Other words borrowed from the Land of the Rising Sun are –

OBI JINGSAM WABBIT, I am exceedingly fatigued.

WANNA SUKAT, as in the hospitable invitation 'Do you want a suck at my orange?'

GONNIGEISHASANG? Are you going to favour us with a ballad?

UCHAMSHI, I am somewhat diffident.

WHITWUNNA THREETHURTI? A request for racing information.

OMI WHITATUMMI, a comment made on observing a gentleman's pendulous stomach.

SAMURAI BUNGFU, a lady's rebuke to her bibulous husband, Sam.

THE WOMAN IN GOVAN LIBRARY, 1983
Jimmy Reid

Jimmy Reid (1932–2010) came to prominence in the early 1970s when he was one of the leaders of the Upper Clyde Shipbuilders work-in to try to stop the Conservative Government from closing down shipyards. In a speech that is regarded as one of the most powerful he ever delivered, Reid told workers: 'There will be no hooliganism. There will be no vandalism. There will be no bevvying . . .' Born in Govan, Reid was an autodidact, an avid reader of G.K. Chesterton, George Bernard Shaw and George Orwell. The speech from which this extract is taken was delivered without notes at a Scottish Library Association Conference.

Libraries played a very important part in my own education, if you can call it an education. In terms of formal scholastic qualifications I have none – not even an 'O' level. Not because I was a total 'bampot', as they say, but I left school at fourteen and, to tell you the truth, we did not take exams at that time. I passed my eleven plus. We still had the eleven plus in those days. I think it was out of 150, and I got 148½, which was not a bad pass mark. I am not indicating anything here, because I did not think about the eleven plus at that time. When I grew to maturity I thought even less about it as any kind of guide for measuring the intelligence of human beings, because people, particularly children, develop at different levels.

Anyway, I passed the eleven plus. I don't know what it is now, but they streamed you in those days, and in Govan we were streamed into the academic stream that was based on Oxford and Cambridge. I did Greek, French and Latin, but my expectations never involved higher education. I did not know anybody who went to university from the streets of Govan. You normally assumed that at the first opportunity you were out to work. I must confess I never found the smattering of knowledge about Latin verbs of great assistance in the shipyards, but do not knock it for that reason.

I must also add that I have no recollection of my formal education, particularly at secondary school, stimulating or generating the slightest interest in any subject, in any subject at all, yet at the age of twelve or thirteen I was a voracious reader and pestered the life out of the woman in Govan Library. She swore blind that I could not be reading all the books I was taking out! Now, I was not exactly a bookworm – I used to play football and do all the other things with the lads. The truth is that for whatever reason, I started reading and by the time I was thirteen or fourteen had read every thing that Shaw had ever written, including his novels (which were not very good), and, to this day, I am still a voracious reader.

The importance to me then was considerable. But there is another factor which I want to raise with you which I think is important. The best way of raising it is to ask you to jump forward in time to about 1972–73. I went down to London to do a literary programme for London Weekend Television and Jonathan Miller was there. I introduced the question of the decline and fall of the novel. All the evidence suggests, in my opinion, that that particular art form has gone over the apex of its development. I am saying that now, more in sorrow than in joy, because to me it has made a colossal contribution to human knowledge. Anyway, we went into this in detail and after the programme, having a drink, he said to me, 'Where did you study English Literature?' I said, 'Govan Library', and he said, 'Ah, come on. The library?' And I did realise then that because I had not been reading in order to increase job expectations, or career prospects, or to pass an examination, there was a catholicity in my reading for which I am eternally grateful.

TOM JONES IN GLASGOW, 1983
Billy Sloan

For unfathomable reasons women attending performances by the Welsh singer Tom Jones like to throw their underwear at him. Glaswegians, it seems, were no less afflicted.

Welsh superstar Tom Jones embarked on his first British concert tour in over ten years. I caught his show at Glasgow Apollo, and was impressed by his still powerful tonsils and explosive, sex-charged stage show.

Most of the audience were tipsy women – quarter bottles neatly concealed in handbags – who were determined to have a rerr terr and a good ogle. As Jones whipped off his jacket, exposing his he-man hairy chest and thrust his hips provocatively towards them, the excitement level reached fever pitch. His tight clothes left nothing to their imaginations. Then with 3,000 females simultaneously bursting a blood vessel, one of them rushed up to me and, in a mixture of ecstasy and obvious distress, screamed into my ear.

'Wid ye just look at that boady. He's the only singer in the world I'd haud in a pee fur . . .'

Only in this fair city could twenty years of gold discs, Las Vegas sell-outs, phenomenal riches and international acclaim be summed up by the self-discipline of a wee Glesga wummin's bladder movements.

MILES BETTER – THAN WHERE? 1983
Harry Diamond

If New York could have its image changed by a slogan, why not Glasgow? That was the thinking in the 1980s when the city was in need of a surge of energy and a dose of the feelgood factor. But where to start? As Harry Diamond (1930–99), who ran the City Council's PR operation recounts, it was actually a teenager who helped set the ball rolling, ably abetted by his father, who was in advertising. Thus was 'Glasgow's Miles Better' born. Diamond was the son of a Russian alien called Chatzkind who took the name Diamond because it was the first one an immigration officer saw on the board over a shopfront.

John Struthers, a Glasgow advertising man, and his 14-year-old son Mark were doodling, John's own word, on sheets of paper on a flight to London trying to devise a campaign slogan for their native city.

Page after page was discarded as they wrote things like 'GLASGOW TOPS FOR YOU, GET TO KNOW GLASGOW, GROW WITH GLASGOW, THE GLASGOW SMILE'. They still hadn't quite got it when they arrived in London. Then on a train from the airport to the centre of the city John wrote 'GLASGOW'S MILES BETTER'. When they got home that night they substituted a smiling face for the letter 'O'. And so was born the slogan that swept the world.

Struthers took his idea to Lord Provost Michael Kelly, who had the wit and foresight to see its possibilities. He persuaded the City Council to put up £150,000 towards a full-scale promotional campaign for the city. The business community put up £200,000. Kelly persuaded business leaders that what was good for Glasgow was good for them and businesses too. After all, if a lot of people were attracted to the city because of the things they read they would obviously spend money there.

The Glasgow's Miles Better campaign, which started in 1983, was one of the best promotions ever mounted by a British city. It won the International Film and Television Festival of New York award in 1983, 1984, 1985 and 1987. 'The only reason we didn't win in 1986 is because we didn't enter the festival,' says Struthers.

Struthers devised a series of advertisements based on the things we had been publicising over the years: the city's international hotels, museums, parks, restaurants, sporting facilities. Then came badges, car stickers, umbrellas, tee-shirts, and plastic carrier bags, all carrying the miles better slogan.

No opportunity to spread the word was overlooked. Holidaymakers flying out of Glasgow had the miles better stickers on their luggage in a variety of languages. People like Jimmy Savile and Lulu were recruited by council departments. Even the Queen was pictured with Michael Kelly under a miles better umbrella.

At one point John Struthers devised a miles better advertisement to put on Edinburgh buses during the Edinburgh Festival but we were refused permission by the city's transport authority. We planned to spend about £2,000 on this exercise but the transport authority's refusal was reported worldwide and we received millions of pounds worth of publicity for nothing. I was even quoted on the front page of the *Wall Street Journal*.

In March 1984 Michael Kelly launched the campaign nationally with a breakfast at the Savoy Hotel in London hosted by Britoil. The list of guests from every walk of life was enormous. One of them was Billy Connolly. Mr Connolly was being what he considered amusing for the benefit of the crowd in a reception area when I approached him quietly at Michael Kelly's request and stopped a few feet away. I waited until he acknowledged my existence by looking in my direction and said, 'Would you mind taking your place at the top table Mr Connolly so that we can get started.'

Mr Connolly looked me up and down and said in a voice that carried to Carlisle. 'Whooo are yoooo? Fuck off.' A few self-conscious titters broke out at this brilliant riposte. Mr Connolly had obviously been misled by my immaculate appearance.

I put my hand under his armpit, assisted him to a nearby wall, and whispered in his ear in the idiom which he apparently understood best, 'Listen pal, Ah'm a Glasgow man an' all and if you talk to me like that again I'll rip yer scruffy fucking heid aff and fling it to all yer admirers out there. Get the message, son?' Mr

Connolly was taken aback, abashed and nonplussed. He went in for breakfast.

PURE MINCE, 1984
James Kelman

For many Glaswegians – not to mention many Scots – a plate of mince is as memory-laden as Proust's petite madeleine. Extraordinarily, Alexander Fenton's otherwise comprehensive, The Food of the Scots *(2007) makes no mention of mince or, for that matter, minced beef, but it does contain a couple of references to mince pies, which of course have nothing to do with real mince. Nor, indeed, is there any mention of mince in Annette Hope's* A Caledonian Feast *(2002), though there is a recipe for a dish called minced collops, an essential ingredient of which is a handful of toasted oatmeal. Is this any way to treat a meal that made the lips of generations smack in anticipation? Thankfully, Booker Prize-winning novelist James Kelman (1946–), who was born and brought up in Glasgow, knows how to make the perfect plate of mince and tatties. Follow the instructions the Busconductor Hines delivers to his son, published in Kelman's novel of the same name. Follow them to the letter and you cannot go wrong. Be warned but, Hines is only just avoiding a nervous breakdown.*

¾lb beef links, 1lb of potatoes, 2 onions medium sized and 1 tin beans baked. And that's you with the sausage, chips and beans plus the juicy onions – and they're good for your blood whether you like it or no. This big pot with the grill type container is for the chips, it lets them drip so the fat goes back into the pot. Simple economics. And even if your mummy's sick to death of chips, what should be said is this: she isn't the fucking cook the day so enough said, let her go to a bastarn cafe. 2 nights on the trot is okay as long as it's not regularly the case. Fine: the items should get dished no more than 4 times per week but attempt to space it so that 1 day can pass without. 7 days in a week. What is that by christ is there an extra day floating about somewhere? Best to ignore fixed things like weeks and months and days. The minimum to cover all of the things i.e. breakfast, dinner, tea. Right: chips number 1 day, 3 day, 5 day, 7 day; missing 0 day, 2 day, 4 day and 6 day. Alright 8 times a fortnight. But 7 every 14 days. So there you are you can maybe get left having them twice on the trot but being a chip lover you just ignore it. Let's go then: right; Monday is fish day – rubbish. Monday is mince and potatoes. Simple, get your pot. Item: 1 pot. Item: ¾lb mince. Item: 2 onions medium sized, then a ½lb carrots, a tin of peas and also a no – not at all, don't use a frying pan to brown the mince; what you do is fry it lightly in the same pot you're doing the actual cooking in. Saves a utensil for the cleaning up carry on. So: stick mince into pot with drop cooking oil, lard or whatever the fuck – margarine maybe. Have onions peeled and chopped. Break up mince with wooden spoon. Put pot on at slow heat so that it doesn't sizzle too much. While breaking up mince all the time in order that it may not become too fucking lumpy. Toss in onions. The pepper and salt have been sprinkled while doing the breaking up. Next: have your water boiled. Pour a ½ pint measure in which you've already dumped gravy cube viz crumbled into the smallest bits possible. Stir. When mince brownish add mixture. Stir. Place lid on pot. Having already brought to boil. Then get simmering i.e. once boiling you turn gas so's it just bubbles and no more. Pardon. Once you've got ½ pint gravy water poured in you'll probably need extra. Lid on. Handle turned to inside lest accidents to person. Then sit on arse for following hour apart from occasional checks and stirring. 30 minutes before completion you get the spuds peeled and cut into appropriate sections and fill the other pot with boiling water, having already dumped said spuds in to pot while empty for fuck sake otherwise you'll splash yourself. Stick on at hot heat. Sit on arse for 15 to 20 minutes. Open tin peas of course. The bastarn fucking carrots. At the frying mince and onion stage you've got them peeled and chopped and you add to same. The peas get placed in wee saucepan and can cook in matter of moments. When time's up you've got mince, potatoes and peas set to serve from a trio of pots.

ALASDAIR GRAY'S *LANARK*, 1984
Anthony Burgess

First published in 1981, Alastair Gray's debut novel, Lanark, *was immediately recognised as a significant contribution to Scottish literature. Many years in the writing, it combines realism, surrealism and science fiction, introducing a hero called Duncan Thaw, who may or may not be based on the author, and a city called Unthank, which doubtless owes a lot to Glasgow. The most quoted passage in the novel is that in which one of the characters asks: 'What is Glasgow to most of us? A house, the place we work, a football park or golf course, some pubs and connecting streets. That's all. No, I'm wrong, there's also the cinema and library. And when our imagination needs exercise we use these to visit London, Paris, Rome under the Caesars, the American West at the turn of the century, anywhere but here and now. Imaginatively Glasgow exists as a music-hall song and a few bad novels. That's all we've given to the world outside. It's all we've given to ourselves.' One of* Lanark*'s many fans was the English novelist, Anthony Burgess, who cited it in his book,* Ninety-nine Novels: The Best in English since 1939.

A big and original novel has at last come out of Scotland. Gray is a fantastic writer (and his own fantastic illustrator) who owes something to Kafka but not much. He has created a mythical city called Unthank, a kind of lightless Limbo where people succumb to strange diseases and then are transformed into crabs, leeches, dragons before disappearing without trace. This nonplace has a vague resemblance to contemporary Glasgow. Lanark, one of its citizens, indeed eventually its Provost, suspects that he is a metamorphosis of an earlier life-form, consults the Oracle in a strange place called the Institute and is granted a vision of the life of a young man named Duncan Thaw, growing up in a real Glasgow, preoccupied with the problem of reconciling his artistic ambitions with the maintaining of ordinary human relationships. All this is good traditional naturalism. Thaw dies, and it is not clear whether his death is accidental or suicidal. He finds himself in Unthank, which nightmarishly reproduces aspects of his past life. His identification with Lanark is vague. Lanark sets out now on a mad journey 'through the mist and time chaos of the Intercalendrical Zone', visits a city called Provan, where the citizens drink rainbows and are oppressed by security robots. Gray attempts no linguistic innovations, though his footnotes and marginal glosses recall *Finnegans Wake*. Whether his intention is satirical is not clear. It is best to take this novel as the emanation of the fancy of a Celt with a strong visual imagination and great verbal power. Scotland produced, in Hugh MacDiarmid, the greatest poet of the century (or so some believe); it was time Scotland produced a shattering work of fiction in the modern idiom. This is it.

COME AND SEE MA BLUE HOOSE, 1984
Ian Jack

Glasgow is not by any means unique in being a city of contrasts. Like Paris, or for that matter New York or London, rich and poor have always lived within its precincts. Perhaps, though, the two are more obviously demarcated in Glasgow. Taking his lead from George Orwell's novel Nineteen Eighty-Four, *journalist Ian Jack imagined what a day in the life of a Glaswegian might be in the not-too-distant future.*

It is the best of times, it is the worst of times, and there are two Glasgows. Perhaps the Burrell Collection exemplifies the city at its best; a fine and genuinely popular modern building, set among woods and parkland, which attracted a million visitors within the first ten months of its opening. It cost £20 million to build but entrance is absolutely free. Here the people worship art, or merely gawp at the results of one man's gobbling hunger for rare and precious artefacts. Sir William Burrell made his fortune by the simple expedient of ordering ships cheap during slumps and selling them dear during booms. The profits went into salerooms. A great man for a bargain, Sir William would buy almost anything, from any period, from any culture, if the price was right. Glaswegians are celebrating a belated monument to the city's old wealth and self-confidence.

Glasgow at its worst can be found in the housing estates, the famous 'peripheral estates' which have changed in twenty years from a solution to a problem to a problem without any solution in sight. Unemployment rates in the estates can rise as high as fifty or sixty per cent. Many of the houses are damp; Glasgow Council received more than 17,000 complaints of dampness last year and spent more than £8 million trying to dry out its tenants' homes. According to a recent medical report, children who grow up there are more likely to be hospitalised for diseases such as whooping cough and gastroenteritis than children born in the more privileged parts of the city. Heroin-taking increases by the week. Large numbers of people want to get out.

I took a taxi to Possilpark, a pre-war estate built on a hill above the derelict wharves of the Forth and Clyde canal and only a mile or so from the city centre. Here, quite coincidentally, Sir William Burrell owned the boatbuilding yard which laid the foundations of the Burrell fortune in the middle of the last century.

'Possilpark,' said the driver, 'that's a helluva place to get into. It's a maze, no joke. They've built all these barriers across the roads to stop the boys pinching cars. Not, mind you, that it stops them.'

We passed abandoned factories and then began to rumble up and down streets full of wild dogs and wild children. Many houses had hardboard nailed over the windows.

'Christ knows what the folk do in a place like this,' said the driver. 'I think they must stay in doors and just screw the arse off one another.'

I got out and walked through the children ('Hey look, there's a funny man in a taxi') and called on Mrs Betty Collins to ask her if Glasgow had improved. 'Oh aye,' she said, 'miles better if you don't have to live in this damned place.' The Burrell Collection, the Citizens' Theatre, Scottish Opera; to Mrs Collins they seemed hopeless fripperies, possibly located on Mars. She helps run a local tenants' group. The majority of tenants, she said, were 'decent people trying to do their best' in the face of formidable problems which people who don't live in a place like Possilpark could never hope to understand. Take the woman who lived across the street. She was a 'wee bit simple', not quite right in the head poor girl, and frequently taken advantage of. She's been raped once. Then children had broken into her house and painted it blue – with hands not brushes, blue paint daubed on every wall. The woman came home and was delighted. 'Come and see ma blue hoose,' she'd told Mrs Collins, who didn't know whether to laugh or cry.

Housing estates, as a Glasgow councillor remarked, live in a 'peculiar psychological isolation'. Mrs Collins defined it as frustration bred from lack of hope and solved, temporarily, by alcohol, vandalism, theft and heroin. Kids, she said, were beginning to take junk (heroin spliced with Vim or sugar) at the age of twelve. Dirty needles had given the boy next door three separate doses of hepatitis. You could recognise heroin-users by the fact that they went into pubs and sat there clueless, without a drink. Mrs Collins remembered that as a teenager in the Fifties she'd had a choice of dancehalls, cafés, cinemas. Now there was nothing but pubs and bookies' shops. Nearly every local factory had closed and gangs of teenagers wandered aimlessly about the streets.

Within ten minutes of leaving Mrs Collins I was sitting in a restaurant and inspecting a menu which advertised not only food but also the manner of its recent capture. Oban-landed monkfish, creel-caught langoustines. All around happy diners talked about interesting personal developments.

'I hear Andrew's bought a wee weekend place on Loch Fyne.'

'I hear he's off the drink.'

'Heard that one before though.'

Here is an interesting change. Glasgow restaurants, unlike their London counterparts, were once filled with whispering customers who deferred both to the waiters and the food; an abnormal treat, eating expensive food, and an experience clearly devised for the luxury races to the south. But now people eat, drink and talk with unabashed enjoyment, as though, indeed, their custom made the owner's profits.

We ordered food. The Wild East Coast Salmon was especially recommended. My friends, none of them rich but all of them doing all right, discussed the peripheral estates. They had heard – heard perhaps too often – about the unemployment, the damp and the heroin. But what was going to be done? 'I mean, let's face it, the Clyde is never going to build Cunarders again . . . and it's difficult to see how the bears will ever work again.' ('Bears' is a Glasgow word for yobs or *lumpens*.)

In future, then, the Glaswegian will come in two types. Here is a day's timetable for each:

The Aspirer

7.30 Rise; muesli and orange juice

8.00 Jog.

9.30 Office; work on new software deal.

13.00 Meet Roddy, Fergus and Diarmid in Gertrude's wine bar. Discuss scheme to open print shop in disused railway signal cabin.

15.00 Festival shopping with the wife. Shiver while eating hot croissant and watching imitation of Marcel Marceau.

19.30 To see Scottish Opera's new production of *Rigoletto*, updated to the Gorbals of 1935.

22.30 Supper with lawyer friends at the Café de Paris. Oban-landed monkfish off.

23.50 Home; remember to adjust burglar alarm.

The Non-Aspirer

11.00 Rise; Wonderloaf and PG Tips.

12.00 Dress.

13.00 Watch *Pebble Mill at One.*

15.00 Watch *Willy Wonka and the Chocolate Factory* for the fourth time.

18.00 Meet pusher, buy £5 bag.

22.00 Wonder what happened during the past three hours.

24.00 Steal car for purposes of burglary elsewhere, to finance purchase of more £5 bags.

Meanwhile the most considered judgement on the new Glasgow comes from Alasdair Gray. For thirty years Gray painted Glasgow and its people without making a fortune doing so. Then, three years ago, he published his first novel, *Lanark*, which attracted notice and praise from London and even further afield. Many remarked on its length, ambition and anarchic brilliance.

I asked Gray the old question. Had Glasgow improved? He didn't rush to answer.

'Och, ha, hum, quack-quack,' said Gray, who often turns a mysterious phrase. 'Well, if you're middle-class, like I am, and if you're middle-aged, like I am, and if you work in a luxury trade, like I do, and if you've had a bit of luck recently, like I have, then yes, Glasgow is a better place.'

JOCK STEIN, 1985
Alex Ferguson

In 1967, Celtic football club, managed by John 'Jock' Stein (1922–85), became the first British team to win the European Cup, defeating Inter Milan in the final. Stein, who was born in Burnbank, Lanarkshire, left Celtic in 1978 for a brief period as manager of Leeds United, returning north the same year to manage Scotland, where one of his assistants was Alex Ferguson (1941–).

Everybody in the game knows that Jock Stein's record as Celtic manager was as triumphant as any ever achieved in the history of club football. The best tribute to his genius is not the winning of nine successive league championships, the countless other trophies he collected or even the historic breakthrough that made Celtic the first British club to lift the European Cup. What sets him apart more than anything else is the fact that the team who devastated Inter Milan on a magical evening in 1967 consisted of ten players born within a dozen miles of Celtic Park and one outsider, Bobby Lennox, who came from thirty miles away in Ayrshire. Jock won the European Cup with a Glasgow and District Select. At no other time, before or since, has one of the greatest competitions of world football been blitzed by such a concentration of locally produced talent. It was as close to a miracle as management can go. So who could blame me for being excited by the prospect of working with the man who created it?

Stein had just about every attribute required of a great manager, but none of his talents was more significant than his judgement of people. Whether a man was playing for him, or against him, Jock specialised in probing assessments of strengths and weaknesses. He had worked underground in the pits until he was twenty-seven and he had a wider, richer experience of human nature than is readily available to somebody confined since schooldays to the enclosed, insulated world of professional football. I am sure I have been helped by the fact that I spent a full apprenticeship as a toolmaker, that in my formative years I was exposed to the values of the workplace other than the training ground and the football field. His talent for dealing with all kinds of men probably counted as much as his technical knowledge and his advanced ideas on the game in enabling him to establish himself as a manager. He matured to greatness very quickly.

Stein was a big man in every sense. When he came into a room he dominated it. You always knew Jock was present. He seemed to know everybody's first name and that's a wonderful asset. Matt Busby had it. When Jock left Dunfermline to manage Hibs he had a wee share in a bookie's in Dunfermline and I remember going into the betting shop one day when he was there. He said: 'Hello Alex, are you enjoying playing at Dunfermline?' It made me feel really important. When people treat you that way you are instantly in favour of them. I had never spoken to Jock in my life but he knew me.

My first assignment as Jock's assistant with Scotland was a friendly match against Yugoslavia in September 1984, and I felt the preparation was good. Well, it couldn't have been too bad – we won 6–1, with Kenny Dalglish and Graeme Souness both at their majestic best. I revelled in the opportunity to operate from an assistant's position, blissfully free of all the extra responsibilities that crowded in on me as a club manager. I did not have to handle the press, deal with directors or cope with the countless obligations that go with being in overall charge of a group of players. Big Jock was a master in all those departments, so I was able to concentrate on working with some great footballers in training and studying how they applied themselves.

The Scotland get-togethers were an absolute revelation for me, priceless access to the mind and personality of Jock Stein. I am sure there are times when he got fed up with my incessant barrage of questions. I was so determined to find out as much as I could about one of the greatest managers of all time that I used every moment to draw enlightenment from him. On general football matters he was always forthcoming and educational but the brick wall went up if there was a hint of a negative about Celtic. I felt – and it wasn't exactly an isolated opinion – that Celtic had treated him disgracefully in failing to reward the years of inspired management that had brought the club the greatest run of success in its history. So I could not resist asking him how he had felt about the insult of being offered a job supervising the Celtic development pool, which amounted to reducing a supreme football man to a fund-raiser. His reaction was astonishingly low-key and devoid of bitterness. He said: 'When you are successful it is fine for a time and then they maybe think you are too successful and that the success wasn't really due to you at all.' End of story.

Another subject that Jock consistently refused to expand upon was how he went about making Celtic the first British club to win the European Cup. Everybody knows that his contribution – in finding and developing the players and then supplying them with tactics brilliantly devised to suit their skills – was utterly crucial, but he shrugged off any attempt to give him a substantial share of the glory. His modesty was extraordinary, and it was sincere. When the European Cup was mentioned, he would eulogise the players who won it and launch into some of the marvellous human stories surrounding that great team. We would be sitting in the reception lobby of the hotel at 2 a.m. with one hilarious tale following another. Many involved wee Jimmy Johnstone. According to Jock, when his phone rang at home late on a Friday night a picture of Jimmy would leap instantly into his mind and his first thought would be: 'Which police station this time?'

Having lost the second of our World Cup [qualifying] matches with Spain by 1–0 in Seville three months earlier, we now found that qualification for Mexico would hinge on our final group fixture against Wales at Ninian Park on 10 September 1985. We needed at least a draw to earn a play-off with the winner of the Oceanic group, Australia ... There were, naturally, signs of nerves at the start of the game. I don't care what anybody says, when the crowd at Cardiff start singing that Welsh national anthem it creates some atmosphere. There were 35,000 in the ground that night and when they gave it voice it was bound to stir their players. That was real motivation. The Welsh team were revved and in the first half they gave us a hard time. Wales went ahead when the ball was driven in from the left-hand side and Sparky Hughes took the goal brilliantly. So at half-time we were down 1–0 and in the dressing-room Jock got stuck into wee

Gordon Strachan. He was going to take Strachan off and bring Davie Cooper on at that point. Gordon was upset but there was nothing new in that.

Then all of a sudden Jock left the main part of the dressing-room. Hugh Allan, the physiotherapist, had called him into the bathroom area. I went across and sat down with Gordon.

'What Jock is saying is for the sake of the team. You're not playing as well as you should.'

'I can't believe he is saying that to me,' Gordon responded.

'Look,' I said, 'he's right. Just settle down. You're not coming off. He'll give you ten minutes. Get your game together.' Then big Jock called.

'Alex, come here.'

I walked into the bathroom area and I'll never forget the scene that greeted me. There was a kind of wooden plinth and Jim [Leighton, Scotland's – and Aberdeen's – goalkeeper] was half-sitting on it with an expression that told me straightaway there was a serious problem.

'He's lost his contact lens.'

Jock said it in a way that suggested he was assuming I had known about the lenses and hadn't told him. I swear I had absolutely no idea that Jim used them. I was so dumbfounded and there was such a swirl of anger and embarrassment going through me that at first I didn't say a word. When I did speak it was to ask him if it would be better to take the second lens out and play without any. 'I wouldn't be able to see the ball,' he told us. That meant we had to put Alan Rough in goal for the second half . . .

As everybody knows, we didn't lose the match. With ten minutes left, David Speedie was going through on a ball when it bounced up and hit David Phillips on the arm and we were given a penalty. The contact was accidental but it was blatant handball and the Dutch referee, Mr Keizer, did not hesitate over the decision. Davie Cooper stayed cool and directed the ball low away to Neville Southall's left and into the corner of the net and we were on our way to the next summer's World Cup finals in Mexico.

When the equaliser went in, Jock didn't say a word. Shortly afterwards the referee blew for a free kick but Jock thought it was the full-time whistle. There were actually a couple of minutes to go but the Big Man rose to move towards Mike England, the

Wales manager. Jock was annoyed about a lot of the stuff England had been quoted as saying about the Scotland team and I am sure the idea was to go across and say, 'Hard luck, son.' It would have been a touch of the old sharp-edged commiserations, doing things right by letting Mike know he didn't fancy somebody running off at the mouth. But as he rose from the bench he stumbled. I had been keeping an eye on him throughout the second half and when he began to fall I grabbed for him and shouted to Hughie Allan to do the same. The doctor joined us and the medics came out of the tunnel immediately. Hughie and I held him up until the others took over and helped him inside. I went back to the bench and at the end of the game I told the players to stay on the pitch. We didn't know whether Jock was in the dressing-room or what was happening. We were given the signal that it was all right to go in and when we asked how he was the first impression we received was that he was recovering. There were no real celebrations in the dressing-room but I felt reassured enough to start saying 'well done' to the players and telling them that the Boss had suffered a heart attack but was going to be all right. Everything appeared to be OK and when I was told I would have to deal with the press, I was starting to warm to that job. Some of the reporters had been a bit critical of Jock and I was relishing addressing a few words to them. But when I came out I saw Graeme Souness at the door of the medical room and he was crying.

'I think he's gone,' Graeme said. I couldn't believe it.

THE PATTER, 1985
Michael Munro

Following the success of Stanley Baxter's Parliamo Glasgow, *Michael Munro published* The Patter: A Guide to Current Glasgow Usage, *which remains essential for daily discourse. Described dismissively by the* Scottish National Dictionary *as 'impoverished and bastardised Scots', Glaswegian is a unique and dynamic tongue with its own extensive vocabulary and distinctive grammar. Students of language have suggested that Irish immigrants may have influenced its development. Another significant influence may have been the author John Joy 'J.J.' Bell (1871–1934), whose incredibly popular novel* Wee Macgreegor *(1902) and its sequels are replete with Glaswegianisms. The language, if such it is, is remarkable for its 'notorious' glottal stop and the absence of the initial 'th' which has a tendency to change 'that' to ''at' and 'there' to ''err'.*

Arab In Glasgow this has been a term of abuse since even before the rise of the oil sheikhs: 'Get lost ya Arab ye!'

bampot *or* **bamstick** An idiot, fool, or sometimes a nutcase. This is often shortened to **bam**, and any eccentric named Thomas risks being dubbed 'Tam the Bam'.

coup *or* **cowp** To spill, overturn, or dump: 'I've couped a pint over my good denims', 'The big eejit couped the table ower', 'You're no meant tae coup yer rubbish here.' A **coup** is a dump or rubbish tip. It can also be applied insultingly to an untidy place: 'His bedroom's a right coup.'

Dan A nickname for a Roman Catholic: 'Are you a Billy or a Dan?'

electric soup Vivid term for a mixture of meths and red biddy as drunk by alcoholic down-and-outs.

finger Often pronounced to rhyme with singer.

gaun A local pronunciation of go on. Used on its own or with an insulting name it is a term of rude dismissal: 'Gaun ya daft eejit ye!' **Gaun yersel** is a phrase of encouragement or approval, perhaps coming from football in the sense of a player making a lone run. I was once present at a rally in Queen's Park which was addressed by Tony Benn. Amidst the applause and cheering that followed his speech a wee Glasgow wifie was heard to cry: 'Gaun yersel Mr Bogeyman!'

hackit Ugly, unattractive, most often applied to girls: 'Chic got aff with the big blonde and Ah wis left wi her hackit wee mate.'

ile A Scots pronunciation of oil. The phrase **away for ile** means wasted, useless, finished, etc: 'His brain's away for ile.'

jiggin, the A dance: 'Are ye goin tae the jiggin the night?'

keepie-uppie Footballing game of juggling with the ball using feet, knees, head – anything other than hands. One of the legends attached to the Scotland–England fixture is that during Scotland's 1967 Wembley victory Scotland's dominance of the World Cup holders was so complete that Jim Baxter was able to play keepie-uppie with the ball.

laldy To **give someone laldy** is to give him a thrashing or a beating. To **give it laldy** is to do something vigorously or enthusiastically: 'The band's been givin it laldy the night.'

mince Mysteriously enough this prosaic word for humble fare has blossomed into one of the most versatile words in the dialect. It is used to mean nonsense, rubbish: 'Yer heid's full a mince', 'He talks a lot a mince'. It is also a general term for anything unpleasant that finds its way to somewhere it shouldn't be: 'The back a ma jeans is aw mince!' Extremes of denseness are also measured by it: 'He's as thick as mince.' Someone who is listless or lacking in animation may attract a comment like: 'What's up wi you? Ye're sittin there like a pun a mince.' If a person succeeds in spoiling something for someone else, taking the wind out of someone's sails, etc., he might say: 'That's sickened his mince for him.'

nippy-sweetie A jocular term for a drink of spirits: 'How about a nippy-sweetie to finish off?' Also used to describe a bad-tempered person: 'Just keep out of that yin's road; she's a bit of a nippy-sweetie.' The derivation is from the sense of nippy meaning sharp-tasting, burning to the taste, etc.

ooyah An exclamation of pain: 'Ooyah! Get aff ma fit!'

plootered Drunk.

quoted Well-quoted means highly-regarded, well-esteemed: 'I hear the challenger's well-quoted.' **Not quoted** means given no chance, unimportant or useless: 'Never mind what that balloon thinks – he's no quoted.'

run-out To **do a run-out** is to eat a meal in a restaurant and then abscond without paying; a most unsavoury practice.

scratcher One's bed: 'Ach, Ah'll away tae ma scratcher.'

Teddy Bears Nickname for Rangers FC. The fact that this is rhyming slang becomes clear when you know that Bears is pronounced Berrs and thus rhymes with Gers.

urny Local version of aren't, as in 'Youse urny gaun', 'We urny comin', 'They urny here'.

vicky A local term for a rude V-sign: 'We gied them the vicky an got aff wur mark.'

wee man A friendly title for a small person: 'Look who it is – how's it gaun wee man?' Someone wishing to register disgust, amazement, exasperation, etc. without resorting to profanity may say: 'Aw in the name a the wee man!' Perhaps this is a euphemism for the Devil.

yin A local form of one: 'That yin's mines.' It can be applied to a person ('She'll come to no good, that yin') and is often used in nicknames or terms of address, as in **big yin, wee yin, auld yin, young yin.** The fact that Billy Connolly is known as The Big Yin has occasioned some confusion down south and I remember hearing him introduced by an English TV announcer as the big *Yin*. No doubt millions assumed this was some kind of derogatory term for a Scotsman.

THE MATTER OF SHIRT-TAILS, 1989
Anne Simpson

For a city that has long had a reputation for dreariness, Glasgow is surprisingly fashion conscious. The phrase 'dressed to kill' may be ambiguous but it is one Glasgow men and women embrace in a manner that makes the rest of Scotland look like scruffs. For men, a sharp suit, a loud tie and a Borsalino fedora are just the ticket, even if it makes them look like one of Al Capone's gunslingers. Women are even more apt to put on the style. Come the weekend, they are to be seen wandering around the designer boutiques of the Merchant City trying desperately to stay aloft in heels so high they turn midgets instantly into giraffes. Moreover, when the thermometer plunges, they would rather discard clothes than add layers. Necklines plunge, hems rise and the bling is blinding. This is not a new phenomenon but, as Anne Simpson notes in this piece from The Glasgow Herald Book of Glasgow, *it became more noticeable towards the end of the 1980s, when there was influx of French and Italian labels. Until then, no one surely would have dared to call Glasgow effete. Theda Bara, by the way, was a star of the silent screen and one of cinema's earliest sex symbols.*

Now this may surprise you, while the English businessman abroad is still too often identified by a certain seedy fatigue about the waistline, the Scotsman, or more specifically the Glaswegian, emerges, in any pinstripe throng, as elegant and taut, the owner of twenty shirts in fashionable working order, the possessor of a fine gold chain around his neck and on his wrist, most probably, a Rolex denoting upward mobility in in circles highly serious about time. These are not the ramblings of a deranged fashion writer but the findings of various solid market research studies carried out over recent years on behalf of the British menswear industry. At its most detailed such data reveals not just the Glaswegian's superiority in the matter of shirt tails – the average man here owns more than his equivalent brother anywhere else in Britain – but also the sparkling role ornamentation plays in his life. No matter how discreet, his cuff-links are meant to be observed.

Glasgow, of course, has always dealt brazenly in superlatives, sending shivers of disapproval down Edinburgh's prim spine. Yet one leading jeweller with outlets in both cities once disclosed that he lost more items through theft in the capital than he did forty miles away in the west. In general he suffered one break-in a month in Glasgow while in Edinburgh some costly bauble was lifted almost every week by professional gangs up from the South whose ultimate refinement was the elderly fur-coated lady acting as a decoy. In Glasgow the raw ebullience of smash-'n'-grab prevailed. But while Edinburgh men disguise what they spend on clothes by sheltering in the safe tradition of tweeds and sober suits, Glasgow men listen to the language of fashion, its code of status signals, and rapidly respond. Does all this prancing around, this looking sharp in the definitive leather blouson or the draped Numero Uno jacket suggest that effetism is now sweetening Glasgow's macho armpit? Who can be sure? But much has changed utterly and much has to do with a new attitude of mind which doesn't ask men to become dandies but requires that they be less repressed about sensuality and self-expression.

Among Glasgow's daughters, of course, visual panache has always been the thing. Long before the city's remarkable revival, Recession Chic cohabited here quite naturally with multiple deprivation. By cultivating a strong, personal style, Glasgow women defied their turf's ugly reputation. Keeping up appearances welded body and soul together and thus the city of the hard shoulder became the city of the fast turnover, one of the first centres in Britain to sustain two mobbed Marks and

Spencers, two bustling C & A's. So this battered old place became the rag trade's lingering *amour*, meticulously coiffed and enamelled, ready to strut through the dark with all the beckoning relish of sin. The other night a raven-haired girl in a silk romper suit and black stockings was seen running for a Springburn bus. Scoffing chips from a poke, she appeared like some wild alliance between Theda Bara and a kindergarten. Where had she been, this self-regarding *ingénue*? Fury Murry's . . . the Sub Club . . . shaping with her pals in all that pagan House music, practising her panda-eyed gaze and desire to look silently profound?

Today new money seeks the pedigree of international labels from The Warehouse, Ichi Ni San and Princes Square. Mappin and Webb in Glasgow sell a Rolex at around £2,000 practically every day of the week. Sax is the only shop in Scotland to stock Romeo Gigli and through the adventurous buying spirit of David Mullane at The Warehouse, Jean-Paul Gaultier, the most anarchic designer in Paris, can claim to have a Scottish chapter in the Merchant City.

Much tested in resilience, Glasgow's earthiness is never likely to allow *poseurs* to gain the upper hand. Even so one already detects certain little *arriviste* snobberies, a sniffy suspicion that in fashion (as in the general arts) the only good things are those that are imported. This is the reverse of that tedious London myopia about anything north of NW1 and equally as ill-founded. In fact it does nothing except mark out the truly provincial, but more seriously it also puts at risk the very creative possibilities of those indigenous designers whose talent requires sustained investment rather than the smug tokenism of ineffectual start-up grants.

GLASGOW'S MILES DAVIS, 1989
David Belcher

Is – was? – Glasgow, music-wise, the new Liverpool? Or Manchester? There is surely a case to be made. The city's musical heritage is, of course, illustrious. Did not Chopin play here? Indeed, he did, in the Merchant City in 1848, a year before he expired. Alas, few turned out to witness his performance and one ungenerous report noted that he was 'a man of weak constitution and seems labouring under physical debility and ill-health'. More recently, in 1990, Frank Sinatra wowed the crowd even though he too, then in his seventies, was unable to perform at the highest level. As music journalist David Belcher points out in this extract from The Glasgow Herald Book of Glasgow, *as the Year of Culture approached, Glasgow was in the grip of a 'rockbiz' resurgence which, a quarter of a century on, shows no sign of abating.*

Beware, children, of those who would adopt the authentic, multi-hued mantle of cred and try to tell you where to go in pursuit of the hippest, hip-hoppiest pleasures after sundown. Shun those who would claim to know what's ah, shakin' out there on the street and on the dancefloor, who would insist that they are in tune with 'The Kids'. Anyone who claims to be able to tell you all about the clubs has not been enjoying himself in any of them sufficiently enough to know whether or not they are worth attending. Me? I'm just going to give you a few gnomic pointers: like most of the rest of 'The Kids', I spend the bulk of my time re-inventing myself at home in private, not paying £5 admission to try and do it in public, in the dark, over someone else's choice of pounding beat. Bomp-bomp, bompitty-bomp, excuse me, I feel my head spinning . . . spinning . . .

Glasgow's Miles Davis: there isn't one, we'd have told him to learn how to play in tune. Glasgow's Miles Kington: nope, there isn't one of those either, far too consciously-absurd and clever-clever. Glasgow's Miles better . . . ah, yes, my head is clearing and I remember that line from somewhere . . . what does it mean again? While the city of Glasgow is in many and varied ways miles better than it was (rather than actually being better than anywhere else), in what might be termed youth culture (whatever that is), Glasgow is simply miles better than most places in the rest of Britain, outside London.

If youth culture is how young people address one another, dress, enjoy themselves, measure one another, chart their aspirations, articulate their desires, and pretend to be more youthful than they are, then Glasgow has got a lot of it. Not the most inventive, innovative, or original brands of youth culture, but lots of it, lots definitely and derivatively if not definitively, most of it music-related. Glasgow presently likes to think of itself, with some justification, as Rock City, UK. To employ rockbiz parlance, Glasgow-based bands such as Wet Wet Wet, the Blue Nile, Deacon Blue, Hue and Cry, the Silencers, the River Detectives, and Texas, have all, along with émigrés like Simple Minds, done mega-business in the charts.

Quite why there are so many bands from Glasgow, more bands than from any other UK city of comparable size, is one question (as is their quality): what is indisputable is that rock music, live or recorded, plays a vital practical role in the city's perception of itself and in its cultural identity. We rock, therefore we do not have to seek unavailable joinery apprenticeships which we did not want in any case. We rock because we might as well, because in the post-industrial first city of Europe we stand more chance of getting a number one hit single than we do of securing gainful long-term employment as a warehouseman or invoice clerk.

DIARY OF A SHOP ASSISTANT, 1989
Ajay Close

Shopping is something Glaswegians approach with the utmost seriousness and for which they prepare appropriately. It is an event, like the storming of the Bastille. Over the decades, the epicentre of bargain hunters and fashion victims has changed. Time was when Argyle Street was where those who had money to burn flocked. Later, Sauchiehall Street was retail heaven, and to some extent it still is. More recently, however, Buchanan Street has become the prime location. As you stand at its top, on the steps of the Concert Hall, you look down on a sea of adrenalin-fuelled humanity which belies any notion of recession or retrenchment. For while Edinburghers may put their money into property – preferring to inherit clothes, even undergarments, rather than purchase new items – Glaswegians display their wealth on their backs. Christmas, of course, is when the shops hope to do their best business. In 1989, journalist and novelist Ajay Close spent four days at John Lewis experiencing what it feels like to be on the other side of the counter. What follows is her account of day three.

9 a.m.

Christmas is high season for crime, so I am assigned to Store Security (sensitive to police teasing, they avoid the term detective). As security manager, David Macklin (known among Glasgow's shoplifting fraternity as 'Carrot') is responsible for everything from ejecting mischief-making children to arresting light-fingered drug addicts. None of this compares with the trauma of having to shut out customers at 5 p.m. on Christmas Eve. 'Suddenly you're the most unpopular man in Glasgow.'

He encounters every type of criminal, from Dippers (pickpockets) to professional shoplifters who make a handsome living out of store theft. 'They steal anything of value: from top of the range £300 to £400 suits, down to a £20 bottle of perfume. You can pick the good ones, they'll come in clean-shaven, with a smart suit – perhaps Christian Dior – but you look at their shoes and you know,' he says. 'Their heels are worn down.' ??? 'Have you ever tried to steal a pair of shoes?' Then there are the regulars: Shorty, Gumsy – who takes his false teeth out in a vain attempt at disguise – and the Salmon Man, bane of the Food Hall, who only steals tinned fish. In an average day the team spots 30–35 of them on the video monitors, fed by overhead cameras which a surprising number of thieves assume to be dummies. Drug addicts, known as desperadoes, are a major problem, accounting for 75 out of the 180 prosecutions this year. Every store detective dreads having a needle pulled on him.

Not everyone is prosecuted. 'We've got nothing to achieve by putting 60 and 70-year-olds into court. You could kill a person of that age,' he says. 'It can cause a lot of bad publicity for the store: "Granny shoplifting takes a stroke and dies – security man last seen heading for the Costa del Sol" . . .'

12.30 p.m.

I grab my coat and take a tour round the store with Aileen, a former sales assistant who moved sideways into security. Dressed in jeans and an outdoor jacket, she mingles convincingly with the customers, although the regulars aren't fooled. On the streets of Glasgow it is not unknown for them to say hello and offer to buy her a drink.

Since Lewis's insists on three months' training before security staff are unleashed on the shop floor, mine is strictly a watching brief. I listen for unfamiliar accents and keep my eyes peeled for prams (which can have false bottoms), duvet anoraks (perfect for poacher's pockets), big carrier bags and sports holdalls. Amazingly, given this list, they insist they have never stopped a genuine customer. A common trick is for men to take two suits into the changing room and come out with one (embarrassing if you're caught in the cubicle next door, peeking under the partition to see if the suspect is tucking a pair of trousers into his socks). Hiding booty up a jumper is another favourite. ('You get women coming in and the next time you see them they're nine months pregnant.') 'Watch their eyes and their hands,' Aileen advises. 'Everything else about them is normal.'

Unfortunately, I find it difficult enough to negotiate the crystalware displays and avoid toppling shelvesful of stuffed hippos in wedding dresses without having to spot shoplifters as well. After countless top-to-bottom tours of the store, all I have to show for my efforts is a mysterious ache in my kidneys.

3 p.m.
Christmas Stationery. Underneath a speaker blaring out jazzed-up carols, I am instructed to tidy the card racks. I soon know just how Sisyphus felt. For some reason, no slot contains an equal number of cards and envelopes. In the time it takes me to straighten one row, another three are messed-up. Periodically I am asked if we have a card specifically for a boss/nephew and wife/cousin and husband. I rifle through cards for mothers, fathers, brothers, sisters, aunts, uncles, in-laws – every permutation of human bonding except the one the customer wants.

If by some miracle I find the right relation, the rhyme inside is unsuitable. One woman looking for a card 'to a special brother and his wife' isn't keen on: *Here's a Xmas wish for you/With more love than before/To bring you happiness on this day/And throughout the year in store.* I take her point. Still, it's preferable to *It's Xmas, so let's make music together: you shake your maracas and I'll play with my organ.*

I go home to a nightmare about mismatched envelopes and wake with a stabbing pain between my shoulder blades.

À LA MODE, 1990
Roy Jenkins

One of the 'Gang of Four' who left the Labour Party in 1981 for the newly-formed Social Democratic Party – the others were Shirley Williams, David Owen and Bill Rodgers – Roy Jenkins (1920–2003) won Hillhead from the Conservatives in a by-election the following year. Though he subsequently lost the seat, he retained his affection for Glasgow and when he entered the House of Lords took the title Baron Jenkins of Hillhead. He gave this paean to the Royal Philosophical Society of Glasgow to mark the city's year as European City of Culture.

There is only one word of warning that I must give to Glasgow. Glasgow has ridden high on a mounting wave of fashion in the 1980s. It amuses me to look back over the change in the outside perception of Glasgow during the period that I have been closely associated with the city. When I became Member of Parliament for Hillhead in 1982 I derived a lot of pleasure from surprising people all over the world with the wholly accurate information that my Glasgow constituency was, according to the census, the most highly educated in the whole of the United Kingdom. And I added for good measure that, while it was geographically only one-eleventh of the City of Glasgow, it contained at least fifteen institutions or monuments of major cultural, intellectual or architectural fame. That was all in the days before the Burrell Collection was open. The Burrell (not in Hillhead but three miles away on the South Side), while it is a fine heterogeneous collection, housed in perhaps the best building for a gallery created anywhere in the past quarter-century, adds to what was previously in the Kelvinside Gallery and other Glasgow collections before but does not qualitatively change it. 1982 was also the beginning of the 'Glasgow's Miles Better' slogan, and before there was much thought of Glasgow being either an important centre of aesthetic tourism or the European City of Culture.

What has changed since then has been that for three or four years everybody has come to accept these earlier facts without the previous surprise, while for me the sad fact amongst them is that Hillhead has ceased to be my constituency. My warning is that fashion is a fickle jade. Glasgow has been tremendously *à la mode* for the past five years. But *la mode*, by its very nature, cannot remain constant. Last week, for the first time in my experience, someone said to me that he thought Glasgow had achieved an exaggerated reputation, and went on to add that he thought Edinburgh – admittedly he lived these – was the cultural as well as the political capital of Scotland. I rocked on my heels in amazement. No one had said such a thing to me for years.

I do not happen to believe that it is true. Edinburgh has of course great cultural assets, the Festival, the National Gallery of Scotland, the Portrait Gallery, and the copyright library, but they are none of them strictly indigenous. They come from outside or by virtue of capital status rather than arise out of the life of and work of the inhabitants of the city itself, as is the case here. None the less, I think Glasgow must be prepared for the going to be a little harder in future. Having caught and mounted the horse of fashion in the early eighties and dashingly ridden it for seven years or so, Glasgow must be ready for its vagaries soon to take the horse veering off in another direction . . .

When in 1982 I first came to know Glasgow well, and in particular its West End, what most struck me was not so much the warmth as the quiet self-confidence. It was not a complacent or narrow or inward-looking self-confidence. It was not based on a desire to keep strangers out, or I would not have been made nearly so welcome. What it was based on was a consciousness of the contribution which this strip of river and hills had made to the advancement of civilisation throughout and beyond Britain, and on a feeling that while it was desirable to go outside the West End from time to time it was as good a place to live as anywhere in the world. It was based neither on complacency nor on any sense of compensating for inferiority, but, as true self-confidence always is, on a desire to learn of outside things accompanied by a contentment within one's own skin. That is the dominant impression that I retain of Hillhead and of Glasgow as a whole.

A PINT OF TENNENT'S, 1993
Bill Bryson

Ever wondered what it must feel like to be an alien in Glasgow? Or an American? That's the impression one has of Bill Bryson, who arrived in Glasgow towards the end of a tour of Britain in 1993. Not only did it feel foreign, it sounded it. This was not his first visit. He had been two decades earlier, when no one beat a path to its door. In the intervening years, however, it had been transformed, or so it appeared. Grimy buildings had been sand-blasted, Princes Square had been built and the Burrell Collection had been opened. Moreover, 'In 1990, Glasgow was named European City of Culture, and no one laughed.' What hadn't changed was the argot. *Apologising to a taxi driver for not speaking Glaswegian, Bryson was told: 'D'ye dack ma fanny?' Later he got lost in the Gorbals and decided to seek refuge in a pub. There have been worse ideas, but not many . . .*

I wandered along a series of back lanes and soon found myself in one of those dead districts that consist of windowless warehouses and garage doors that say NO PARKING – GARAGE IN CONSTANT USE. I took a series of turns that seemed to lead even further away from society before bumbling into another short street that had a pub on the corner. Fancying a drink and a sitdown, I wandered inside. It was a dark place, and battered, and there were only two other customers, a pair of larcenous-looking men sitting side by side at the bar drinking in silence. There was no one behind the bar. I took a stance at the far end of the counter and waited for a bit, but no one came. I drummed my fingers on the counter and puffed my cheeks and made assorted puckery shapes with my lips the way you do when you are waiting . . . I cleaned my nails with a thumbnail and puffed my cheeks some more, but still no one came. Eventually I noticed one of the men at the bar eyeing me.

'Hae ya nae dook ma dooky?' he said.

'I'm sorry,' I replied.

'He'll nay be doon a mooning.' He hoiked his head in the direction of a back room.

'Oh, ah,' I said and nodded sagely, as if that explained it.

I noticed that they were both still looking at me.

'D'ye hae a hoo and a *poo*?' he repeated. It appeared that he was a trifle intoxicated.

I gave a small apologetic smile and explained that I came from the English-speaking world.

'D'ye nae hae in May?' the man went on. 'If ye dinna dock ma donny.'

'Doon in Troon they croon in June,' said his mate, then added: 'Wi' a spoon.'

'Oh, ah.' I nodded thoughtfully again, pushing my lower lip out slightly, as if it was all very clear to me now. Just then, to my small relief, the barman appeared, looking unhappy and wiping his hands on a tea towel.

'Fuckin muckle fucket in the fuckin muckle,' he said to the two men, and then to me in a weary voice: 'Ah hae the noo.' I couldn't tell if it was a question or a statement.

'A pint of Tennent's, please,' I said hopefully.

He made an impatient noise, as if I were avoiding his question. 'Hae ya nae hook ma dooky?'

'I'm sorry?'

'Ah hae the noo,' said the first customer, who apparently saw himself as my interpreter.

I stood for some moments with my mouth open, trying to imagine what they were saying to me, wondering what mad impulse had bidden me to enter a pub in a district like this, and said in a quiet voice: 'Just a pint of Tennent's, I think.'

The barman sighed heavily and got me a pint. A minute later, I realised that what they were saying to me was that this was the worst pub in the world in which to order lager since all I would get is a glass of warm soap suds, dispensed from a gasping, reluctant tap, and that really I should flee with my life while I could. I drank two sips of this interesting concoction, and, making as if I were going to the Gents, slipped out a side door.

'WILLIE LYNCH IS NO' A GRASS', 1996
Nick Danziger

Few writers spend as much time getting to know a place as Nick Danziger. Fewer still are prepared to venture into those bleak backwaters that are well off the tourist trail. Glasgow's East End has long had an unenviable reputation but as Danziger reveals, there are within its insalubrious precincts individuals, many of whom are women, who are doing what they can to get by and make of life what they can. The streets described here are of the meanest, where drugs, violence and theft are endemic. Few

Glaswegians, let alone foreigners, ever visit them. They are Glasgow's equivalent of what in Paris are called 'banlieus', vast high-rise housing estates with few amenities, and even fewer reasons to linger.

I left the far north of Scotland in July, having discovered that social intimacy comes at the price of privacy: everybody knows your business. The day I arrived in Glasgow the rotting body of a pensioner was found in his flat eight months after he died. Neighbours hadn't seen the quiet eighty-two-year-old for months, but no one had reported him missing. Council officials only took an interest in Malkie when his rent fell into arrears and they moved to evict him. When police battered down his door the Christmas cards were still on the mantelpiece.

It is difficult to speak of Glasgow. In 1990 it found new prestige as the cultural centre of Europe, but at first sight it is not a pleasant place, this sprawling metropolis with its grim tenements and claustrophobic closes. For many Glaswegians it is not cheerful, or easy, or safe, or reasonable; it is, however, a passionate place, where both young and old, the hopeful and the disillusioned, find a life constantly on the edge. The city breathes with a vitality like no other city in Britain. In this Glasgow has much in common with New York.

I drove into Christine's close at a snail's pace, through toddlers playing in the street oblivious to the traffic. As I pulled my bag out of the car a young man called up to a third-floor window, 'Do you want any rugby balls?' In Newcastle they were known as jellies or wobbly eggs because of their soft centre; here the prescription sleeping pill Temazepam is also nicknamed after its shape. I was soon to discover that this drug was almost as popular as oxygen.

Appearances can be deceptive. Christine's sandstone tenement in the East End is framed by a thin border of pleasant shrubs, but a steady stream of young drug addicts, both men and women, use the pavement for making their deals. They are rarely older than their late twenties, and often as young as fifteen and sixteen. In Christine's presence they were not malicious, and they often asked her, as a former local community activist, for advice on rehabilitation centres.

When I telephoned Christine ahead of my arrival she asked me, 'Wherr ur gawn tae stop?' I wasn't sure. Less than two miles out of Glasgow city centre, there were no boarding houses or hotels. When I said I would find something in town she told me off. 'Ach don't annoy me! You're gawn tae stay with me.'

'What about your son?' She lived in a compact two-bedroom flat.

'Duncan is in Tenerife and is no home till Saturday week and Alistair lives with Patricia and the wean.'

So I pitched up with a bottle of malt whisky, knowing that with this pillar of strength in the community, who had enough energy and bounce to make an active person dizzy, there wouldn't be a dull moment. I was not to be disappointed.

Christine is one of those larger-than-life figures like so many women I was to meet in Glasgow. Like many of them, too, she had discovered the nation is too big to look after the little things and too small to take care of the big things. Like more and more people living in small communities, Christine was one of those who recognised and dealt with problems at a local level without recourse to the state. Politics had, in her words, become like the supermarkets, 'More for less'. She took her battles to the male-dominated local councils, which she saw as impenetrably bureaucratic and chauvinist as well as hopelessly irrelevant and out of touch with the day-to-day reality of local people. She had won battles to help set up a creche, a drugs advice centre and a family flat for young children and their parents. The women were the driving force, but success also bred resentment, petty jealousies and envy, particularly from men who were out of work. When the women had fought successfully for funds to set up support groups, the men wanted a piece of the action; they wanted to be given the job of running them.

Having helped set up the community's self-help groups, Christine had moved on to working with street women. At the end of the week, after four two o'clock to midnight days, she was ready to try and obliterate her clients' harrowing lives from her mind; but, as I was to discover, everyone knew Christine and wherever she went they brought their troubles to her. She had, however, learnt to set the problems to one side and allow herself to have a good time.

'Tonight we're rockin',' she said soon after I arrived at her place. 'It's Patricia my daughter-in-law's twenty-fifth birthday and we're goin' to the pub to meet Catherine, Jenny, Olive and Little Frances. I hope you dain't mind.'

'Why should I mind?'

'They're only women, no men.'

As we prepared to go to the pub, her son Alistair came banging at the door. 'Where's my fookin' giro?'

'Sorry, Alistair?'

'Where's my fookin' giro?' he screamed. He stormed into the flat, took one look at me. 'Meet Nick, Alistair,' said Catherine.

'Fook you.'

'Leave me alone.'

Alistair left the flat cursing his mother. 'Bitch! Cunt! Fucking cow! Liar!'

His wiry bicycle-frame of a body was spry and wan, and he looked older than his twenty-eight years. For years he had been abusing his body with sachets of smack and capsules of jellies.

'I wish he were dead. I don't want him to die. I love him because I'm his ma, but I don't like him. Can you understand that? I'm so tired, he must be so tired.' Christine had lived through a marriage to a violent husband and had two sons who were like chalk and cheese. One had inherited the violence of her deceased husband, fuelled by an addiction that had driven him to steal her wedding ring; the other son, Duncan, was as polite, supportive and helpful as could be dreamed. 'Alistair has his father's insane jealousy. If I'd had an argument with his da or a fight he'd go out and hit someone out of spite. I had a girlfriend to stay last month and Alistair accused her of being a lesbian. He smashed her car window and slashed her tyres.' I cringed at the thought of my borrowed car parked right outside her tenement and I had reason to be worried: the neighbour found his new car's tyres slashed the following morning.

When Patricia came to collect us, she was agitated. She knew Alistair as well as her mother-in-law did, and yet she continued to show unstinting devotion to her husband. As Christine readied herself, Patricia confessed that, 'The best birthday present from Alistair would be if he went away for eight weeks. I hardly ever get a shag, he's so wasted. And I'm afraid to be out at the pub because I'm worried about leaving the wean in his care.' The two women joked about his behaviour: Christine laughed off the threats Alistair made whenever he saw her drinking in a pub with a male friend, and Patricia did an imitation of Alistair promising to give up his habit. She called to Christine in the bathroom. 'Are you using that new mouthwash I bought you?'

'It's not mouthwash I need, it's sheep dip.'

We left the tenement and passed the teenagers in scrums on street corners hustling their deals. We passed the railings to the factor's office hung with bunches of flowers in memory of Willie Lyle, victim of a gangland execution two days before in broad daylight in the middle of the street. An official sign on the factor's door read, 'A look on the bright side of town.' Daubed on a wall close by were the words: 'Willie Lyle is a grass' and 'Willie Lyle is a police snout'. I read some of the cards on the bouquets: 'Proud to be your pal', 'All the lads from the Apple' (local wine alley), and 'You were many things, but never a grass'.

Glasgow is a tale of two cities, 'Cathlicks and Proddies', Celtic and Rangers, Green and Blue. Christine looked at several of the bouquets. 'It's terrible,' she said. 'Even in death they won't leave it alone', pointing to the orange lilies tied with red, white and blue ribbon. 'Willie would have liked that and laughed.' Everyone knew Willie Lyle and in the pubs they were still talking about his death, but the dozens of witnesses weren't talking to the police.

'He'd gie his last penny,' said Catherine over a pint.

'It wasn't his money, he'd robbed it,' said Christine.

'I was staring down the barrel of a gun. Two men in masks – I thought it was a joke. I thought they were raising money for charity. I put my hand in my purse for a couple of quid. Realised they were for real. Jenny started shouting at one of them. I realised one of them was Willie. Afterwards I told him, don't you ever point a gun at me. He said, "You know I would never have pulled the trigger." You never know, and his partner who had the gun at Jenny is a fucking psycho. He's in Barlinnie for murder.'

I went to the bar to buy a round of drinks. The barman wouldn't take my English £10 note. 'We don't take £10 and £20 English notes, there are too many sniders floating around.'

'But I don't have any Scottish money,' I pleaded.

'Are you from New York, the city that never sleeps? Ha, try changing Scottish money in the Big Apple.'

As we talked, the pub filled. Like all the pubs I was to visit with Christine, the windows were bricked up and no natural light penetrated inside other than from the entrance. Men played snooker, others hung around the electronic gaming machines or watched the races on the television set while a steady stream of shoplifters hawked their merchandise. A man found no buyers for a pair of size eight brown suede shoes. An extremely attractive woman Christine worked with, who was facing five years for the possession of 932 jellies, offered several blouses and woollen skirts still on their hangers. Another had pairs of designer sunglasses: she crouched in a corner next to Christine in a foetal position, her young, pretty face ravaged by her addiction, with deeply drawn lines and hollow eyes. Christine tried to comfort her in the only way she knew, but the lure of the next fix was greater than Christine's powers of persuasion, and she disappeared into the ladies to keep her appointment with the needle. After the clothes and the accessories came other merchandise, including a joint of meat and bottles of perfume.

Catherine was one of the many who had witnessed Willie's murder. She had been shopping with her four- and six-year-old nieces.

'Willie left the factor's and was walking across the road, five guys started running after him. Willie started to run, he nearly got away, one of them got hold of his jacket. The first one slashed him across the stomach, the second into his neck, the third into his side, four of them kept stabbing, they screamed, "Willie Lyle grassing b—!" Sorry, I don't like swearing. The women in the street started shouting "Cowards!" They screamed, "Lyle, you're going to die, bastard!" God forgive me for swearing. It was all over in a second, so quick that when they ran off they knocked into my sister's two weans. I don't know what they saw. The lassie next to me said she knew first aid, but she was too scared to go over. I said, "hold my hand". He was lying in so much blood, his face was so white. I think he was still alive when the ambulance arrived, but I knew he was going to die. We took the weans home – one had blood on her dress. I recognised one of the murderers, he hangs around here, but I couldn't tell the polis, they'd get one of my family, George or someone else.' Catherine had witnessed four murders in sixteen years, including a mistake when the man they were aiming for jumped out of the way of the car that was to have run him down and it killed his girlfriend instead.

She had been a bus conductress, a wages clerk, a telephonist and a shop assistant. 'When I was a kid you could change jobs like changing your socks. Now I can't find work. I could have got redundancy if I hadn't left my last job to look after my dying husband. The supermarket closed when I wasn't working. I had worked there fifteen years. They want young women now, but I'm thinking of getting educated on computers.' We were interrupted by a young man who pulled a handful of vacuum-packs of smoked salmon out of his coat pocket. 'Half price for youse,' he touted and for the first time that afternoon there were takers.

Two foot soldiers from the Salvation Army were hawking their newspaper the *War Cry*. 'I'll give,' said Catherine, 'but when I'm giving I want to make sure it's going into the weans' bellies, not to the maggots. They're lining their pockets with thousands of pounds.

'Look at the way things are going. There's nothing for us. My granda sweated to build them ships. My granda worked for eleven and six a week. Now they've closed the yards. The great cranes along both banks of the Clyde are gone. The yuppies have moved in. I'm greetin'. There'll be anarchy, and I'll be honest with you, I'm for the anarchy, I hope there'll be trouble. I'm all for a revolution, there needs to be, to renew, to start again.

'The lottery is our only hope. The working classes need hope. Surviving is not enough! The only industries we've got left here is football and rock. And I'm no spending me money on lottery when they're giving £58 million to opera, to the fuckin' toffs. I'll pay for half a ticket, and I begrudge even that.'

Christine fetched a birthday cake that had been held behind the bar. Everyone sang 'Happy Birthday' and Patricia was about to start greetin'. 'I feel A bubble coming on.' As Patricia cut into the cake, Catherine told me, 'My first birthday cake was at forty-five. My da had a dumpling for my birthdays, and I've not yet been to a pantomime.'

Double-jointed, rail-thin Little Frances took to the pub floor and did an erotic snake dance, then used one of the pub's concrete pillars as a tango partner. We laughed so hard we nearly split our sides. Helen, Little Frances's sometimes partner, started to greet from helpless laughter. 'She's got no teeth, but she's shit hot.' And she was.

We all tumbled out of the pub at closing time. 'D'ye fancy a curry?' asked Christine.

'Yeah.'

'Right, c'mon.'

Christine, Patricia, Olive and I walked home. We passed a group of ten- and eleven-year-olds too busy skinning up on the steps of the Social Services to take notice of us. We ordered our curry at the Chinese takeaway which, like much of the neighbourhood, had been daubed with the words: WILLIE LYLE IS A GRASS.

I slept fitfully. As the sound of the traffic died down I could hear the children playing outside. Tin cans were being kicked, skateboards were being used to hurdle the curb. The night air was still, making the sounds all the more raw. A child screamed and another started crying. I lay there turning it over and over in my mind. How old could the child have been? Five, six, possibly seven years old. That child's bleating continues to haunt me.

Next morning I woke to the clatter of the police helicopter. It hovered over the tenements like a gigantic bee, moved this way and that, the beat of its rotor blades chopping against the sandstone walls. It hovered again, and eventually moved away – it had either found its prey or had moved on to another quarry.

Christine cooked me an enormous breakfast. There was a knock on the front door. 'That'll be Alistair coming to apologise for last night.'

Alistair stood in the hall, his emotions playing volcanically on his face. 'My giro! Where's my fucking giro!'

'Alistair,' she tried to reason with him. 'The post hasn't come.'

'You were out drinking in the pub last night.' Alistair accused her of talking to a man. 'Do you remember your marriage vows?'

'Yes,' Christine started to smile, but she daren't relax. '"Till death do us part." So there. You're father's dead.'

'But you're not dead.'

2001–

BLOW UP

SMEATON AS SUPERMAN, 5 JULY 2007

Lawrence Donegan

In the first terrorist attack on Scottish soil since the Lockerbie bombing in 1988, two men crashed their Jeep Cherokee loaded with propane canisters into the glass doors of the terminal of Glasgow International Airport. Among the first to react was John Smeaton, an off-duty baggage handler, who set about one of the terrorists with selfless zeal, for which he was awarded the Queen's Gallantry Medal. Later, he reflected: 'If any more extremists are still wanting to rise up and start trouble, know this: We'll rise right back up against you. New York, Madrid, London, Paisley . . . we're all in this together . . .'

When asked if he had a message for the bombers, John Smeaton, the baggage handler who helped thwart Saturday's 4x4 attack on Glasgow airport, said, 'This is Glasgow. We'll just set aboot ye.'

The city of Glasgow's marketing department, which has spent 20 years trying to obliterate Glasgow's 'No Mean City' reputation, might have winced at the sentiment. But the rest of the world was enchanted, and Scotland – and the internet – had found a new hero.

Smeaton confronted one of the men from the 4x4, who was fighting with a police officer. 'I got a kick in,' he said. 'Other passengers were getting kicks in. The flames were going in two directions . . . You know when you're younger, you put a can of Lynx [aftershave] on the fire, and it's like a flame thrower.' And: 'Me and other folk were just trying to get the boot in and some other guy banjoed him.' (To banjo is Scottish slang for to hit someone as hard as you can.)

Another day, another paean to the man: yesterday's contribution came from Michael Kerr, whose own efforts at tackling one of the would-be terrorists were rewarded with a couple of smashed teeth, a broken leg and a supporting role in a worldwide phenomenon henceforth known as Smeatomania. 'I flew at the guy a few times but he wouldn't go down. Then he punched me so hard he knocked my teeth out and sent me flying so hard I broke my leg,' Kerr said with a commendable lack of machismo. 'I landed next to the burning Jeep and thought it was going to explode. That was when John Smeaton dragged me to safety. He's a hero.'

With crews working hard yesterday to restore the fire-damaged terminal, it seems the moment might have passed for building a plinth and commissioning a statue of Smeaton. Nevertheless, some form of official recognition is surely on its way. Scotland's first minister, Alex Salmond, says so, and so does the *Scottish Sun,* which yesterday launched an in-your-face campaign to 'Give John a Gong'. (Rumours that the airport is to be renamed Smeaton International Airport appeared to be unfounded at time of going to press.)

Still, our hero has plenty of other things to occupy his mind while awaiting the call from the Palace, not least the demands that come with being the latest in a long line of everyman heroes delivered by Scotland to a grateful world, from William Wallace to Sean Connery.

In Australia, his remarks were broadcast accompanied by subtitles – the sort of accolade usually reserved for the likes of *Gregory's Girl* and *Trainspotting*. And on Fox News in the US, Smeaton has received the fawning treatment normally reserved for Dick Cheney.

It is a similar story in cyberspace, where a large corner of the internet is now devoted to the great man. One website gives visitors the chance to put a pint for Smeaton behind the bar of the Glasgow airport Holiday Inn. So far, 1,035 fans have taken up the offer. Elsewhere, the Photoshop enthusiasts have been hard at work. There is Smeato as Superman; Smeato as a Jedi knight; Smeato as Bruce Willis in *Die Hard*; Smeato as the man who made Osama bin Laden say, 'You told me John Smeaton was off on Saturdays!' Another shows Smeaton midair performing a flying kick with the words, 'This is Glesga, mate.'

Just one thing, though. The great man is not actually from Glasgow. He is from Erskine, a nice little suburb about 10 miles north of the city. Still, at this stage of the game, who in their right mind would want to argue with John Smeaton?

EARLY CLOSING TIME, 4 DECEMBER 2013
Sunday Herald

Late on a Friday night, a police helicopter crashed into the Clutha Vaults, a popular pub on the north bank of the Clyde, killing ten people and injuring many more. A subsequent inquiry confirmed that the tragedy was due to pilot error. Less than two years later the Clutha reopened.

The uncle of former Rangers player Steven Naismith became a reluctant hero when he went to the rescue of shocked revellers trapped in the crumbling building. Retired senior fire officer Douglas Naismith helped pull casualties to safety within minutes of the police helicopter crashing on to the pub roof but afterwards was too modest to speak about his actions.

He had been walking past the Clydeside pub with another retired fireman and immediately went to the aid of frantic drinkers who had been trapped when the roof collapsed. A friend said: 'Douglas just happened to be passing by with another experienced fire fighter. Instinct took over and he went straight into the building to help in the rescue operation and bring people out to safety. It was a brave thing to do, but it just came naturally to him. He definitely helped bring people out and ended up injuring himself by either fracturing his collar bone or dislocating his shoulder. But he took it in his stride.

'Douglas was a senior fire officer until he took early retirement. He had attended a lot of major incidents in his time. It just so happened he was walking by the pub with another retired colleague when it all happened.'

Former fire fighter Edward Waltham also ran into the pub to help with the rescue effort. He said: 'I helped grab a couple of people. One gentleman in particular was completely covered in dust, who had very shallow breathing and appeared to be quite badly injured. My initial reaction for him – from my experience – was to try not to move him because he had been in a crush situation. However, as we were lying there, other people were literally being pulled out of the pub and more or less thrown on top of us.'

Reveller Grace MacLean was inside The Clutha at the time of the crash and relived the horror when she said: 'There was a ska band on in the pub just at the back and it was fairly busy. We were all just having a nice time and then there was like a "whoosh" noise. There was no bang, there was no explosion, and then there was some smoke – what seemed like smoke. The band were laughing and we were all joking that the band had made the roof come down.

'They carried on playing and then it started to come down more and someone started screaming and then the whole pub just filled with dust. You couldn't see anything, you couldn't breathe. It was a real testament to the people of Glasgow. Everyone in that pub was shouting "Here's the door" – they were helping each other out.'

Another pub drinker caught up in the mayhem was Brendan Riordan who told how The Clutha had been 'packed' and said: 'It was quite hard to move in there with the amount of people enjoying the gig.' He remembered hearing 'a very loud bang' before a cloud of dust filled the pub and recalled: "I was on the right side of the pub where the band were performing and if you look at the pictures which have come out now, you will notice that the right side of the pub did not collapse. It was more the central bit and the left side.

'After I exited the pub I saw people coming out covered in blood and covered in dust. There were people quite desperate and just before I left the inside of the pub I noticed that the ceiling had fallen towards the bar. People were not aware that a helicopter had crash-landed on the pub.'

Esperanza, a nine-piece Glasgow band known for its high-tempo ska numbers, were playing when the helicopter crashed on to the roof of the pub. Band members managed to flee the scene unscathed and last night a management spokesman said: 'The band have made a collective decision not to do any interviews at this time. Hope you understand.'

Newspaper editor Gordon Smart watched in horror as the helicopter plummeted on top of the pub. The editor of the *Scottish*

Sun was 250 yards away from the crash scene in a car park when he spotted the helicopter. He said: 'It was just a surreal moment. It looked like it was dropping from a great height at a great speed.' Smart added: 'There was no fire ball and I did not hear an explosion. It fell like a stone. The engine seemed to be spluttering.'

GLASGOW SCHOOL OF ART, MAY 2014
Alan Taylor

Charles Rennie Mackintosh (1868–1928) is to Glasgow what Antoni Gaudí is to Barcelona, and the best evidence of his genius is Glasgow School of Art. It was the result of a competition held in 1896. In the early stages of planning and construction, there was no indication, or excitement, that the building would be anything special. Local papers, for example, were less than overwhelmed. 'The plans,' remarked one, 'are of the most complete description and embrace all recent ideas and improvements.' Another added: 'The building appears to be in every way suitable for the requirements of art education.' Encouraged by the School's energetic and ambitious head, Francis 'Fra' Newbery, who appreciated Mackintosh's talent, the result was a work of art and a place of work. Nevertheless, it took time for the 'Mac' to become an accepted and much-loved part of Glasgow's landscape. In particular, it has an emotional bond with those who have studied in its extraordinarily beautiful surroundings. Unlike other such buildings, the School of Art has always been a building to use as well as admire. In 2014, however, it was seriously damaged by a fire which, had it not been for the swift action of firefighters, would have led to its destruction. As it was, much of it did succumb, including its wonderful library.

A few days after the fire that threatened to reduce Glasgow School of Art to ash, I went to see for myself how bad the damage was. My trip took me up unlovely Sauchiehall Street into that part of the former Second City of Empire called Garnethill, at the summit of which, after an almost vertical ascent, is Charles Rennie Mackintosh's masterpiece. It was a morning remarkable for its dankness, the hills to the west enveloped in mist, the pavements greasy with drizzle. Access to the school's entrance was cordoned off and men in hard hats, steel toe-capped boots and fluorescent jackets hung around eating bacon rolls and slurping tea, while a photographer captured the scene. The air smelled nippily of barbecue. From the outside, the building looked to be in decent shape. Some stonework was blackened by smoke and many windows had been melted by the furnace. But to an untutored eye there appeared to be nothing that was beyond restoration.

As I looked, I was joined by a middle-aged couple. They were from Manchester, it transpired. Assuming them to be tourists, I said I was sorry they wouldn't be able to see inside the 'Mac', as it's fondly known. 'Oh, we know it well,' said the woman, 'our son's a sculpture student. He's in his final year. We came for his degree show. All his work's been destroyed.' Her lower lip quivered. Shortly after the fire broke out, she added, her son had called home, weeping copiously, in part because of the loss of his work, but also because of his fear for the future of the place where he had spent much of the last four years. Now he was in limbo, not knowing when or whether his degree might be awarded; and, if it was, what kind of a degree it would be.

There was not much I could say by way of consolation. In the hours after news of the fire broke, I heard from many people who had either studied at the Mac or taught there, or who simply loved the building, recognising in it that which is inspirational and irreplaceable. Rare for such an institution, it was open to the public and one often wandered in, marvelling anew at Mackintosh's inventiveness and thoughtfulness. What made it particularly special was its functionality, its user-friendliness, its ergonomics. It was designed not as a museum piece or a showcase but as a workshop which was to be subject daily to wear and tear. My daughter was a student there and whenever I visited she would take me on a tour, acting as if she were the chatelaine of Balmoral Castle. Others of its tenants said it was like being given permission to use a Ming vase in which to display daffodils or to have a Meissen porcelain plate on which to eat baked beans.

There was always something outside or inside the building to please the eye. No matter where you turned, it seemed that Mackintosh, who designed it in the first decade of the twentieth century, had anticipated your gaze and offered you the wherewithal to satisfy it. From the mullioned windows one could look across the urban sprawl of Glasgow to the countryside beyond. The internal perspective was no less beguiling. Everything in the Mac was designed by Mackintosh himself: light fittings, bookshelves, easels, rattan-cover chairs, magazine stands, desks and clocks. Even his rather Presbyterian basement lecture theatre drew admiration. Panelled with stained timber, it has long been the bane of students, most notably the narrowness of the benches on which they sat, leading some architectural historians to surmise that a century ago students' backsides must have been rather leaner. An accomplished artist himself, Mackintosh knew instinctively what was required. For him natural light was as essential as oxygen is to a scuba diver and it pours in at every opportunity. But equally important were private spaces, nooks and crannies and window seats where one could read and think and daydream free from interruption.

By common consent, the school's library was Mackintosh's *pièce de resistance*. I say 'was' because it is no more. Situated on the first floor, it must have been directly in the line of the flames, and while the firefighters arrived within four minutes of being summoned they were unable to save it. I remember it well. My friend Dugald Cameron, the Mac's erstwhile director, was ever eager to show it off. Dugald had been a student before he became a member of staff. As with Mackintosh, drawing is at the heart of his art. On our strolls he'd stop and examine a student's work, pointing out where it was on course or where it was going awry. Dugald draws trains and planes in forensic detail. His equivalent of Michelangelo's *David* is Concorde's engine or the Flying Scot's, and he brought to his exposition of Mackintosh the sensitivity of a Glaswegian whose memory of the heyday of the Clyde and its throbbing shipyards is still fresh. With Dugald, one is reminded that art schools are not just about turning out Turner Prize-winners, but also the designers of useful – and beautiful – objects and machines.

It was in the 'wondrous' library, Dugald recalled, that forty-five years ago he first met his wife Nancy, who had joined the school's staff as a librarian. Spatially, it was small, but it never struck me as such. Rather, as the editors of the Glasgow volume of *The Buildings of Scotland* series point out, the double-storeyed room had 'a decidedly Japanese character'. In less accomplished hands this might have felt fey or affected or pastiche; in Mackintosh's, the perfection of the proportions, the attention to detail and the play of light and dark make it the kind of place in which the drudgery is taken out of study. 'This is justly considered one of the finest rooms in Glasgow', *The Buildings of Scotland* editors concluded.

That it is no more is cause for national lamentation. All, however, is not lost. While the earliest generations of students never learned the name of the person who designed the building to which they were attached, that has not been the case for several decades. Consequently, the Mac and its furniture and fittings have been photographed endlessly and Mackintosh's drawings are all said to be extant. Once the insurers have examined the contracts, administrators will know how much money they have to begin the reconstruction. Meanwhile, the Scottish and British governments have indicated that they are ready to help when required.

What no one can say, though, is how long it may take to recreate what Mackintosh achieved in a few astonishing years and what fire destroyed in a matter of minutes. When I was told what had happened, I recalled the weekend I spent with the sculptor Kenny Hunter – a graduate of the Mac – at Maryhill Fire Station in the north of the city. He'd been commissioned to produce a sculpture of firefighters and had embedded himself with a number of them, the better to understand their job. It seemed like a good idea for a newspaper article and so I allowed myself to undergo some basic training and don a uniform. Glasgow, I soon discovered, is a highly inflammable city, especially on a Saturday night. Kenny's sculpture, which is called *Citizen Firefighter*, now stands outside Glasgow Central Station, in salute to those redoubtable men and women who take the heat on our behalf.

LET THE GAMES BEGIN, 24 JULY 2014
Hugh MacDonald

When the 2014 Commonwealth Games was awarded to Glasgow one thing was certain, that spectators and participants would receive the kind of embrace unique to a city which prides itself on wit and irreverence . . .

The city of Benny Lynch, the haven of the eternal wee man, has always punched above its weight. Glasgow last night took a small budget and came up with a big idea.

It is what Scots do. The land that brought the world penicillin, television, the square sausage, the Enlightenment, slagging as a way of declaring love, the novel, ships that sailed the world, quips that nailed the moment, modern engineering, the carry-oot and the philosophy of economics, toyed with the idea of a conventional opening ceremony in the way that Jim Baxter once played with an English midfield. It then gave it a body swerve.

Glasgow 2014 came up with a move that burst the net at a packed Celtic Park. It asked for financial generosity and matched that with a generosity of spirit that is part of the Scottish DNA. Arms of more than 40,000 spectators were raised inside the stadium, with mobile phones providing a glittering mosaic. Numbers were texted inside the ground and across the globe. Each message pledged £5 to Unicef, which had come together with Glasgow 2014 to save children's lives across the world. Early figures indicated that more than £2.5 million had been raised.

This spirit of charity was complemented by the themes of reconciliation with an imperial past and the promise that no one should fear a Scotland of the future. The most dramatic articulation of this act of faith came from Pumeza Matshikiza, the South African soprano whose rendition of Hamish Henderson's 'The Freedom Come All Ye' would be seen both as a hymn to liberty and an acceptance that the more sinister history of the Commonwealth has to be confronted before it can be consigned to the past.

There was the heady glamour of celebrity inside Celtic Park, but there was also sobering sentiment too. Billy Connolly, the greatest comedian in a city teeming with them, devoted his appearance to recalling the Clyde-built link forged with Nelson Mandela, the South African freedom fighter.

This, then, was an opening ceremony that was not content to entertain. It had a message of Glasgow gallusness and an undeniable theme of freedom from poverty, from illness, from the lingering fall-out from history. And it had Caledonian ambition. In the manner of John Logie Baird, Alexander Fleming, Sir Walter Scott, David Hume and Adam Smith, it sought to change the world.

A budget of approximately £20 million – about a quarter of that at the fabulous London Olympic ceremonies – was spent on a party that threatened to put the K of kitsch into kulture and kliché. But it all succeeded, though the Duke of Wellington, sitting in statue in the stadium with the mandatory cone on his head, might have observed: 'It was a damn close-run thing.' An early profusion of kilts, sporrans and Nessie was in danger of also putting the K in kringe. It was lightened by a self-deprecatory irony that saw cans of Irn-Bru holding up the Forth Bridge, a scattering of outsized Tunnock's teacakes littering the ground, and shortbread standing for the Callanish Stones.

John Barrowman, the darling of international audiences, was joined by Karen Dunbar, whose sincerity of welcome was moving, as was, oddly, the section that owed most to Danny Boyle's London extravaganza: the glimpses of the shipyards and their workers caused a craving for the Scotland of full employment and multiple trades.

The ceremony blossomed into something irreverent but strangely wonderful with Amy Macdonald kicking off a raucous 'Rhythm of My Heart' with a series of unlikely accompanists, including Rod Stewart. There was even a ballet version of The Proclaimers' 'I'm Gonna Be (500 Miles)', stepped out in front of the screen that stretched so far it would have taken even Usain Bolt ten seconds to race across it.

There was also Susan Boyle reprising 'Mull of Kintyre' and Nicola Benedetti giving the world a version of 'Loch Lomond' that would have brought a tear to a moneylender's eye. The energy was raised further by Andy Stewart, resurrected from The White Heather Club, singing its eternal theme of 'Come In, Come In'.

Brilliantly and dramatically, it was turned into a soaring chorus by use of the mash-up. People of a certain age may regard a mash-up only as a process that requires potatoes, a large dollop of butter and a pummelling, but it became something breathtakingly modern and extraordinarily powerful.

The teams entered to a tumult behind Scottish terriers. Their owners lifted the odd reluctant pooch who had discerned almost immediately that a circuit around Celtic Park constituted a lot of Scottie steps.

The atmosphere was one of welcome rather than politically charged, though the singing of 'Freedom Come All Ye' could be interpreted to suit a variety of purposes, including one of Scottish independence. The song has been described as a Scottish national anthem but, crucially, it also anticipates a nation free of a past where it played a significant role in imperialism.

In 2014, the athletes of a Commonwealth once seized and shaped by the forces of a small island danced, cavorted and swayed to a series of tunes, having been welcomed from afar by the astronauts of the International Space Station. They were also greeted in a more down-to-earth manner by the words of Burns, which proclaim: 'Wi' joy unfeign'd, brothers and sisters meet'. But Henderson's words, too, had an import: 'Broken families in lands we've herriet, will curse Scotland the Brave nae mair, nae mair'.

The Queen spoke of 'shared ideals and ambitions'. She said: 'The baton relay represents a calling together of people from every part of the Commonwealth and serves as a reminder of our shared ideals and ambitions as a diverse and resourceful family. And now, that baton has arrived here in Glasgow, a city renowned for its dynamic culture and for the warmth of its people, for this opening ceremony of this Friendly Games ... It now gives me great pleasure to declare the 20th Commonwealth Games open.'

THE GLASGOW EFFECT, 26 JULY 2015
Kevin McKenna

How long you can expect to live in Glasgow depends very much on your postcode. Glaswegian men ought on average to make it to 73 while women can look forward to a further five and half years. If you live in an affluent part of the city, your survival rates rise considerably; if you live in one of the poorer parts there's a fair chance you won't see out your sixties. Such statistics show that Glasgow has the lowest life expectancy rates in Scotland. The reasons for this are generally rather obvious: lack of exercise, poor diet, excessive drinking, dodgy genes, addiction to cigarettes, stress, poverty. Here journalist Kevin McKenna, who is as Glaswegian as a tattie scone, describes his own close encounter with the Grim Reaper.

Somewhere over the Indian Ocean at 30,000 feet a couple of weeks ago, I had an encounter with the Glasgow Effect and almost added another number to my city's grim mortality index. The Glasgow Effect is the curious phenomenon that sends the city's dwellers to their grave earlier than their brothers and sisters in those other major UK cities with large, working-class communities.

Not that I was aware of the physiological drama that had begun to unfold around my heart on Etihad flight No. 88888 from Abu Dhabi to Perth, the second leg of three in a 23-hour trip to visit my daughter in Melbourne.

You become aware of a slight tightening around the chest and the breaths that had previously emerged cleanly from the back of your lungs were now coming up a wee bit jaggy.

You immediately put it down to a bit of delayed anxiety rooted in the long haul between continents and a lifelong aversion to flying. And you resolve to locate the smoking shelter at Perth airport and fire up a couple of Bennies for the purposes of settling everything down again and regaining your cardio-composure. Throw in a couple of swift Bacardis in the airport lounge and everything would surely be tickety.

By the time I met Clare in Melbourne three hours later though, things were most definitely untickety in the ticker vicinity and I was struggling to walk the length of myself.

Being Glaswegian, though, you feel you have to deploy insouciance in the face of adversity and so, safely ensconced in my friend David's apartment in the Collingwood area an hour or so later, I had convinced myself it was just a touch of that deep-vein thrombotulism malarkey and resolved to get something for it the next morning from a chemist. I just needed to pull myself together and get a decent night's sleep fortified by another Benson's and a chilly sauvignon. That, I felt certain, would see off the collywobbles rapidamente. Instead, the collywobbles proceeded to give me a right good kicking for my folly and so, somewhat shamefaced, I shuffled the next day into the nearby St Vincent's hospital.

You've had a minor heart attack, they said, and so we'll need to look after you for a few days. Thus my first holiday in years, during which I was to offer some paternal consolation to a daughter who'd recently encountered some emotional unpleasantness, had ended as soon as it had begun 10,000 miles from home on a critical-care ward hooked up to the sort of machinery you had previously only seen in ER.

Never having been treated for anything in hospital, I had imagined it to be a crucible of stainless-steel terror and old men shuffling about in slippers and those bare-arse smocks they insist on everyone wearing.

Yet the only aspect of St Vincent's hospital to which I struggled to become accustomed was the unremitting kindness, compassion and good cheer of the nursing and medical staff. I had seen this phenomenon on many Scottish NHS wards while visiting stricken friends and relations; to encounter it at first hand, though, is a truly humbling experience. It may only have been a minor heart attack which I felt sure was at the infinitesimal end of the scale but in the medics' lexicon the word 'angiogram' started to recur with some frequency.

I had initially heard this as 'anziogram' and wondered if it was some kind of strippogram wearing the Aussie flag whom the Australians, in that direct way of theirs, would send on to the ward to keep everyone's pecker up. Instead, though, it was that queasy procedure by which they light up your heart to determine whether you need the full hacksaw and staples treatment or simply some medication.

Fortunately, they determined that a few tablets and a couple of wee lifestyle tweaks would be the best way of dealing with this. Of course, everyone says that an event like this is a 'warning' and that the ramifications can be 'life-changing'. So the consultant cardiologist decided to have a wee chat with me.

'The thing I don't understand,' I said, 'is that I was beginning to train for the Glasgow 3.5k in October and was taking lots of citrus fruit with my Bacardis and vodkas. I was even down to fewer than 10 Bennies a day. My temple may not exactly be a body but I was heading in the right direction. And this is the result. It's all a bit dispiriting.'

'Well, it could have been a lot worse if you hadn't been making those lifestyle changes,' he said.

'I take it the smokes are completely out now?'

'Yes; if you do nothing else but stop smoking you'll be rocking and rolling. How many units of alcohol do you drink per week?'

'It's actually only about 12–16 units.'

'That's not bad.'

'Occasionally, though, I might do them all in a single sitting; you know, like at a wedding.'

'That's binge drinking and puts your heart under enormous pressure.'

He also told me that the angiogram had also revealed something quite startling: there was evidence of a heart attack many years ago at a time in my life when I was jouking up Munros and doing three-peak challenges and 'Tough-Mudder' assault courses all over the shop. Looking back, I can now say with some certainty that this cardiac event seems to have occurred at some point during Celtic's Anton Rogan period.

When I returned home, I was startled to discover that the males on the McKenna side of the clan have been going down like skittles with heart failure for centuries. And you wonder if 30 years of a smoke-free, low-alcohol, high-broccoli, Munro-bagging, flower-arranging existence instead of 10 years ripping the arse out of it is actually a fair swap. And will it matter a jot if your heart already has the black spot on it?

END OF AN ERA, 15 OCTOBER, 2015

Alison Irvine

The Red Road flats were finally demolished, or at least partly demolished, some fifty years after the first residents moved in. It had been suggested that they might be reduced to rubble as part of the Commonwealth Games opening ceremony a year earlier but this was eventually, and wisely, rejected as insensitive and tasteless. Glasgow writer Alison Irvine, author of This Road is Red (2014), *marked their passing.*

The morning after the demolition of the Red Road flats, children trotted past the rubble to the nursery, and pensioners waited at the doors of the Alive & Kicking day centre. It was at this day centre in 2009 that I interviewed John McNally, 89, a former shop steward at the Provan Gas works. He had been a widower for more than twenty years and had lived in the same home in Red Road since 1969, 27 floors up, with views west to the Isle of Arran. He remembered seeing men at work on the former cabbage fields: 'I watched them getting built every day as I was passing. Steel, steel, steel.'

Here, too, I interviewed Jean McGeogh, who put her hand in a ballot box to get the keys to her flat in 1966. Like others whose former homes were inspected by the Corporation before a flat was allocated, she moved from a tenement. She did cleaning and bar work: Red Road rent was high. The flats were 'immaculate' and a welcome solution to the city's overcrowded and squalid housing. Designed by Sam Bunton, and built between 1964 and 1969, the two 28-storey 'slab' blocks and the six 31-storey 'point' blocks were once the tallest residential structures in Europe.

For the children of the Red Road in the 1960s and 1970s, the concrete walls were climbing frames, the surrounding fields football pitches. Games of chap door, run away, giant headers (a football thrown from a tower window and headed at the bottom), den making and squash matches were popular. Kids messed about in the lifts and rode bikes to the nearby Campsie Fells. Inspired by the Ken Loach film *Kes*, one of my interviewees, Matt Barr, kept a kestrel on a homemade perch on his veranda. For the adults, there was the underground pub – the Brig Bar – and the adjacent bingo hall, the electric heating, floor-cleaning rotas, grocery vans and community spirit.

But even in the 1970s, the flats' reputation was going downhill. Concerns about asbestos, antisocial neighbours, vandalism and lifts that broke down led many families to seek accommodation elsewhere. A fire in 1977 at 10 Red Road Court, in which a boy died, was a catalyst for change. Many residents refused to return to their homes.

From the 1980s, two of the blocks housed students. Louise Christie moved into Red Road in 1987 and stayed for five years. She remembered students arriving from the Western Isles, India and Indonesia. She was a student Labour Party activist and gave talks at residents' meetings, advising new students on Red Road life. 'You didn't use the ice-cream van, you didn't buy drugs from anyone in the area, you stayed out of the pubs, and you stayed out of the bookies,' she said.

In 1999, the first asylum seekers, from Kosovo, arrived and a new chapter in Red Road's history began. Locals, horrified at the destitution of the arrivals, donated clothes, toys and furniture. In 2009, I interviewed a Zimbabwean teenager who had stayed for two weeks while her application was processed. I also met a 17-year-old Iranian who had lived at Red Road much longer. Unable to study medicine because she did not have leave to remain, she raged against the asylum system, seeing its effects on the physical and mental health of her parents. I interviewed boys who played the same games as their counterparts in the 1960s and 1970s. 'Blacks v Scottish' became a popular football match.

In 2007 Didier Pasquette attempted to walk a high wire between two point blocks but had to abandon the effort because of high winds. Residents told me their bath water would slosh about in windy weather.

As many tenants were being rehoused from 2005, the last Red Road block remained home to asylum seekers. In 2014, when it was announced that the flats would be demolished live during the Commonwealth Games opening ceremony, asylum seekers were still living there – just one of the reasons the idea was dropped.

Before he was due to be uprooted from his home of forty years, McNally passed away. He would have hated the demolition. The feelings of others are more contradictory.

The woman who was afraid for her young children when they encountered drunk men in the lifts reminisced about the days on the grass with other families, playing music and having picnics while the kids played. The man in his forties who left Red Road in order to stay out of trouble had happy childhood memories and lifelong friends. The 74-year-old who couldn't wait to move to a 'front and back door' said she missed the 'neighbourliness' of her high rise.

Ade Kearns, professor of urban studies at Glasgow University, told BBC Radio Scotland: 'High rise works in some contexts but they don't work in situations where you build them in rather large numbers, often in quite isolated locations, without many amenities. You put up the most expensive structures to look after and then you put the people in them with the least amount of money. It's a circle you can't square.'

The demolition on Sunday was a little anticlimatic, with two of the point blocks only partly destroyed. It was a final twist in a complex history: they built them up, they blew them up, but they couldn't quite knock them down.

BIBLIOGRAPHY

Baird, John Logie, *Sermons, Soap and Television: Autobiographical Notes* (Royal Television Society, London, 1988)
Baxter, Stanley, *The Concise Parliamo Glasgow Dictionary of Current Glaswegian* (Paul Harris Publishing, Edinburgh, 1982)
Beech, John; Hand, Owen; Mulhern, Mark A. and Weston, Jeremy, eds., *Scottish Life and Society: A Compendium of Scottish Ethnology* (John Donald, Edinburgh, 2005)
Bell, J.J., *I Remember* (The Porpoise Press, Edinburgh, 1932)
Berry, Simon and White, Hamish, eds., *Glasgow Observed* (John Donald, Edinburgh, 1987)
Betjeman, John, *Betjeman's Britain* (The Folio Society, London, 1999)
Billcliffe, Roger, *The Glasgow Boys* (Frances Lincoln Ltd, London, 2008)
Blake, George, *The Shipbuilders* (B&W Publishing, Edinburgh, 1993)
Bogarde, Dirk, *A Postilion Struck By Lightning* (Chatto & Windus, London, 1977)
Borthwick, Alastair, *Always a Little Further* (Faber & Faber, London, 1939)
Boswell, James, *Life of Johnson* (Oxford University Press, London, 1969)
Boyle, Jimmy, *A Sense of Freedom* (Canongate, Edinburgh, 1977)
Brown, P. Hume, ed., *Early Travellers in Scotland* (David Douglas, Edinburgh, 1891)
Bryson, Bill, *Notes from a Small Island* (Doubleday, London, 1993)
Buchan, John, *Memory Hold-the-door* (Hodder & Stoughton, London, 1940)
Burkhauser, Jude, ed., *Glasgow Girls: Women in Art and Design 1880–1920* (Canongate, Edinburgh, 1990)
Burgess, Anthony, *Ninety-nine Novels: The Best in English Since 1939* (Allison & Busby, London, 1984)
Burgess, Moira, *Imagine a City: Glasgow in Fiction* (Argyll, Glendaruel, 1998)
Calder, Angus and Sheridan, Dorothy, eds., *Speak for Yourself: A Mass-Observation Anthology, 1937–1949* (Oxford University Press, London, 1985)
Campbell, T.C. and McKay, Reg, *Indictment: Trial By Fire* (Canongate, Edinburgh, 2001)
Carlyle, Alexander, *The Autobiography of Dr. Alexander Carlyle of Inveresk, 1722–1805* (TN Foulis, London & Edinburgh, 1910)
Carswell, Catherine, *Lying Awake* (Secker & Warburg, London, 1950)
Cleland, James, *Description of the City of Glasgow: Comprising an Account of Its Ancient and Modern History, Its Trade, Manufactures, Commerce, Health and Other Concerns* (John Smith and Son, Glasgow, 1840)
Cobbett, William, *Rural Rides* (A&C Black, Edinburgh, 1856)
Cockburn, Henry, *Memorials of His Time* (Penguin, London, 2001)
Collier, Paul, *Stairway 13: The Story of the 1971 Ibrox Disaster* (Bluecoat Press, Liverpool, 2007)

Colpi, Terri, *Italian Migration to Scotland* (Oxford: The Author, *c.* 1986)
Cooke, Anthony, *A History of Drinking: The Scottish Pub Since 1700* (Edinburgh University Press, Edinburgh, 2015)
Cowan, James, *From Glasgow's Treasure Chest: A Miscellany of History, Personalities and Places* (Craig Wilson Ltd, Glasgow, 1951)
Craig, Carol, *The Scots' Crisis of Confidence* (Big Thinking, Edinburgh, 2003)
Craig, Carol, *The Tears That Made the Clyde: Well-Being in Glasgow* (Argyll Publishing, Glendaruel, 2010)
Crawford, Robert, *On Glasgow and Edinburgh* (The Belknap Press of Harvard University Press, Cambridge, Massachusetts, 2013)
Cunnison, J. and J.B.S. Gilfillan, eds., *The Third Statistical Account of Scotland: Glasgow* (Collins, Glasgow, 1958)
Daiches, David, *Glasgow* (Grafton, London, 1982)
Danziger, Nick, *Danziger's Britain: A Journey to the Edge* (HarperCollins, London, 1996)
Defoe, Daniel, *A Tour Through the Whole Island of Great Britain* (Folio Society, London, 2006)
Devine, T.M., *To the Ends of the Earth: Scotland's Global Diaspora, 1750–2010* (Allen Lane, London, 2011)
Devine, T.M. and Jackson, Gordon, eds., *Glasgow: Volume 1: Beginnings to 1830* (Manchester University Press, Manchester, 1995)
Devine, Tom and Logue, Paddy, eds., *Being Scottish: Personal Reflections on Scottish Identity Today* (Polygon, Edinburgh, 2002)
Devine, T.M., ed., *Recovering Scotland's Slavery Past: The Caribbean Connection* (Edinburgh University Press, Edinburgh, 2015)
Diamond, Harry, *Can You Get My Name in the Papers?* (Neil Wilson Publishing, Glasgow, 1996)
Dunn, Douglas, ed., *Scotland: An Anthology* (HarperCollins, London 1991)
Ferguson, Alex, *Managing My Life: My Autobiography* (Hodder & Stoughton, London, 1999)
Eyre-Todd, George, ed., *The Glasgow Poets: Their Lives and Poems* (William Hodge and Company, Glasgow and Edinburgh, 1903)
Faley, Jean, *Up Oor Close: Memories of Domestic Life in Glasgow Tenements, 1910–1945* (White Cockade, in association with Springburn Museum Trust, Wendlebury, Oxon, 1990)
Fenton, Alexander, *The Food of the Scots* (John Donald, Edinburgh, 2007)
Ferguson, Alex, *Managing My Life* (Hodder & Stoughton, London, 1999)
Ferguson, Hugh, *Glasgow School of Art: The History* (The Foulis Press of Glasgow School of Art, Glasgow, 1995)
Fontane, Theodor, *Beyond the Tweed: A Tour of Scotland in 1858* (Libris, London, 1998)
Fyfe, J.G., ed., *Scottish Diaries and Memoirs, 1746–1843* (Eneas Macaky, Stirling, 1942)
Gaitens, Edward, *The Dance of the Apprentices* (Canongate, Edinburgh, 1990)
Gale, George and Johnson, Paul, *The Highland Jaunt* (Collins, London, 1978)
Gallacher, Tom, *Apprentice* (Canongate, Edinburgh, 2003)
Gibbon, Lewis Grassic and MacDiarmid, Hugh, *Scottish Scene: Or the Intelligent Man's Guide to Albyn* (Jarrolds, London, 1934)
Gifford, Douglas, *The Dear Green Place? The Novel in the West of Scotland* (Third Eye Centre, Glasgow, 1985)
The Glasgow Herald Book of Glasgow (Mainstream, Edinburgh, 1989)
Glasser, Ralph, *Growing up in the Gorbals* (Chatto & Windus, London, 1986)
Goring, Rosemary, *Scotland: The Autobiography* (Viking, London, 2007)

Grant, Elizabeth, of Rothiemurchus, *Memoirs of a Highland Lady* (Canongate, Edinburgh, 1992)
Gray, Alasdair, *Lanark: A Life in Four Books* (Canongate, Edinburgh, 1981)
Hanley, Clifford, *Dancing in the Streets* (Hutchinson, London, 1958)
Harper, Marjory, *Adventurers & Exiles: The Great Scottish Exodus* (Profile Books, London, 2003)
Herman, Arthur, *The Scottish Enlightenment: The Scots' Invention of the Modern World* (Fourth Estate, London, 2001)
Hind, Archie, *The Dear Green Place* (Polygon Books, Edinburgh, 1984)
Honeyman, T.J., *Art and Audacity* (London, 1971)
House, Jack, *The Heart of Glasgow* (Hutchinson, London, 1978)
House, Jack, *Music Hall Memories* (Richard Drew Publishing Ltd, Glasgow, 1986)
Irvine, Alison, *This Road is Red* (Luath, Glasgow, 2014)
Jack, Ian, *Before the Oil Ran Out* (Vintage, London, 1997)
Jenkins, Roy, *Portraits and Miniatures* (Macmillan, London, 1993)
Jephcott, Pearl (with Hilary Robinson), *Homes in High Flats* (Oliver and Boyd, Edinburgh, 1971)
Kaplan, Wendy, ed., *Charles Rennie Mackintosh* (Glasgow Museums and Abbeville Press, New York, 1996)
Keay, John and Julia, eds., *Collins Encyclopaedia of Scotland* (HarperCollins, London, 1994)
Kelman, James, *The Busconductor Hines* (Polygon Books, Edinburgh, 1984)
Kemp, Arnold, *The Hollow Drum: Scotland Since the War* (Mainstream Publishing, Edinburgh, 1993)
King, Elspeth, *The Hidden History of Glasgow's Women* (Mainstream, Edinburgh, 1993)
Kohli, Hardeep Singh, *Indian Takeaway: A Very British Story* (Canongate, Edinburgh, 2008)
Laing, R.D., *Wisdom, Madness and Folly: The Making of a Psychiatrist, 1927–57* (Canongate Classics, Edinburgh, 1998)
Lindsay, Maurice, *Thank You for Having Me* (Robert Hale, London, 1983)
Liverani, Mary Rose, *The Winter Sparrow: A Glasgow Childhood* (Michael Joseph, London, 1976)
Lockhart, John Gibson, *Peter's Letters to His Kinsfolk* (Scottish Academic Press, Edinburgh, 1977)
McArthur, A and Long, H. Kingsley, *No Mean City* (Corgi Books, London, 1986)
McArthur, Tom and Waddell, Peter, *Vision Warrior: The Hidden Achievement of John Logie Baird* (Century Hutchinson, London, 1986)
McCormack, Cathy (with Marian Pallister), *The Wee Yellow Butterfly* (Argyll Publishing, Glendaruel, 2009)
MacDiarmid, Hugh, *Selected Prose* (Carcanet, Manchester, 1992)
MacDougall, Carl, *Painting the Forth Bridge: A Search for Scottish Identity* (Aurum Press, London, 2001)
MacFarlane, Colin, *No Mean Glasgow: Revelations of a Gorbals Guy* (Mainstream, Edinburgh, 2008)
MacGill, Patrick, *Children of the Dead End: The Autobiography of a Navvy* (Herbert Jenkins, London, 1914)
McGinn, Matt, *McGinn of the Calton: The Life and Works of Matt McGinn, 1928–1977* (Glasgow District Libraries, Glasgow, 1987)
McGonigal, James, *Beyond the Last Dragon: A Life of Edwin Morgan* (Sandstone Press, Dingwall, 2010)
McIlvanney, Hugh, *McIlvanney on Football* (Mainstream, Edinburgh, 1994)

McIlvanney, William, *Laidlaw* (Coronet Books, London, 1984)
McIlvanney, William, *The Papers of Tony Veitch* (Coronet Books, London, 1983)
McIlvanney, William, *Surviving the Shipwreck* (Mainstream Publishing, Edinburgh, 1991)
McLaren, Moray, *The Scots* (Penguin, London, 1951)
MacLean, Colin and Veitch, Kenneth, eds., *Scottish Life and Society: A Compendium of Scottish Ethnology – Volume 12: Religion* (John Donald, Edinburgh, 2006)
McLean, Jack, *The Bedside Urban Voltaire* (Lochar, Moffat, 1990)
McNaught, Thomas P., *The Recollections of a Glasgow Detective Officer* (Simpkin, Marshall & Co., London, 1887)
Maan, Bashir, *The New Scots: The Story of Asians in Scotland* (John Donald, Edinburgh, 1992)
Marr, Andrew, *The Battle for Scotland* (Penguin, London, 1992)
Martin, David, *The Glasgow School of Painting* (George Bell & Sons, London, 1897)
Maver, Irene, *Glasgow* (Edinburgh University Press, Edinburgh, 2000)
Morton, H.V., *In Search of Scotland* (Methuen, London, 1929)
Muir, Edwin, *An Autobiography* (Canongate, Edinburgh, 1993)
Muir, Edwin, *Scottish Journey* (Flamingo, London, 1985)
Muir, James Hamilton, *Glasgow in 1901* (William Hodge and Company, Glasgow and Edinburgh, 1901)
Munro, Michael, *The Patter: A Guide to Current Glasgow Usage* (Glasgow District Libraries, Glasgow,1985)
Munro, Neil, *The Brave Days: A Chronicle of the North* (Porpoise Books, Edinburgh, 1931)
Murray, Bill, *The Old Firm: Sectarianism, Sport and Society in Scotland* (John Donald, Edinburgh, 1984)
The New Statistical Account of Scotland, Vol VI, Lanark (William Blackwood and Sons, Edinburgh and London, 1835)
Oakley, C.A., *The Second City: The Story of Glasgow* (Blackie, Glasgow, 1990)
Osborne, Brian and Armstrong, Ronald, eds., *Mungo's City: A Glasgow Anthology* (Birlinn, Edinburgh, 1999)
Patrick, James, *A Glasgow Gang Observed* (Eyre Methuen, London, 1973)
Pennant, Thomas, *A Tour in Scotland 1769* (Birlinn, Edinburgh, 2000)
Peter, Bruce, *100 Years of Glasgow's Amazing Cinemas* (Polygon, Edinburgh, 1996)
Phelan, Jim, *The Name's Phelan* (The Blackstaff Press, Belfast, 1993)
Phillips, Alastair, *Glasgow's Herald: Two Hundred Years of a Newspaper, 1783–1983* (Richard Drew, Glasgow, 1982)
Pieri, Joe, *The Scots-Italians: Recollections of an Immigrant* (Mercat Press, Edinburgh, 2005)
Pieri, Joe, *Tales of the Savoy: Stories from a Glasgow Café* (Neil Wilson Publishing, Glasgow, 1990)
Pritchett, V.S., *Build the Ships* (HMSO, London, 1946)
Reid, Jimmy, *As I Please* (Mainstream, Edinburgh, 1984)
Reid, R. ('Senex'), *Glasgow Past and Present* (Nabu Press, Charleston South Carolina, 2010)
Reid, R. ('Senex'), *Old Glasgow and Its Environs, Historical and Topographical* (Longman, London, 1864)
Robertson, George Gladstone, *Gorbals Doctor* (Jarrolds, London, 1970)
Rosie, George, *Curious Scotland: Tales from a Hidden History* (Granta Books, London, 2004)

Roy, Kenneth, ed., *The Best of Scotland on Sunday* (Carrick Publishing, Ayr, 1990)

Royle, Trevor, ed., *Isn't All This Bloody: Scottish Writings from the First World War* (Birlinn, Edinburgh, 2014)

Royle, Trevor, ed., *Jock Tamson's Bairns: Essays on a Scottish Childhood* (Hamish Hamilton, London, 1977)

Savage, Hugh, *Born Up a Close: Memoirs of a Brigton Boy* (Argyll Publishing, Glendaruel, Argyll, 2006)

Smout, T.C., *A History of the Scottish People, 1560 1830* (Collins, London, 1989)

Smout, T.C., *A History of the Scottish People, 1830 1950* (Collins, London, 1989)

Southey, Robert, *Journal of a Tour in Scotland in 1819* (J. Murray, London, 1929)

Spence, Alan, *Its Colours They Are Fine* (William Collins Sons & Co Ltd, Glasgow, 1977)

Spottiswoode, John, *The History of the Church of Scotland* (Scolar Press, Menston, Yorkshire, 1972)

Spring, Ian, *Phantom Village: The Myth of the New Glasgow* (Polygon, Edinburgh, 1990)

Strang, Dr John, *Glasgow and its Clubs* (London, 1856)

Theroux, Paul, *The Kingdom By the Sea: A Journey Round the Coast of Great Britain* (Penguin Books, London, 1984)

Tweed, John, *Tweed's Guide to Glasgow and the Clyde* (Molendinar Press, Glasgow, 1979)

Waugh, Evelyn, *Sword of Honour* (Penguin Books, London, 1999)

Weir, Molly, *Best Foot Forward* (Hutchinson & Co, London, 1972)

Weir, Molly, *Shoes Were For Sundays* (Hutchinson & Co, London, 1970)

White, Kenneth, *Travels in the Drifting Dawn* (Mainstream, Edinburgh, 1989)

Who Belongs to Glasgow? 200 Years of Migration (Glasgow City Libraries, Glasgow, 1993)

Whyte, Hamish, ed. *Noise and Smoky Breath* (Third Eye Centre, Glasgow, 1983)

Williamson, Elizabeth; Riches, Anne and Higgs, Malcolm, *Glasgow: The Buildings of Scotland* (Penguin Books in association with the National Trust of Scotland, London, 1990)

Wordsworth, Dorothy, *Recollections of a Tour Made in Scotland A.D. 1803* (David Douglas, Edinburgh, 1894)

Wormald, Jenny, ed., *Scotland: A History* (Oxford University Press, Oxford, 2005)

Worsdall, Frank, *The Tenement* (W & R Chambers, Edinburgh, 1979)

Worsthorne, Peregrine, *Tricks of Memory* (Weidenfeld & Nicolson, London, 1993)

SOURCES AND PERMISSIONS

Every effort has been made to trace the rights-holders of material which appears in this book. The editor and publisher will be happy to rectify any omissions and print appropriate acknowledgements in future editions.

Prologue

'Glasgow Got Its Name', from *Collins Encyclopeadia of Scotland* by John and Julia Keay (HarperCollins, London, 1994)

1597–1700 An Archbishop's Seat

'Witchcraft', from *History of the Church and State of Scotland* by John Spottiswoode (London, 1655)

'A Closet Lined with Iron', from *Travels in Holland, The United provinces, England, Scotland, and Ireland* by Sir William Brereton (The Chteham Society, 1844)

'O Glasgow!' from *Skene's Succinct Survey of the Famous City of Aberdeen* by (John Forbes, Aberdeen, 1685)

1701–1750 Pretending To Be Gentlemen

'A Fishy Tale', from *A Short Account of Scotland* by Thomas Morer (Newborough London, 1702)

'Cleanest and Beautifullest City in Britain . . .', from *A Tour Through the Whole Island of Great Britain* by Daniel Defoe (London 1724–27)

'Nothing But Good Looks and Fine Clothes', from *The Autobiography of Alexander Carlyle of Inveresk 1722–1805* (TN Foulis, London and Edinburgh, 1910)

1751–1800 What To Do with Dung

'The Saracen's Head', by Robert Tennant, from *The Glasgow Courant*, 1755
'Best of the Second Rate', from *A Tour in Scotland 1769* by Thomas Pennant (John Monk, Chester, 1771)
'A Mediocrity of Knowledge', from *Journey to the Western Isles of Scotland*, by Samuel Johnson (W. Statham and T. Cadell, London, 1775)
'Have You Ever Seen Brentford?', from *The Journal of a Tour to the Hebrides with Samuel Johnson, LLD* by James Boswell (Charles Dilly, London, 1785)
'Dung Moving', from *The Glasgow Mercury*

1801–1850 Haunts of Vagrancy

'Glasgow Green', from *Recollections of a Tour Made in Scotland A.D.1803* by Dorothy Worsdworth (David Douglas, Edinburgh, 1894)
'Indescribably Underbred', from *Memoirs of a Highland Lady* by Elizabeth Grant of Rothiemurchus (Canongate, Edinburgh, 1992)
'The National Jealousy of the English', from *Rob Roy* by Sir Walter Scott (Constable and Co., Edinburgh, 1817)
'Glasgow Invades Edinburgh', from *Memorials of His Time* by Henry Cockburn (T.N. Foulis, Edinburgh & London, 1856)
'The Ritual of Punch-making', from *The Life of Sir Walter Scott* by J.G. Lockhart (Robert Cadell, Edinburgh, 1837–39)
'An Invincible Nose', from *Journal of a Tour in Scotland in 1891* by Robert Southey (J. Murray, London, 1929)
'The Rogueries of the Broomielaw', from *Peter's Letters to His Kinsfolk* by J.G. Lockhart (William Blackwood, Edinburgh, 1819)
'Molly's History', quoted in *The Hidden History of Glasgow's Women* by Elspeth King (Mainstream, Edinburgh, 1993)
'Bread, Beef and Beer', from *Rural Rides* by William Cobbett (A&C Black, Edinburgh, 1856)
'Willie Winkie', from *Scottish Nursery Songs and Poems* by William Miller (Kerr & Richardson, Glasgow, 1863)
'Cock-fighting', from *The New Statistical Account of Scotland, Volume VI, Lanark* (Wm. Blackwood and Sons, Edinburgh & London, 1835)
'A Reckoning', from *The New Statistical Account of Scotland, Volume VI, Lanark* (Wm. Blackwood and Sons, Edinburgh & London, 1835)
'Less wet than Edinburgh', from *Description of the City of Glasgow: Comprising an Account of Its Ancient and Modern History, Its Trade, Manufactures, Commerce, Health and Other Concerns* by James Cleland (John Smith and Son, Glasgow, 1840)
'Glasgow Observatory,' (Thomas de Quincey) quoted in *The Opium-eater: A Life of Thomas de Quincey* by Grevel Lindop (OUP, Oxford, 1985)
'Wretched, Dissolute, Loathsome and Pestilential', by Captain Miller, from Reports on the sanitary condition of the labouring population of Scotland, ... Presented to both houses of Parliament, by command of Her Majesty, July, 1842

1851–1900 City of Merchants

'The Trial of Madeleine Smith', from *The Illustrated London News*, 30 June 1857
'A Suburb of the Dead', from *Biographic and Descriptive Sketches of Glasgow Necropolis* by George Blair (M. Ogle, Glasgow, 1857)
'Not Waving But Drowning', from *Glasgow Sentinel*, 3 March 1860
'The First Football Match' (Robert Gardner) quoted in *Scottish Football: A Pictorial History* by Kevin McCarra (Polygon, Edinburgh, 1984)
'A Noble Park' (John Tweed) from *Tweed's Guide to Glasgow and the Clyde* (Molendinar Press, Glasgow, 1973)
'Maryhill Barracks', from *Groome's Gazetteer*, 1876
'School for Cookery', from *The Baillie*, 22 March 1876
'Doon the Watter,' from *I Remember* by J.J. Bell (The Porpoise Press, Edinburgh, 1832)
'Kennedy Jones', from *The Brave Days: A Chronicle of the North* by Neil Munro (Porpoise Books, Edinburgh, 1931)
'Brief Lives', from (J.B. Russell) from *Public Health Administration in Glasgow: A Memorial Volume of the Writings of James Burn Russell* (J. MacLehose & Sons, Glasgow, 1905)
'A Vexed Question in Sanitation', from *The Builder*, 4 August 1888
'Unlucky with Ships', from Lying Awake by Catherine Carswell (Secker &Warburg, London, 1950)
'Glasgow' from *Poetic Gems Selected from the Works of William McGonagall, Poet and Tragedian with Biographical Sketch by the Author and Portrait* by William McGonagall (Winter, Duncan and Co., Dundee, 1890)
'A Minor Episode', from *Memory Hold-the-Door* by John Buchan (Hodder & Stoughton, London 1940)
'Steel Drops', from *I Remember by* J.J. Bell (The Porpoise Press, Edinburgh, 1932)
'Glasgow Boys' (Francis 'Fra' Newbery), from *The Glasgow School of Painting* by David Martin (George Bell & Son, London, 1897)

1901–1925 Fighting Women

'The City Man', from *Glasgow in 1901* by James Hamilton Muir (W. Hodge, Glasgow, 1901)
'George Square', from *Glasgow in 1901* by James Hamilton Muir (W. Hodge, Glasgow, 1901)
'The Bone Factory', from *An Autobiography* by Edwin Muir (Hogarth Press, London 1954)
'Kate Cranstonish', from *The Brave Days: A Chronicle of the North* by Neil Munro (Porpoise Press, London, 1931)
'Baird Remembers Reith', from *Television and Me*, by John Logie Baird, edited by Malcolm Baird. Copyright © Malcolm Baird. Reprinted by permission of Birlinn Ltd.
'At the Pickshers', from *The Name's Phelan* by Jim Phelan (Blackstaff Press, Dublin, 1948)
'A Room and Kitchen in Springburn', (Marian Smith) quoted in *Up Oor Close: Memories of Domestic Life in Glasgow Tenements, 1910–1945* by Jean Faley (White Cockade, in association with Springburn Museum Trust, Wendlebury, Oxon, 1990)

'Suffragettes at War', by Helen Crawfurd, from an unpublished memoir made available through the Marx Memorial Library and Workers' School

'Bearded Like a Man', from *Children of the Dead End: The Autobiography of a Navvy* by Patrick MacGill. Copyright © the Estate of Patrick MacGill. Reprinted by permission of Knight Features on behalf of the Estate of Patrick MacGill

'Rent Strike', from *In the Rapids of Revolution: Essays, Articles and Letters by John Maclean*, ed. Nan Milton (Allison and Busby, London, 1978)

'Doctoring in the Gorbals', from *Gorbals Doctor* by George Gladstone Robertson (Jarrolds, London, 1970)

'Close Encounters', from *Dance of the Apprentices* by Edward Gaitens. Copyright © the Estate of Edward Gaitens, 1948. Reprinted by permission of Canongate Books Ltd

1926–1950 Canoodling

'Built by the Picts', from *Dancing in the Streets* by Clifford Hanley (Hutchinson, London, 1958)

'Springburn Sinners', from *Shoes Were for Sundays* by Molly Weir (Penguin Books, 2012). Copyright © Molly Weir, 1970. Reproduced by permission of Penguin Books Ltd

'A Crate of Apples', from *Thank You for Having Me* by Maurice Lindsay. Copyright © The Literary Executor of Maurice Lindsay. Reprinted by permission of the family of Maurice Lindsay

'A Razor Attack on Mosley', from *Harold Nicolson's Diaries and Letters* by Harold Nicolson (William Collins, Glasgow, 1966–68)

'Not Even a Scottish Slum' (Lewis Grassic Gibbon) from *Scottish Scene* by Hugh MacDiarmid and James Leslie Mitchell (Jarrolds, London, 1934)

'Naming the Yards', from *The Shipbuilders* by George Blake. Copyright and permission for use courtesy of Black & White Publishing Ltd

'A Tree in Argyle Street', from *Glasgow's Treasure Chest: A Miscellany of History, personalities and Places* by James Cowan (Craig Wilson Ltd, Glasgow, 1951)

'An Anti-Social Neighbour', (Agnes Muirhead) quoted in *The Hidden History of Glasgow's Women* by Elspeth King (Mainstream, Edinburgh, 1993)

'A Cocktail Bar at Ibrox', from *Born up a Close: Memoirs of a Brigton Boy* by Hugh Savage. Copyright © Capercaillie Books. Reprinted by permission of the publishers, Capercaillie Books

'More a Dummy Than a Mummy', from *A Postilion Struck By Lightning* by Dirk Bogarde. Copyright © by the Estate of Dirk Bogarde. Reprinted by permission of United Agents on behalf of the Estate of Dirk Bogarde

'Coupling', from *Growing up in the Gorbals* by Ralph Glasser. Copyright and permission for use courtesy of Black & White Publishing Ltd

'You Say "Polis"; I Say "Police"', from Report on Glasgow Speech: common errors in language usage in elementary schools by the Educational Institute of Scotland (Educational Institute of Scotland, Glasgow Local Association, 1934)

'The Art of Tapping Lifts', from *Always a Little Further* by Alastair Borthwick. Copyright © the Estate of Alastair Borthwick. Reprinted by permission of the Estate of Alastair Borthwick

'Swastikas in Sauchiehall Street', from *The Jewish Echo*, November 1939

'A Mongrel among the Dustbins', from *Sword of Honour* by Evelyn Waugh. (Penguin Books, 2002). Copyright © Evelyn Waugh, 1965. Reproduced by permission of Penguin Books Ltd

'Mob Rule', from *The Scots Italians* by Joe Pieri. Copyright © the Estate of Joe Pieri. Reprinted by permission of Birlinn Ltd

'The Clydebank Blitz', from *The Glasgow Herald*, 13 March 1941

'An Old-style Amputation', from *Wisdom, Madness & Folly: The Making of a Psychiatrist, 1927–57* by R.D. Laing (Macmillan, London, 1985)

'Riveting Stuff', from *Build the Ships* by V.S. Pritchett. Copyright © the Estate of V.S. Pritchett Reprinted by permission of Peters Fraser & Dunlop (www.petersfraserdunlop.com) on behalf of the Estate of V.S. Pritchett

'The Lowest of the Low on *The Glasgow Herald*', from *Tricks of Memory* by Peregrine Worsthorne (Weidenfeld & Nicolson, London, 1993)

'The Quest for Woodbines', from *The Winer Sparrow: A Glasgow Childhood* by Mary Rose Liverani (Michael Joseph, London, 1976)

'Horsing Around', from *Music Hall Memories* by Jack House. Copyright © the Estate of Jack House. Reprinted by permission of Derek House

'The Citizens' Theatre' (James Bridie (O.H. Mavor)) from *A Conspectus To Mark the Citizens' 21st Anniversary as a Living Theatre in Gorbals Street, Glasgow* (Citizens' Theatre Limited, Glasgow, 1964)

1951–1975 Hello, Dali

'A Tale of Two Cities', from *The Scots* by Moray McLaren (Penguin, London, 1951)

'The Dali Story', from *Art and Audacity* by T.J. Honeyman (Collins, London, 1971)

'The Dour Drinkers of Glasgow', from *Selected Prose* by Hugh MacDiarmid (edited by Alan Raich). Copyright © Carcanet Press Ltd. Reprinted by permission of the publishers, Carcanet Press Ltd

'Armageddon in George Square', from *Curious Scotland: Tales from a Hidden History* by George Rosie. Copyright © Granta Books. Reprinted by permission of the publishers, Granta Books

'Learning about Colours', from *Its Colours They Are Fine* by Alan Spence (William Collins & Co. Ltd, Glasgow, 1977). Reprinted by permission of the Author

'Rite of Passage', from *Apprentice* by Tom Gallacher (Sceptre, London, 1983)

'Paraffin Dressing', from *No Mean City* by Alexander McArthur and H. Kingsley Long (Longmans, Green & Co., London, 1935)

'Are Ye Dancing?', from *Music Hall Memories* by Jack House (Richard Drew Publishing, Glasgow, 1986). Copyright © the Estate of Jack House. Reprinted by permission of Derek House

'North and South of the River', from *The Heart of Glasgow* by Jack House (Hutchinson, London, 1978). Copyright © the Estate of Jack House. Reprinted by permission of Derek House

'Bud Neill', from *Dancing in the Streets* by Clifford Hanley (Hutchinson, London, 1958)

'A Cupboard for Coal and Marmalade', from *Betjeman's Britain* by John Betjeman. Copyright © Candida Lycett Green. Reprinted by permission of United Agents on behalf of Candida Lycett Green

'Glasgow, 1960' from *Selected Poetry* by Hugh MacDiarmid (edited by Alan Riach). Copyright © Carcanet Press Ltd. Reprinted by permission of the publishers, Carcanet Press Ltd

'The Art of Stabbing', from *A Sense of Freedom* by Jimmy Boyle (Canongate, Edinburgh, 1977). Copyright © Jimmy Boyle. Reprinted by permission of the author c/o Peters Fraser and Dunlop

'King Billy' from *Collected Poems* by Edwin Morgan. Copyright © Carcanet Press Ltd. Reprinted by permission of the publishers, Carcanet Press Ltd

'Teeth to Teeth', from *Music Hall Memories* by Jack House (Richard Drew Publishing, Glasgow, 1986). Copyright © the Estate of Jack House. Reprinted by permission of Derek House

'Where is the Glasgow?' by Adam McNaughtan. Copyright ©Adam McNaughtan. Reprinted by permission of the author

'Sunday Blues', from *Travels in the Drifting Dawn* by Kenneth White (Mainstream, Edinburgh, 1989). Copyright © Kenneth White. Reprinted by permission of the author

'The Road to Wembley', From *Surviving the Shipwreck* by William McIlvanney (Mainstream, Edinburgh, 1991). Copyright © the Literary Estate of William McIlvanney. Reprinted by permission of Jenny Brown Associates on behalf of the Literary Estate of William McIlvanney

'"John, You're Immortal"', from *McIlvanney on Football* by Hugh McIlvanney (Mainstream, Edinburgh, 1994)

'Wee Tam's Breakfast', from *The Bedside Urban Voltaire* by Jack Mclean (Lochar, Moffat, 1990)

'A Super Yo-yo', from *Homes in High Flats* by Pearl Jephcott with Hilary Robinson (Oliver & Boyd, Edinburgh, 1971)

'City of Razors' by Eddie Linden. Copyright © Eddie Linden. Reprinted by permission of the author

'Cholesterol' by Adam McNaughton. Copyright ©Adam McNaughtan. Reprinted by permission of the author

'Stairway 13' (Andy Ewan) quoted in *Stairway 13: The Story of the 1971 Ibrox Disaster* by Paul Collier (Bluecoat Press, Liverpool, 2007)

'Gorbals Memories', from *Glasgow News*, 1972

'Never Sit with Your Back to a Door', from *Indictment: Trial by Fire* by T.C. Campbell and Reg McKay. Copyright © T. C. Campbell and the Estate of Reg McKay, 2001. Reprinted by permission of Canongate Books Ltd

'The Most Foreign Town Britain', from *The Highland Jaunt* by George Gale and Paul Johnson (Collins, London, 1978)

'Connollymania', from *No Mean Glasgow: Revelations of a Gorbals Guy* by Colin MacFarlane (Mainstream, Edinburgh, 2008)

'The Biggest Housing Scheme in Europe', from *The Wee Yellow Butterfly* by Cathy McCormack (with Marian Pallister). Copyright © Capercaillie Books. Reprinted by permission of the publishers, Capercaillie Books

'The Only Sane Man in Glasgow', from *McGinn of the Calton: The Life and Works of Matt McGinn* by Matt McGinn. Copyright © the Literary Executor of Matt McGinn, Janette McGinn. Reprinted by permission of Janette McGinn

1976–2000 Deserts wi' Windaes

'An Indian Sunday', from *Indian Takeaway: A Very British Story* by Hardeep Singh Kholi. Copyright © Hardeep Singh Kholi, 2008. Reprinted by permission of Canongate Books Ltd

'The Bargain' from *Dreaming Frankenstein and Collected Poems 1967–1984* by Liz Lochhead. Copyright © Liz Lochhead. Reprinted by permission of Polygon

'Latin or French?', from *Lanark: A Life in Four Books* by Alasdair Gray. Copyright © Alasdair Gray, 1981. Reprinted by permission of Canongate Books Ltd

'A Strangled Peevish Hiccup', from *The Kingdom by the Sea: A Journey Round the Coast of Great Britain* by Paul Theroux. Copyright © Paul Theroux. Reprinted by permission of the Wylie Agency on behalf of the author, Paul Theroux

'Lingua Glesca', from *Parliamo Glasgow* by Stanley Baxter. Copyright © Jayne Maxwell. Reprinted by permission of Birlinn Ltd

'The Woman in Govan Library', from *As I Please* by Jimmy Reid. Copyright © the Estate of Jimmy Reid. Reprinted by permission of Eileen Reid

'Miles Better – Than Where?', from *Can You Get My Name in the Papers?* by Harry Diamond. Copyright © Neil Wilson Publishing Ltd, 1996. Reprinted by permission of the publishers, Neil Wilson Publishing Ltd

'Pure Mince', from *The Busconductor Hines* by James Kelman. Copyright © James Kelman. Reprinted by permission of the author c/o Rogers, Coleridge & White Ltd., 20 Powis Mews, London W11 1JN

'Alasdair Gray's *Lanark*', from *Ninety-nine Novels: The Best in English Since 1939* (Allison and Burgess, 1984) by Anthony Burgess. Reprinted by permission of David Higham Associates Ltd on behalf of The International Anthony Burgess Foundation

'Come and See Ma Blue Hoose', from *Before the Oil Ran Out* by Ian Jack (Vintage, London, 1977)

'Jock Stein', from *Managing My Life: My Autobiography* by Alex Ferguson. Copyright © Hodder and Stoughton. Reprinted by permission of the publishers, Hodder and Stoughton

'The Patter', from *The Patter: A Guide to Current Glasgow Usage* by Michael Munro. Copyright © Michael Munro. Reprinted by permission of the publishers, Birlinn Ltd

'The Matter of Shirt Tails' (Anne Simpson), from *The Glasgow Herald Book of Glasgow* (Mainstream, Edinburgh, 1989)

'Glasgow's Miles Davis' (David Belcher), from *The Glasgow Herald Book of Glasgow* (Mainstream, Edinburgh, 1989)

'Diary of a Shop Assistant' (Ajay Close), from *The Best of Scotland on Sunday* ed. Kenneth Roy (Carrick Publishing, Ayr, 1990)

'À La Mode', from *Portraits and Miniatures* by Roy Jenkins (Macmillan, London, 1993). Reprinted by permission of Peters Fraser & Dunlop on behalf of the Estate of Roy Jenkins

'A Pint of Tennents', from *Notes from a Small Island* by Bill Bryson. Copyright © Bill Bryson. Reprinted by permission of the author, Bill Bryson

'"Willie Lynch is No' a Grass"', from *Danziger's Britain* by Nick Danziger. Reprinted by permission of the publishers, HarperCollins Publishers LLC

2001– Blow Up

'Smeaton as Superman' (Lawrence Donegan), *The Guardian*, 5 July 2007

'Early Closing Time', *Sunday Herald*, 4 December 2013

'Glasgow School of Art' (Alan Taylor), *The Times Literary Supplement*, May 2014

'Let the Games Begin' (Hugh MacDonald), *The Herald*, 24 July 2014

'The Glasgow Effect' (Kevin McKenna), *The Observer*, 26 July 2015. Reprinted by permission of the author

'End of an Era' (Alison Irvine), *The Guardian*, 15 October 2015. Reprinted by permission of Guardian News & Media Ltd. 2016.

INDEX

Note: Page numbers in **bold** refer to complete extracts by the author listed.